Lilibet

ALSO BY CAROLLY ERICKSON

The Records of Medieval Europe
Civilization and Society in the West
The Medieval Vision
Bloody Mary
Great Harry
The First Elizabeth
Mistress Anne
Our Tempestuous Day
Bonnie Prince Charlie
To the Scaffold: The Life of Marie Antoinette
Great Catherine
Her Little Majesty: The Life of Queen Victoria
Josephine
Arc of the Arrow
Alexandra
Royal Panoply
The Girl from Botany Bay

Lilibet

AN INTIMATE
PORTRAIT
OF ELIZABETH II

Carolly Erickson

DOUBLEDAY LARGE PRINT HOME LIBRARY EDITION

ST. MARTIN'S PRESS ❧ NEW YORK

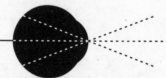

This Large Print Book carries the
Seal of Approval of N.A.V.H.

A Queen's life is hard. Yet a Queen reigns
Over the dream of her people, or nowhere.

—TED HUGHES

Lilibet

ONE

Crowds of theatergoers spilled out into the streets on a rainy night in April, 1926, the women pulling on thick coats over their skimpy short dresses and the men stamping their feet and rubbing their arms to keep warm. "The Student Prince" had just ended at His Majesty's, Ruth Draper had completed her monologue at the Garrick, the stars of George and Ira Gershwin's "Lady Be Good" and Jerome Kern's "Show Boat" had taken their last bows. The cinemas too were closing for the evening, and the variety shows and concert halls, until by eleven o'clock the sidewalks were full and it was nearly impossible to find a cab. Many couples gave up trying, and ended up at the Piccadilly Hotel where Jack Hylton's band was playing, or at the Queen's Hotel in Leicester Square where the Ladies' Russian Orchestra held forth, in peasant costume, with balalaikas and black boots. Some set off for the cabaret at the Café de Paris, or for Elsa Lanchester's nightclub, the Cave of Harmony, in Seven Dials.

Celebrity hunters looked in at the Embassy Night Club where a sofa table was set aside for the Prince of Wales, a regular visitor, or at Ciro's, where the prince sometimes played drums with the band, his explosive rimshots setting off an inevitable wave of applause. There was gossip about his brother Prince George, who was said to be having an affair with the American singer Florence Mills; it was always possible that George and Florence might be having a quiet cocktail in the darker recesses of the Silver Slipper or the Hambone Club, or even at the Fifty-Fifty in Wardour Street, where Gertrude Lawrence and Beatrice Lillie and Noël Coward went after the theater, to see and be seen.

One man in the vast crowd was hurrying through the clogged traffic on an important errand. Sir William Joynson-Hicks, Home Secretary in the Conservative government, had been deputed to represent the cabinet at the birth of a royal child. He was on his way to Mayfair, to the town home of the Fourteenth Earl of Strathmore in Bruton Street, where the earl's daughter the Duchess of York was in labor—indeed she had been in labor for more than a day—and he was impatient to fulfill this obligation and return to more pressing duties.

As his cab made its way along the rain-slick streets with their carefree merrymakers Joynson-Hicks turned from the sight with indignation. As far as he was concerned, the capital was in the grip of a destructive hedonism that brought in its wake lax morals, decaying values and a pervasive ennui. The postwar society of London, he was convinced, had far too many women—indeed, because of the immense loss of life in the Great War, far more women than men—and they seemed to be everywhere, unescorted, in their alarmingly short dresses and bobbed hair under cloche hats, their cigarettes in long holders, their gaze bold and direct and provocative. Modesty, Joynson-Hicks believed, had gone the way of the dinosaur. A jungle ethic prevailed, catering to primitive urges. One had only to note the pervasiveness of liquor (the sale of which the Americans, in their wisdom, had prohibited), the loud jazz music, the sordid nightclubs, the pornographic "modern" books that extolled adultery and unnatural sexuality, modern art with its formlessness and lack of proper aesthetic standards, above all, the rampant illicit sex that seemed to be the besetting vice of the postwar world.

As Home Secretary, Joynson-Hicks was on a crusade to quash the evils he deplored, sending in the police to shut down nightclubs, arrest drinkers and jail partygoers, confiscating books and closing art galleries, campaigning in speech after speech against the decline of principles and urging his hearers to aid him in the cause of holding the line of civilization against the encroaching barbarism. Such was his mission—but not on this night, when civilization, or at least the Conservative government, with which he often confused it, was under attack on another front.

Britain's miners had been locked out for months, engaged in a bitter dispute with the mine owners (among them Lord Strath-more, toward whose house on Bruton Street the Home Secretary was traveling), who had cut their wages. A million miners were out of work, while the government, trying in vain to mediate the conflict, subsi-dized the industry at great cost. But the subsidies were at an end, for a royal com-mission, appointed to look into the entire situation, had issued a report saying that the miners' wage cuts were unavoidable, and the decision had been made not to re-new the government's financial support to the industry.

Talks were continuing, in an atmosphere of growing tension. But the miners' leader, R.J. Cook, was refusing to accept any com-promise on the wage issue and the Trades Union Congress, which represented some five million workers throughout Great Brit-ain, was threatening to call a general strike in support of the miners.

The prospect of a general strike was a formidable challenge. Not only would such a strike make the ordinary operations of daily life impossible, for there would be no food in the stores, no police, no functioning banks, no newspapers, no public transport, but it might trigger a financial panic and an avalanche of crime. It might even, pessimists were predicting, bring on a social revolution.

For in Joynson-Hicks's mind, as in the minds of most middle- and upper-class Britons, labor agitation of any kind was linked to political radicalism, which at its most extreme meant Bolshevism. Everyone knew what had happened in Russia only a few years earlier, in 1917, when Czar Nicholas's government had been overturned by Bolshevik revolutionaries who had ultimately executed the czar and his wife and children. The terrors of the Red Menace made frightening reading in the daily papers. And had not R.J. Cook, the miners' spokesman, admitted that he was "a humble follower of Lenin"? What was that if not an admission of Bolshevism?

Unless the miners' strike was settled favorably, and soon, Britain might well go the way of Russia.

Given the labor crisis, the Home Secretary's journey to Bruton Street was little more than a detour in his very full agenda, a pause between crucial negotiating sessions. His presence was required, he would do his duty and attend the birth. But at the earliest possible moment he would be away again, his mind on more pressing matters.

In the room set aside for the Duchess of York's delivery, the surgeon, Sir Henry Simpson, kept watch over his exhausted patient. It had been decided that a normal birth was not possible. The baby was in the breech position and after so many hours of labor, the mother was near the end of her strength. Preparations had been made for a cesarean, a relatively rare and dangerous procedure that carried a high risk of hemorrhage and sepsis. An operating theater had been improvised, and made as hygienic as possible. The duchess's obstetrician, Walter Jagger, stood by and other physicians were available should complications arise.

Elizabeth of York continued to struggle with labor pains, as she had since the previous evening. She was twenty-six, and despite her small stature she was hardy—and did not lack courage, as her doctors had observed. She had shown grit and bravery on safari in Africa two years earlier, when she shot a rhino with her Rigby .275 game rifle and found the outdoor life of sleeping in tents, traveling on rough roads and stalking dangerous game bracing.

And now she was prepared to undergo the ordeal of a cesarean operation, since she wanted her baby very much, having had a miscarriage earlier in her marriage. Specifically, she wanted a daughter. There were too many males in the immediate family; another girl would be welcome.

Judging that further delay would be perilous, the surgeon attended to his task, as the rain poured down in the street outside and the Home Secretary, who had arrived and been made comfortable, waited for the announcement of the birth. Prince Albert, Duke of York, worried about his wife and unborn child, fretted and chain-smoked and tried to soothe his nerves with drink.

At last there came a thin cry from the delivery room. In a few moments the doors were opened, and the news given out. It was a girl, Elizabeth Alexandra Mary. Mother and child were well, though the doctors waited some hours before making a formal announcement to the world, and to the crowd that had gathered outside the house, in the rain, that both mother and baby were out of danger.

A great shout went up along Bruton Street when the word was passed. A girl. A princess. Three cheers for Princess Elizabeth Alexandra Mary! God save the king!

The doorbell at 17 Bruton Street was rung so often in the next twenty-four hours that it broke, and had to be replaced. So many telegrams were delivered, so many sprays of flowers, gifts for the baby, messages of congratulations. Every time a visitor arrived, the crowd cheered.

King George and Queen Mary, who had been awakened at four in the morning with the good news of Princess Elizabeth's birth, came that afternoon from Windsor to greet their granddaughter. The crowd went wild at their approach, police had to make way for them to pass, and for the footman who followed behind them, wearing the blue and red Windsor livery and carrying an immense bouquet of purple lilac and pink carnations.

"Such a relief and joy," the queen wrote in her diary after hearing that her daughter-in-law had been delivered safely. Queen Mary, an intensely shy, private and reserved woman who had had six children herself, belonged to a generation that felt distaste for the mess, immodesty and indignity of childbirth, but she had followed the course of the duchess's pregnancy with much concern and worry. She had looked forward to the baby's arrival, helping to sew the layette, inquiring after the arrangements for a nurse and nanny, satisfying herself that the best medical men were in attendance at the birth.

She was no doubt pleased that the baby had been given her name, Mary, along with that of her mother Elizabeth and that of her great-grandmother, Edward VII's widow Queen Alexandra, who had died at eighty only five months earlier.

Certainly the queen was pleased at the appearance of the tiny princess, "a little darling with lovely complexion and pretty fair hair."[1] Her eyes were large and blue, her skin as white as porcelain. As she grew older she would be an attractive child, maybe even a beautiful one.

Day after day the well-wishers in the street continued to watch the door, hoping for a glimpse of the new baby. But her nurse, the tall, formidable Scot Clara Knight, avoided the onlookers, taking the baby out for walks around Berkeley Square or through St. James's Park via a concealed door at the rear of the house. After two weeks the numbers of those keeping vigil dwindled from a crowd to a cluster, and then to a few hopeful stragglers. The royal drama on Bruton Street was at an end, and the greater drama, the grand spectacle of London caught up in the tumult of a general strike, was just beginning.

TWO

The first of the strikers walked off their jobs at midnight on May 2, and by noon on May 3, 1926, business after business was shutting down. The breweries in Brick Lane and Mile End Road, the Ford plant at Dagenham, the Vickers aircraft works at Erith and Dartford closed their doors, along with chemical factories, metalworks, department stores and pubs. Schools closed, theaters remained dark, buses and the trains of the Underground stopped running and in the great mercantile and shipping enterprises in the City, clerks shut their desks and closed their ledgers. The vast human tide that flowed into work in the morning and ebbed outward to the suburbs at the end of the day ceased. Upward of three million workers were out, including ambulance drivers and firefighters, hospital workers and the electricians who ran the power plants, and it looked as though before long the whole working population would be idle, bringing the entire country to a halt.

But long before that threat could take effect, the government moved to counteract the impact of the strike by calling in troops and tens of thousands of special constables to take over essential services and asking for volunteers to haul foodstuffs and drive trucks, unload ships and operate switchboards. Within days the capital and other major cities were functioning once again. Mail was being delivered and the power plants operated by naval ratings. Brigades of guards took charge of the docks, doing the work of the striking dockworkers. Hyde Park became the hub of an informal food distribution network, with supplies of flour, milk, meat and fish brought in from the countryside and loaded onto volunteer-driven cars and trucks to be delivered throughout the capital. A special daily information sheet put together under the supervision of the Home Secretary took the place of the daily papers.

For the upper classes, the titled ladies who ran canteens and drove wagons, the debutantes who measured out foodstuffs and packed them into trucks, the Cambridge undergraduates and medical students (they quickly acquired the label of "plus-four boys" after the fashionable short pants they liked to wear) who drove buses and Underground trains, the days of pitching in and helping out were a pleasurable diversion, a novel interruption in their lives. Their cheery nonchalance offset the grim, determined faces of the picketers and marchers and helped to lighten the general mood. Had the strike been prolonged, however, the few incidents of violence that occurred might well have grown more frequent and deep resentments could have led to rioting and assaults on people and property.

As it was, precautions had to be taken—troops stationed near picket lines, police guards riding volunteer-driven buses, barbed wire strung across the hoods of trucks to prevent sabotage. Hundreds of strikers were arrested. But after nine days of controlled excitement and upheaval, the Trades Union Congress came to terms, and the strike ended. The miners did not return to work, but the other unions did. Many of their members, as it turned out, had never gone on strike at all, and the widespread fear of social chaos, political extremism and financial panic passed.

Thanksgiving services were held in churches all over Britain, and the hero of the hour was Prime Minister Stanley Baldwin, the unflappable, unhurried Conservative leader, calm to the point of languor, cultivated and invariably civil, who was a symbol of stability with his cherrywood pipe and his overworn, baggy suits. Baldwin was saluted as "the man who led the nation through the crisis," and middle- and upper-class Londoners, by and large, resumed their usual lives, reassured about the future.

Within the working class, however, the pain and humiliation of the unsuccessful strike lingered, evident in the ongoing grievances of the underpaid workers and the blight of chronic unemployment. Every town had its highly visible complement of idle laborers, shabby and dispirited, rousing themselves from time to time to march and sing or distribute pamphlets; in London they massed in Hyde Park, many wearing campaign medals from the Great War pinned to their threadbare jackets, and went on to stand silent in their thousands opposite Buckingham Palace, their presence a rebuke to the nation that could provide them no work.

All the upheaval and dislocation of the first weeks of May passed over the house at 17 Bruton Street like a spring squall, intense at times but no more threatening than a sudden rainstorm bending the stems of the daffodils in Berkeley Square. The center of the household continued to be the newborn princess, "Princess Betty," as the press called her, the object of absorbing interest on the part of her parents and grandparents.

The Duke of York, invariably self-effacing, announced proudly that his only claim to distinction was that he was Princess Elizabeth's father. Queen Mary sent a car to Bruton Street to fetch her infant granddaughter to Buckingham Palace for tea. King George, who usually found children to be a nuisance and who had taken scant interest in his two grandsons, George and Gerald Lascelles, the children of his daughter Mary, was delighted with baby Elizabeth and followed her progress with great attention. And her mother, Elizabeth, Duchess of York, who had wanted a daughter so badly, ordered endless photographs taken of the little princess, for the family and for the large, adoring public that clamored for images of her.

The baby was photographed in her heavy satin and lace christening gown, a gown made for Queen Victoria's firstborn in the 1840s. She was photographed again lying on a fringed satin pillow, on a coverlet with embroidered flowers, her mother gazing down at her lovingly. There were pictures of her at three months or so, when she began to sit up by herself on a sofa, and more pictures when she began to crawl. The newspapers reproduced everything they were given, photographs and written descriptions, calling the baby "Princess of a million hearts," and printing details of her daily life.

Little Elizabeth was a phenomenon, an infant celebrity. Already the papers were beginning to build her into a star, as they had her uncle David, Prince of Wales.

Waiflike, boyish good looks, a lighthearted zest for pleasure, above all devastating charm had made David (christened Prince Edward), George V's oldest son, the darling of the press for years. Physically small, even fragile, he had great appeal to women and men liked him nearly as well for his everyman quality, his nonthreatening manner. Far from demanding respect for his exalted birth, the prince was ingratiatingly modest, wore cloth caps and informal, somewhat zany modern clothes—Fair Isle sweaters were his trademark—and spoke with a slight cockney accent instead of in the clipped tones of a royal.

Ever since his service in the Great War, David had been traveling, to Egypt, Australia, Canada, America, India, Japan, Borneo, and most recently, in 1925, to West and South Africa and South America. Wherever he went he drew enormous crowds, overwhelmingly favorable; he had become the British monarchy's roving ambassador to the world, and especially to the Commonwealth countries.

Vanity Fair summed up the Prince of Wales's banjo-playing, polo playing, steeplechasing appeal by quoting a list of mock statistics: the prince had been proposed to by more than four thousand women, had

had his picture taken nearly three million times, had fallen off his horse twenty-five hundred times, kissed twenty-three hundred blonds, and drunk nearly twenty thousand quarts of champagne.

"Hats off to the indestructible Dancing Drinking Tumbling Kissing Walking Talking and Sleeping—but not Marrying—Idol of the British Empire!" was the magazine's triumphant accolade.

None of George V's three other surviving sons came anywhere near David in popularity. (The king's youngest son John, an epileptic, had been separated from his brothers and sister and had spent most of his short life in isolation, dying at Wolferton in 1919, in his fourteenth year.) All had been overshadowed by their famous brother, but none more so than the king's second son, Prince Albert (always called "Bertie" in the family), Princess Elizabeth's father.

If reporters followed David eagerly, avid for pictures and stories, they shunned Bertie, who though he was tall and handsome and athletic, lacked his famous brother's charisma and had a terrible stammer that not only made communication awkward but acutely embarrassed the prince and everyone around him. Bertie did not photograph well; the camera could not capture his mercurial temperament and was merciless in revealing his everpresent nervousness, the fear in his wide eyes and the tense muscles in his bony face. Slight, diffident, self-effacing, Bertie was elusive, not at all the sort of glamorous, outwardly gregarious character his brother was.

Bertie came by his nervousness honestly, for his childhood and young manhood had been a time of emotional torment. Shy, sensitive, high-strung and lacking his older brother's intellect, Bertie had suffered by comparison to the gifted David, and their father, instead of showing compassion to the younger boy and endeavoring to draw him out, shouted at him and tried to shame him into asserting himself and conquering his fears and his deepgoing feelings of unworthiness.

Having survived a tough childhood himself, and having watched his weaker older brother Eddy falter again and again for lack of grit, George V showed Bertie no mercy and even encouraged his other children to make fun of Bertie for his painful stammer.

"Get it out! Get it out!" George would bellow again and again when Bertie tried in vain to speak coherently, reducing the shaking boy to tears. The terrible scene between father and son was often repeated, deepening Bertie's humiliation and exhausting him in the futile effort to overcome his impediment. By the time he reached his teens he had become permanently overwrought, overemotional, easily frightened and given to violent outbursts. Unpredictable and volatile, Bertie fought with David, or cavorted so exuberantly that he risked injuring himself, or withdrew into dark moods from which nothing could rouse him.

His miserable school career worsened Bertie's suffering without helping him find a way to adapt to the stresses of life. Beaten by the other boys, who called him "Bat Lugs" (Bat Ears), he blundered and stuttered his way along from term to term, bullied, criticized, and largely unenlightened by his years of fruitless study. Bertie followed the successful, popular David through Osborne Naval College and the Royal Naval College at Dartmouth, his grades abysmal and his attitude penitent. Stomach aches and an inability to concentrate made learning nearly impossible, and when, with the outbreak of war in 1914, the prince went aboard the battleship *Collingwood*, his gastric attacks became so acute that he had to be hospitalized.

Depressed over his unfitness for duty, desperate to be useful—for Bertie was always well intentioned and dutiful—he spent much of the war battling illness, having his stomach pumped nightly, slow to recover from repeated attacks of what was eventually diagnosed as a duodenal ulcer. His brief moment of glory came at the Battle of Jutland in 1916, when he courageously fought an oncoming attack from enemy torpedo craft. His reward could not have been more precious: six words from his father, "I am pleased with my son." But soon after Jutland the gastric attacks resumed and an operation was necessary to remove the ulcer.

After the war, Bertie languished, studying fitfully at Cambridge, excelling at tennis and golf but morbidly depressed when he lost matches, full of worries and self-criticism— and always hampered socially by his stammer. From this trough of despair he was rescued, providentially, by falling in love with and marrying the Earl of Strathmore's lovely daughter Elizabeth Bowes-Lyon, whose kindness and solicitous acceptance of him, stammer, shyness, depression and all, brought him a large measure of peace and deep contentment.

Two things brought Bertie even more happiness in 1926, the birth of his daughter and hope that his stammer could be overcome.

In October of that year Bertie met Dr. Lionel Logue, an Australian specialist in treating speech disorders, and began a course of daily therapy. Logue taught the duke to breathe from his diaphragm, to repeat long strings of words ("Let's go gathering heather with the glad brigade of grand dragoons . . .") until he could do so flawlessly, and above all, to relax. Bertie worked hard. Logue called his royal patient "the pluckiest and most determined patient I ever had."[1] Day by day Bertie grew in confidence, until the stammer—"the curse which God has put on me," as Bertie called it—began to recede. Logue noticed that the duke's "tired eyes" were beginning to brighten, and that he spoke (without hesitation) of the great improvement he was making.

He was to need his newfound skill in communicating, for he and the duchess were about to embark on a tour of Australia and New Zealand, where there would be many speeches to be made. The baby would not be going along, even though this would mean a separation of many months between parents and child. Elizabeth was to be left in the care of the ever vigilant Clara Knight, with regular news of her growth and development sent to the duke and duchess while they were abroad.

A visitor to the house on Bruton Street met the duchess and her daughter shortly before the leavetaking. She was Anne Ring, a former member of Queen Mary's household, who had been assigned to put together a book about "Princess Betty's" first years. She found the baby princess sitting on a couch, dressed in a filmy white gown, with her mother kneeling on the floor before her. All had been carefully posed, even the baby's curls (Mrs. Knight had begun curling her fair hair). The visitor saw what she was meant to see, a quiet, well-behaved, angelic infant, a doting mother, evidence of an adoring nurse.

"The baby is always good," Anne Ring

wrote afterward, "she has the sweetest air of complete serenity about her—while we were talking her nurse came in to fetch her, and the duchess threw round her daughter's head, to protect her from draughty passages, a filmy veil of gossamer, from which she looked down out of her nurse's arms smiling angelically at her mother, like a cherub out of a cloud."[2]

The scene was contrived, the words sugary. A more revealing description came from the photographer Lisa Sheridan, who made a spontaneous visit to Princess Elizabeth's nursery when no one was expecting her. She was not there to take pictures, merely to visit a family friend who was a member of the staff.

She found a more authentic domestic scene, a large airy nursery with windows overlooking the trees in the park, a warm fire in the grate, Clara Knight sitting in a rocking chair beside the hearth, knitting, the baby's smocks airing and warming on a clothes-horse nearby.

Little Elizabeth, wearing everyday clothes and not dressed, as she had been for Anne Ring, like a "white fluff of thistledown," was crawling across the floor, her small red slippers rubbed white at the toes from constant scraping across the carpet. She stopped to stare at the visitor, and kept her attention on Lisa even after she continued to make her way across the floor and attempted to stand, all the while clutching a large teddy bear.[3]

The nurse kept on knitting and rocking until the baby crawled over to the toy cupboard and managed to open the cupboard door. Then she put down her work and went over to the princess.

"One at a time," she said in a firm voice, helping Elizabeth put her teddy bear in its place before taking a truck from another shelf.

When Lisa left the room, the baby sat back to watch, with a "direct gaze." Clara Knight told her to wave goodbye, and she did.

Independence, venturesomeness, the encountering of firm limits, compliance: a common, and not unhealthy, cycle of behavior in a young child. Yet the baby with the direct gaze and the worn-toed shoes was in fact watchfully controlled, her independence curbed. She would never be allowed to venture far, and as she grew, the limits placed upon her, and her willingness to comply with them, would determine the course of her life.

THREE

Stinging winds carrying shards of icy snow gusted along the river valleys of Northamptonshire in the fall of 1928, shaking the branches of the old elms and forcing sheep to huddle tightly together in the lee of the low walls of fawn-colored stone. Horsemen milled in clusters under the gray sky, waiting for the hunt to begin, hounds ran excitedly here and there, tails up, noses sniffing the wet earth. Flocks of bright yellowhammers dipped and rose over the fallow plowland and pasture, flying low over the green hedgerows to lose themselves in the dense spinneys flanking the dull gray river.

Elizabeth was taken to the site of the

gathering hunt and carried amid the noise and chaos, her eyes alight with excitement as she watched the hounds. Bertie had leased Naseby Hall for the hunting season, and Lilliebeth (or sometimes Tillabet), as she had begun to call herself, loved to run each morning to the stables to pat the horses.

At two and a half she was an agile, graceful child, with her father's fleetness of foot. Winston Churchill, who had met the princess for the first time at Balmoral the previous month, told his wife that she was a "character." "She has an air of authority and reflectiveness astonishing in an infant," he said, and he might have added that she was voluble and extroverted as well.[1] At one gathering of four hundred tenants on the royal estate at Sandringham, toddler Lilliebeth had stood on the dinner table and talked on and on, throwing crackers toward the diners, as she did to the ducks in the park in London, and watching to see whether they ate them.

Bertie was convinced that his daughter had inherited her great-great-grandmother Queen Victoria's pronounced individuality, if not her stern demeanor (Bertie had been terrified of the late queen). "From the first moment of talking," the duke told Osbert Sitwell in an interview, "she showed so much character that it was impossible not to wonder that history would not repeat itself."[2] Like Victoria, Lilliebeth had a "clear ringing voice" and a decided manner, a bright-faced intelligence and strong opinions.

One afternoon at tea-time the princess came into a room and announced to the assembled guests, "You can't think how naughty I've been. Oh, *so* naughty, you don't know."

"Well then tell me," said her grandmother, "and I shall know."

"No," she replied, and would not elaborate.[3]

As a young child Queen Victoria, with her German governess Baroness Lehzen, had made hundreds of dolls, each named and dressed distinctively. Lilliebeth had adopted her mother's personal maid Katta as her preferred companion, and she and Katta maneuvered a pair of dancing dolls to do the Charleston, the Black Bottom and the Lindy Hop—all the dances the duke and duchess liked to do when they went out together.[4]

And like her great-great-grandmother, Lilliebeth loved dogs. Victoria had always had a menagerie of canines, and had worked for the welfare of what she called "our friends the dogs." Lilliebeth loved Glen, the family retriever, and the other labradors, and Choo-Choo, the tiny Tibetan lion-dog that belonged to her grandmother Strathmore. And now she had the hounds of the Pytchley Hunt to admire and befriend.

For weeks she reveled in the companionship of the animals, watching the dogs chasing across the open fields, the powerful hunters jumping the stone fences, and later being taken to the stables and the kennels to observe the grooming, feeding and watering of the horses and hounds. The cold weather did not deter her, any more than it did her father, who took his sport seriously.

Early in November, however, a message came from the palace that the king was ill, and the family returned to London.

George V was suffering from a septic abscess in his chest, and only his strong constitution and curmudgeonly defiance saved him from dying. For a week in December he lay unconscious, his strength ebbing, while a dozen doctors hovered over him. After one of his ribs was removed and the abscess was drained, he began a slow recuperation.

Bad-tempered and impatient, cursing his doctors and refusing to take the medicine they prescribed, the king went to the seaside manor of Craigweil near Bognor, overlooking the Channel, to begin his recovery. And he asked for his granddaughter to join him there.

"I had a party at Bognor," the princess told her mother later on, "and I made sand pies!"[5] For several months she made sand pies and apple cakes on the chilly beach at Bognor with Queen Mary, while the king, whose dark moods she helped to lighten, looked on. During his daily outings in his bath-chair little Lilliebeth walked along beside her grandfather, talking to him, doing her animal imitations (she had learned to bark like a sea-lion), making him smile and laugh.[6] Her vocabulary was growing. She had begun saying "My goodness!" much to her mother's dismay; King George not only didn't mind, he was amused.

"G. delighted to see her," Queen Mary wrote in her diary. When he was well enough, the king got down on all fours with Lilliebeth and pretended to be her horse, while she pulled him along by the beard. It was a game they had played often enough in the past, but at Bognor it gave him particular pleasure.

It may have been during this stay at the seaside that King George began calling his granddaughter Lilibet, his version of Lilliebeth, which was to be her family nickname from then on.

As he improved, the king began to be capable, for short periods of time, of dealing with ministers and attending to public business—and of overseeing, from a distance, the wellbeing of his beloved horses. King George was a knowledgeable owner and breeder whose two best racehorses, in 1929, were the bay filly Scuttle and the swift Limelight. Another promising colt, Glastonbury, had narrowly missed winning a major race, rousing the king's ire; Lilibet must have heard him say something much stronger than "my goodness" when he received the news.

He had taken Lilibet to see his horses at Sandringham many times, and knew how engrossed she was in their care, their silky feel, their look and smell, the sound of their clopping hooves and of their snorts and neighs and whinnies. From earliest childhood she had stood at the window of her parents' London house, looking out at the street below, where horse-drawn traffic mingled with cars. She had admired the well-trained mounts of the police, the strong, shaggy cart-horses, the fine, high-stepping horses of the Life Guards as they rode down Constitution Hill. She adored ponies and liked to pat them and feed them carrots.

Not until her fourth birthday, however, did Lilibet receive a pony of her own.[7] By the time she turned four years old, Lilibet was an international celebrity. *Time* had profiled her at three, and put her on its cover. Photographs of her appeared at regular intervals in publications throughout Europe, the United States and the Commonwealth. Sightseers gathered to catch sight of her when Clara Knight took her out in the afternoon, the spectators becoming so numerous and so bothersome that Mrs. Knight began going all the way to Regents Park in hopes of avoiding them.

On the day of Lilibet's fourth birthday, which she spent at Windsor, people began massing outside the castle gates early in the morning. When the band of the Scots Guards began to play, and the princess appeared, returning the waves of her eager public, the crowd surged forward and the soldier guarding the gates was knocked down.

The princess took the adulation in stride. She was accustomed to noise and applause, to being stared at and photographed. She was aware that children in faraway places knew of her and wanted to contact her. Letters and gifts came from Australia, South Africa, Canada, America. Requests for photographs, birthday congratulations, notes full of personal stories were delivered by the hundreds.

But the best thing to happen by far was that her grandfather presented her with Peggy, a Shetland pony. Seated on Peggy's broad back Lilibet had her first riding lessons, from her parents, from the Crown

Equerry, and then, at Windsor, from the stud groom Owen, who became her hero. From Owen she learned how to hold her seat, grip her mount with her legs, and post. Also how to adjust her saddle girth, how to groom Peggy and massage her after her exercise, and how to watch for galls on Peggy's back or belly from too much friction.

It became a family joke that Owen was all-wise. When Lilibet asked her father about anything, he would say, "Don't ask me, ask Owen. Who am I to make suggestions?"

Horses now became the center of Lilibet's life, the object of her play, the focus of her preoccupations. Her mother had taught her to read, and she read books about horses, and looked through catalogs for more books about them. She rode with Owen, and when not riding, she stood at the window and watched the horses in the road; when with her royal grandfather she asked about his horses, and went to visit his stables.

When Marion Crawford, the new governess chosen by the Duchess of York, met Lilibet for the first time in the spring of 1932, the princess was engrossed in a favorite game: pretending to drive her team of horses around the park.

"A small figure with a mop of curls sat up in bed," the new governess remembered. "She wore a nightie with a design of small pink roses on it. She had tied the cords of her dressing gown to the knobs of the old-fashioned bed, and was busy driving her team."

Clara Knight brought the visitor into the bedroom, and announced her formally.

"How do you do?" said Lilibet, giving the governess "a long, comprehensive look." Then she asked, "Why have you no hair?"

Miss Crawford pulled off her hat, revealing her short haircut, the fashionable cut of the twenties, now slightly out of date. "I have enough to go on with," she said. "It's an Eton crop."

Lilibet picked up her cords again.

"Do you usually drive in bed?" the governess asked.

"I mostly go once or twice around the park before I go to sleep, you know. It exercises my horses." She went on driving, bending over in an imaginary turn.

"Are you going to stay with us?" Lilibet asked.

"For a little while anyway."

Mrs. Knight interrupted the conversation by unhitching the imaginary horses, and put Lilibet under the covers.[8] The interview was over.

When Marion Crawford, who soon became known by her nickname of Crawfie, met Lilibet, she was no longer an only child. A sister, Margaret Rose, had been born in August of 1930, when Lilibet was four. Margaret was a disappointment; the Yorks had wanted a boy. But a son might come eventually, and in the meantime, both girls needed a governess.

That the Duchess of York chose Marion Crawford, when she might have chosen any number of other eligible women to guide and educate her daughters—for she had decided to have them educated at home, as she herself had been—was revealing. Crawfie, though outwardly a brisk, forward-thinking young woman of twenty-two, a graduate of Moray House Training College and with a broad concern for child welfare and child psychology, was in fact a sketchily-educated, small-town girl, provincial in her views, limited in her reading and exposure to higher culture. She knew nothing of intellectual rigor or scholarship, and very little about pedagogy.

Crawfie was chosen, like Golly (Mrs. Macdonald) the cook and Margaret and Ruby Macdonald, sisters who became maids to Lilibet and Margaret Rose, and a number of other servants, because she was a Scot, the product of a venerable yet narrow, and in some ways archaic culture that put a high premium on decency and morality, as the duchess herself did. Her smattering of education aside, Crawfie was a strong, vigorous young woman, healthy, robust and cheerful, accustomed to walking many miles a day and with a direct, no-nonsense approach to life. Not for her the complexities of contemporary childrearing theories, or the dark hints and suggestions of Freud—or the depressive, morally equivocal, erotically charged vagaries of modern literature and art.

In putting her children in Crawfie's hands the duchess was taking her stand against what to her, and to many others, were the disturbing current trends: female emancipation, loud jazz and loose behavior, bo-

hemian attitudes (pacifism, atheism, intellectual rebellion), froth and fun and the delicious, heady wickedness of intoxication
and drug-taking and sexual experimenta-
tion. That the duchess associated learning
with sophistication, and sophistication with
moral decline, was unfortunate, if under-
standable, given her own limited education;
beyond this, the prevailing attitude was that
girls needed far less learning than boys,
since they were destined for marriage and
homemaking—or, in the case of Lilibet and
Margaret Rose, for marriage and lives of
aristocratic service to good causes.

The playhouse built by Welsh carpenters
and thatchers for the princesses on the
grounds of Royal Lodge, the Yorks' weekend house on the grounds at Windsor, em-
bodied the duchess's twin goals for her girls
of domesticity and service. It was called "Y
Bwthyn Bach," or "The Little Thatched
House," and was built to a child's scale, so
that adults had to kneel down to go from
room to room.

The little house was a charming, fully
equipped cottage, with electricity and
working plumbing and curtains of blue
chintz. Miniature cans filled the pantry,

miniature china plates and cups were in the cupboards. Small teakettles, soup pots and saucepans hung from the kitchen walls and towels and linens, embroidered with the initial "E" and a crown, were folded in the linen closet.

Lilibet was encouraged to keep the little house tidy, and she diligently swept the floors and wrapped the silver in newspaper to prevent it from getting tarnished, just as she groomed her toy horses and pretended to feed them. Caretaking and protecting came naturally to her, and because she was praised for these impulses, they were reinforced.

Preparation for domesticity was one pillar of the Duchess of York's childrearing philosophy; another was avoidance of materialism, an almost spartan aversion to displays of wealth. The Yorks lived amid gracious surroundings, but there was no luxurious excess, only upper-middle-class comfort and plenty. Lilibet did have her own pony, to be sure, and gifts in abundance were delivered to the Yorks' residences for both children at Christmas and birthdays. But most of these gifts were returned, or sent to hospitals and orphanages. As for the gifts the family gave one another, they tended to be simple—toy horses and horse books for Lilibet, small silver bracelets or brooches, story books and games. Lilibet was given one shilling a week for pocket money, and she saved most of it, setting aside some of what remained for buying inexpensive Christmas gifts at Woolworth's.[9]

Apart from necklaces of coral and pearls, Lilibet and her sister had no valuable jewelry, and were dressed, always exactly alike, in simple flowered cotton dresses, usually blue, with plain tweed coats, berets and sturdy shoes. When neighbors gave children's parties, Lilibet and Margaret Rose were dressed up in starched pink and blue organdy dresses with bows and rows of lace—much to Clara Knight's satisfaction, for she thought they were dressed far too simply for their status—but such finery was rarely worn.[10]

As with clothing, so with food. Having been raised on a healthy diet of fish and game, fresh vegetables, oat cakes and fruit tarts, the duchess wanted her daughters to be given wholesome food and not tempted with rich fare or cake and candy. Margaret Macdonald ("Bobo" to the children) did make her special fudge from time to time, and the girls treasured it and hoarded it. But for the most part they ate sensibly, and Margaret cut her teeth on hard rusks baked from a particular kind of brown bread the duchess ordered from a bakery in Welwyn Garden City.[11]

The princesses' companionship was as carefully restricted as their education, diet and wardrobes. At age two Lilibet had had a friend, an older boy named Sandy, who came to tea amid great excitement. Then when she was older there was Sonia Graham-Hodgson, daughter of a radiologist, who lived nearby. Sonia was, Crawfie thought, "the only young girl Lilibet ever appeared to rather single out for herself and feel drawn to." But eventually Sonia was sent away to school and the friendship languished.

Cousins Patricia Mountbatten and Margaret Elphinstone came to parties, as did George and Gerald Lascelles and the children of the Yorks' friends. But these encounters were formal and artificial, carefully planned by the adults. Casual acquaintanceships with other children were discouraged—indeed prevented—with the result that, to Lilibet, children outside the social circle of her family and friends were an intriguing mystery.

"Other children always had an enormous fascination, like mystic beings from a different world," Crawfie wrote. Lilibet and Margaret Rose smiled shyly at them, and would have liked to speak to them, but were kept away.

A certain amount of isolation was perhaps inevitable, given Lilibet's celebrity. When she arrived at a children's party, she immediately caused a stir among the nannies and governesses present, for they regarded her as they might a movie star or a well-known flyer or cricketer. The children were well aware of this response, and it made them keep a certain distance.

"She wasn't just another child of friends of my parents," Patricia Mountbatten remembered of Lilibet at the age of five or six. "She created a little flutter."[12]

In Madame Tussaud's wax museum Lilibet, riding a pony, was represented lifesize. Candy boxes carried her picture. Children sang songs written to the princess, or about her, and books were written about her. Reporters and photographers were allowed to watch her play, and take pictures of her, from time to time. She bore an aura of fame, a hint of glamour, which in addition to the fact of her royal birth, set her apart. Her natural reserve and self-contained manner, her undemonstrative exterior, did not encourage close friendships in any case.[13]

Outwardly obedient most of the time, Lilibet had an explosive temper and her personality held an undercurrent of imperious self-regard. Every now and then she abandoned her generally protective attitude toward the much younger Margaret Rose and lashed out at her with what Crawfie called a quick "left hook."[14] After arguing with her French tutor, whom she disliked, Lilibet, "rebelling all of a sudden, and goaded by boredom to violent measures, picked up the big ornamental silver inkpot and placed it without any warning upside down on her own head. She sat there, with ink trickling down her face," while the French tutor, "shattered and transfixed with horror," hurriedly left the room.[15]

Such violent displays of temperament were rare, but barbed comment and pointed remarks arising from a marked self-centeredness were not. Bored at a tea with her mother and a woman friend, Lilibet rang for a footman and announced, "Kindly ring for a taxi. Our guest is leaving." When the Lord Chamberlain met Lilibet in a hallway and said "Good morning, little lady," she shot back, "I'm not a little lady, I'm Princess Elizabeth." She commented rudely on people's ugly names, or ugly faces. Even historical figures came in for attack.

"Who is that funny old man with the beaky nose?" Lilibet asked her grandfather George V when confronted with a painting of Wellington at Waterloo.

"Well, he IS ugly, anyhow!" she insisted when told the funny old man was the Iron Duke.[16]

Often sympathetic and aware of others' needs and comfort, Lilibet nonetheless had a cool, observant side. When her mother's moody, occasionally malevolent corgi, Dookie, bit Lord Lothian's hand, the princess stood by watching, commenting that he was bleeding all over the floor.[17]

When Lilibet showed coldness, hauteur or impudence she was rebuked, or occasionally punished, most often by the firm Queen Mary, but the Yorks were lenient with both their children. Consequently Lilibet, as she grew older, showed more and more of what Crawfie called "her own particularly determined and final manner," and her isolation increased.[18]

By the early 1930s, Britons were caught up in the Great Depression that followed the Wall Street crash of 1929. Unemployment, which had been high throughout the 1920s, reached ever more alarming levels. Nearly three million were out of work—as many people as had gone on strike in 1926—and the industrial regions were completely idle. Hunger marchers converged on the capital, miners, dockers, factory workers, laborers, carrying their few possessions on their backs and living on scraps made into stew. With one in five out of work, and global demand for British products at an all-time low, extreme measures were called for. Protectionism replaced free trade, price fixing was introduced, and, most radical of all, the gold standard was abandoned and the pound, for centuries a stable currency, began to fall in value.

With the economy disintegrating, and the number of defaults and bankruptcies rising, the Labour prime minister, Ramsay MacDonald, resigned and at the king's request a

National government, a coalition of Labour, Conservative and Liberal leaders, was formed. The National government was voted into office in October of 1931, with the economy in ruins and the harsh chill of winter just ahead.

Memories of the general strike were still strong. Resentment against the wealthy rankled, and once again there was talk of a need to redistribute resources more equitably. Inevitably, there was talk of discarding the monarchy, as the crowns of Russia, Germany and Austria had been discarded, or of greatly reducing the expensive pomp and inflated budget associated with the royal family. Workers on government assistance were struggling to support families on fifteen shillings a week, while among the privileged classes, thousands of pounds were spent on mansions with large staffs of servants, garages with dozens of cars and stables with countless valuable horses.

The London home of the Duke and Duchess of York from 1927 on, 145 Piccadilly, was such a mansion, a five-story house of Portland stone with stone steps leading to the front door and a terrace at the back, ornamented with blooming blue hydrangea, overlooking Hamilton Gardens and Hyde Park. Apsley House, Wellington's former home at Hyde Park Corner, was nearby. A large staff maintained the twenty-five bedrooms, reception rooms, ballroom, library and conservatory, kitchens and storage rooms. There were gardeners to trim the weeping willows and maintain the gravel paths, a chauffeur to drive and maintain the Daimlers and Rolls-Royces, a clock-winder, a rat and mole man and a night watchman.

A visitor to 145 Piccadilly stepped into a large, dim entrance hall dominated by two enormous elephant tusks hung on the wall and a statue of an African servant in ornate livery. Pots of flowering geraniums filled the windowsills, the windows framed by lace curtains. A large painting of galloping horses had a caption: "Horses of the Duke of York, 1770."[19]

On the terrace, Lilibet and her mother were feeding ducklings that had wandered in from Hyde Park, oblivious to the row of gawkers who stood watching them through the railings, and of Dookie, who was barking loudly at the onlookers.

The visitor, Lisa Sheridan, watched Lilibet

lift Dookie into her arms and carry him to a garden seat, murmuring into his ear and rubbing her cheek against him. She closed her eyes, and soon Dookie, pacified, closed his. "Their heads were close together and they had quite forgotten everything but their own delicious mutual sentimentality," Sheridan remembered. The tiny ducklings wandered off, the gawkers eventually dispersed, until there was no one in the quiet garden but the observer, the princess and her beloved dog.

FOUR

When the wild geese were on the river, and the forests blazed with gold and scarlet, then Lilibet's grandfather Strathmore would ride his pony into the woods around Glamis and begin to prune the trees. He took one of the keepers with him, and the two men chatted about the migrating birds and the size and color of the berries, the length of the dogs' winter coats and whether the coming winter would be mild or severe. Rural matters preoccupied the elderly Earl of Strathmore, who unlike Lilibet's other grandfather George V was a gentle, soft-spoken countryman, mildly eccentric in his habits and so well versed in the lore of the seasons and the plants and beasts that he almost seemed like a forest creature himself—albeit a forest creature who often carried a cricket bat and was a shrewd—some said ruthless—businessman.

Lilibet, Margaret Rose and Crawfie went walking in the afternoons during the family's autumn visits to Glamis. On their way to Glamis Station to watch for the passing of the Aberdeen Fish Express, they often came across the earl and the keeper sawing off dead branches and felling diseased trees. Besides going for long walks there was little else to do, other than drive to Cortachy or take a picnic lunch to Lumley Den with its carpet of bluebells or search through the old wooden chests in the castle storerooms for gowns and hats worn by Strathmore ancestors and play dress-up.

The long weeks spent at Glamis each August and September were restful, far from the traffic and crowds of London. Lilibet thrived in the bracing air and learned to observe the natural world, the patterns of sky and clouds, the signs of the season's turning, the techniques of grouse-hunting and duck shooting.

She had a strong attachment to Glamis,

and to her grandfather in particular. She liked to sit beside him while he made his cocoa for breakfast, to share the "shooting pudding" he always had with his lunch, to watch him carefully divide his long moustache and brush it back. She enjoyed his subtle humor and responded with affection when he kissed her on the cheek, his whiskers tickling her neck.

The castle itself, with its turrets and towers, its long dim corridors and labyrinth of rooms, was an enduring source of fascination. In the Blue Room, where Grandmother Strathmore presided over tea, large paintings of racehorses surrounded the family. In the banqueting hall, according to (untrustworthy) legend, Macbeth had killed Duncan. Curiosities of all sorts loomed up out of the shadows—the frighteningly tall stuffed bear that stood in the hall, suits of armor, antique machinery and engines of torture.

The Strathmore inheritance was rich in the occult. At least one of Elizabeth of York's brothers was said to be gifted with second sight, having had a vision of his wounded brother, alive and safe, when the latter had been given up for dead during the Great War. Witches were to be found among the Strathmore ancestors. Ghosts were said to haunt the castle: the White Lady, the smiling Gray Lady, Jack the Runner, Old Beardie. One of Elizabeth of York's brothers-in-law swore that he had been tossed out of bed by a disembodied spirit. The legend of the Beast of Glamis, a genetic anomaly of some sort—perhaps a hydrocephalic child—persisted, entering the family mythology. Whatever the basis of these fanciful tales, they seemed to gather substance at night, when the creaks and groans of the ancient walls and the shrieking of the wind made an unholy din that led the imagination in supernatural directions.

After spending the autumn at Glamis, with a trip to Balmoral or nearby Birkhall for the shooting, the Yorks went back to London until Christmas, when the family joined King George and Queen Mary at Sandringham. Easter was spent at Windsor, some birthdays and holidays at St. Paul's Waldenbury, the Strathmores' estate in Hertfordshire, with its lime walk and extensive gardens, beech woods, meadows and expanse of parkland where cattle grazed.

For the most part, however, Lilibet spent her childhood at 145 Piccadilly and at Royal

Lodge, the family estate on the Windsor grounds, which became their weekend retreat. Set in behind tall old oaks and massive elms, the pink Regency-era house with its balustrades and terraces was bright and airy inside, and kept full of flowers, but it was the grounds and gardens which made it unique. Although the house was only a little over a mile from Windsor Castle and the town adjoining it, it had the feel of a country manor, with tall cedars, acres of garden, and a copse of silver birches, the leaves of the slender trees tremulous and glimmering in the sunlight. Beside the jasmine and forsythia, the roses and hyacinths in the formal beds, there was a rock garden with a stream, and a separate flower garden cultivated by Lilibet and Margaret Rose. Blue budgerigars chirped in an outdoor cage that Lilibet herself kept clean, at least on weekends, and bowls of water and food were put out to attract wild birds, so that the garden was full of calls and whistles, trills and bursts of piercing song.

One of the Duke of York's interests was horticulture, he had made a study of plants and had a flair for landscaping. At Royal Lodge, whose grounds were overrun with weeds when the family first moved in, he mandated that Sunday afternoons be turned over to the work of clearing out and preparing beds for new plantings. Not only the family but the staff—Crawfie, the chauffeur, the butler, even the house detective— put on their oldest tweeds and gloves and worked alongside Bertie in uprooting and pulling out dead trees and shrubs, creepers and trailing brambles.

Bertie, according to Crawfie, was "an absolute slave driver, hacking, sawing, pulling out dead wood, heaping up bonfires."[1] He had a collection of razor-sharp tree-cutting implements, and slashed away right and left, worrying his wife.

"Darling?" she remembered the duchess saying, "Darling, do mind . . . Lilibet, get out of the way . . . Margaret, for goodness's sake, look where you are going."[2]

All the strenuous activity produced, over time, a beautiful gardenscape, banks of blooming shrubs, masses of annuals, the whole overbowered by tall cedars and bounded by the copse of silver birches where Lilibet, as a child, liked to lie in the dappled sunlight and muse and dream.[3]

Lilibet was, according to Crawfie, "an immensely interesting child to teach, with a high IQ," "quick at picking things up, and one never had to do a lot of explaining to her."4 Even if one allows for a certain amount of exaggeration in the governess's praise, it seems clear from this and other evidence that the princess possessed not only a quick intelligence but a searching curiosity. She was drawn to reading at a very early age, and she not only collected books about horses but pored over them, time and again, until she absorbed their contents. By the time she reached ten or twelve she knew the various breeds well enough to identify all the horses in the Windsor Horse Show flawlessly, and could judge each one for color, body shape and temperament, just as professional judges did.

But Lilibet's quick mind was not fed adequately in the schoolroom. In theory, mornings were devoted to lessons, but as both princesses began the day playing in their parents' bedroom, sometimes until ten o'clock, and took a break for "Elevenses," and rested from noon to one in the afternoon, the brief lessons in arithmetic, history, grammar and geography were squeezed into a scant hour or at most two. In the af-

ternoons, there was dancing class or singing class at Lady Cavendish's house in
Prince's Gate, long walks, piano lessons or
drawing lessons—or, on occasion, an outing with Queen Mary to a museum or historic site.[5] Cooking lessons with Golly in the
semi-basement kitchen of 145 Piccadilly
were long-drawn-out affairs, with the girls
learning to make scones and cakes, their
arms covered in flour, and cleaning up the
kitchen afterward. The scones and cakes
were eaten at tea-time in Golly's sitting
room.[6]

Queen Mary, whose own childhood had
been rich in exposure to higher culture, and
who had lived for a time in Florence, was
dismayed at the sparse intellectual nurture
Lilibet and her sister were receiving, and
wrote to Crawfie suggesting revisions in the
curriculum. She also advised the Duchess
of York to enlarge her daughters' exposure
to ideas, literature and fine art, and to make
sure they were equipped to speak and write
fluently and, if possible, knowledgeably,
about a large range of subjects. But her
daughter-in-law was nonplussed. After all,
the role of education for girls was to prepare them for marriage, and surely a com-

petent governess could manage that. So the curriculum, with minor modifications, remained in place. As a result, Lilibet emerged from childhood undereducated, her quick mind scantily furnished—except in the lore of horses.

She was growing up in turbulent times. Britain was undergoing economic catastrophe and the political landscape of Europe was darkening, with the emergence of a belligerent Italy and Germany. Elizabeth of York did her best to insulate her family from the stark economic realities and growing political threats, cocooning them in restricted lives lived in fortress-like mansions amid sunny gardens. But as the thirties went on, her efforts became more and more futile, until it became impossible to protect the sunlit garden, and those in it, from the oncoming political and personal storms.

One storm in particular was beginning to swirl around the family's epicenter, the heir to the throne, the charming, much-celebrated Prince of Wales.

David turned forty in 1934, still unmarried, still resoundingly popular, despite his highly visible playboy life. But a change had come over him, his boyish charm had cur-

dled, he had become a hardened volup-
tuary—or so it seemed to those among his
entourage who watched, in horror, as he ignored a summons to his seriously ill father's
bedside in the winter of 1928 in order to
pursue a passing seduction while out of the
country. George V might well have died,
and David would have entered into his royal
inheritance and become king—yet instead
of acknowledging the gravity of his father's
illness and facing his responsibilities, he
chose to disregard the entire situation.

The prince's errant reaction may have
stemmed as much from fear as from negli-
gence, or from a simple preference for dissipation. For beneath his surpassing charm,
David had always been ill at ease in his role,
just as he was ill at ease in his personal life,
particularly with women. Louche, seductive,
avid for pleasure, where emotional intimacy
was concerned David remained constrained. He preferred the company of
older, married women, who made few or no
demands on him. That he would have to
marry in time was understood, and from
time to time princesses from Protestant
royal houses were suggested to him. But instead of choosing one of these appropriate

women, and settling down, the prince pursued his bachelor life, moving into his chosen retreat, Fort Belvedere, in Windsor Great Park, with his wild, handsome younger brother George.

In the fall of 1934 two surprising developments took place. George, the most adventurous and abandoned in his private life of all the royal brothers, was about to get married—to his cousin Marina of Greece, the exotically beautiful daughter of Prince Nicholas, a princess first proposed as a bride for David. And David, who had always kept his emotional distance from his lovers, had fallen deeply in love.

Eight-year-old Lilibet was a bridesmaid in the stylish wedding of Uncle George and Aunt Marina at the end of November. Enormous crowds for whom the royal wedding provided a welcome distraction from severe hard times gathered to cheer the bride and groom—and the king and queen. But both King George and Queen Mary, while gratified by the public approbation, were themselves distracted by a worrisome scene that had taken place two nights earlier.

At a state reception at the palace, David had appeared with two friends, Wallis and

Ernest Simpson—guests whom Queen Mary had specifically ordered removed from the official list of invitees. Ernest Simpson was an Anglo-American businessman, Wallis his Baltimore-born, brashly American wife, who on this night wore an almost theatrically stunning violet gown with a green sash, and drew much attention.

To the king and queen's consternation, David brought Wallis over to them and introduced her.

She was much as they had been led to expect: animated, shallow, chic. Her genuine charm eluded them, her lively talk grated on them. Seen through their eyes, she was vulgar. She wore too much makeup, her clothes were loud, her manner overly forward. And she displayed entirely too much fondness for David, and he for her.

Their evident attachment was worrisome, not only because of Mrs. Simpson's lack of refinement and cultivation, but because it was being said that, having already divorced her first husband, she was about to divorce Ernest Simpson.

In 1934 divorce, though it had become more and more common in the years following the Great War—the divorce rate in

England having multiplied fivefold—was still a deeply shameful state, divorce itself an unmentionable topic in royal circles. Divorced persons were not allowed at court; respectable people shunned them, though this social stigma was slowly beginning to fade. (King George found the restriction irritating when he wanted to meet Edith Day, the star of his favorite show, "Rose Marie." Edith could not be presented at court because she was divorced.)

This, and many other troubling thoughts, ate away at the aging king's always fragile composure as he celebrated his Silver Jubilee in 1935. He was worried about the worldwide depression and the belligerence of Mussolini and Hitler. ("I will not have another war," he insisted, his once-booming voice now weak and quavering. "I will not.") He fretted over David's waywardness, over the vulgar American woman, over the future. He knew, in his seventieth year, that he would not be able to reign much longer. His health was failing, his ability to grasp detail and carry out his duties as king diminishing.

Day after day he rode through the streets in an open landau, taking a different route each time in order to let all of London see

him, and not avoiding the dirty, over-
crowded slums where his ragged subjects
gathered to cheer him. Night after night
there were grand dinners, receptions and
parties at which the Prime Ministers of the
Dominions, princes from India, heads of
state from Africa and Arabia joined with dignitaries and aristocrats and government officials.

Lilibet was very much a part of the celebration. A special Jubilee stamp bore her
picture, she stood in a prominent place in
the Thanksgiving service at St. Paul's, and
she often rode in the royal carriage beside
her grandfather on his London progresses,
waving to the crowds and smiling. She saw
that the king was frail, his habitual vigor
much diminished and his gruff manner, if
not his irritable temper, receding. He was no
longer able to sail or shoot, and though he
still played with Lilibet and Margaret Rose,
it was only for a few minutes at a time. With
Lilibet he had a system of communication
worked out; at a prearranged time she
stood waving at the window of 145 Piccadilly, and from across the park at the
palace, he watched for her through his
binoculars.

By Christmas, 1935, the king could no longer ride at all, needed oxygen to help him breathe and was almost too weak to eat. The entire family was gathered at Sandringham, their holiday overshadowed by King George's very evident decline. Lilibet watched her grandfather sadly, and left reluctantly in mid-January, aware that she might never see him again. On January 20, 1936, he died, his physician giving him drugs in his final hours to ensure that his death could be announced in the morning, rather than the evening, newspapers.

Lilibet, white and shaken, went to the lying-in-state in the huge, echoing vault of Westminster Hall. She stood, a small, slender figure in her black coat and black beret, watching as the long file of mourners passed the coffin on its raised dais surrounded by masses of flowers. Her father, her uncles George and Henry, and her Uncle David—now King Edward VIII—stood unmoving at the four corners of the coffin, their rifles reversed, forming a guard of honor for their late father.

"Uncle David was there," Lilibet told her governess afterward, "and he never moved at all, Crawfie. Not even an eyelid. It was wonderful. And everyone was so quiet. As if the king were asleep."[7]

She was overawed by the dignified spectacle, and by the sight, in the following days, of the funeral procession, the coffin resting on the gun carriage, surmounted by the imperial crown. Weeping crowds watched the late king pass by, the mournful "Dead March" played again and again by a military band. "From time to time I felt anxious about Lilibet," Crawfie wrote, "for she was very white."[8]

She watched as Uncle David followed the gun carriage on foot, looking, many thought, very worried. She had seen little of him in the past two years. Once he had been perhaps the most frequent visitor to 145 Piccadilly, walking over from his house nearby to join the Yorks for tea and staying on to play Snap and Happy Families with his nieces or to read to them from *Winnie-the-Pooh* or *When We Were Very Young*.[9] But in the past two years his visits had become fewer and fewer. And when he did appear, he seemed different, no longer carefree but drawn and distracted, restless and so preoccupied that when he made plans to go out with his nieces, he was apt to forget that he had made them, and disappear again.[10]

Tension began to rise at 145 Piccadilly and at Royal Lodge. The Duchess of York was frequently ill or upset, Bertie nervous about the international situation—Germany reoccupied the Rhineland in March, 1936, an action which seemed at first to threaten war—and about his brother's unkingly attitudes and behavior. David ignored protocol, neglected business and spent a great deal of time away from the palace at Fort Belvedere, where he attacked the untidy shrubbery with a machete and dug up tree stumps. Eschewing formality, he walked rather than rode in a chauffeured car, continued to see his déclassé London friends as well as his aristocratic ones, did not attend church despite his being, as monarch, head of the Church of England, and made ill-judged, politically opinionated remarks at dinner parties. His pro-Hitler bias caused much negative comment, along with some approval. But beyond all this, the new king saw Wallis every evening and spent every weekend with her, and his intimacy with her, well known to officialdom and high society, became the most absorbing topic of conversation and focus of interest.[11]

"David is besotted," his brother George announced. "One can't get a word of sense out of him." Wallis had begun to wear a ring with an immense emerald, David's gift; some saw in it a sort of engagement ring, a pledge for the future, though she was still married to Ernest Simpson.

When David brought Wallis to tea at Royal Lodge, the general discomfort was felt by all, including Crawfie. Wallis's offhand friendliness, her way of speaking to David, as if she owned him, her suggestions to improve the grounds—suggestions made as if she would one day own Royal Lodge as well—created unease.[12]

"Crawfie, who is she?" Lilibet asked one day after the children had left the adults and were outdoors.[13] She knew that something was wrong, though exactly what it was she couldn't have said. Overheard gossip, whispered conversations, Queen Mary's silent disapproval of David all registered with the observant Lilibet.

When the family went to Scotland for their annual holiday in August, the discomfort deepened. At Birkhall, where the Yorks always stayed, the routine was much as usual but when they visited Balmoral, in September, they found Wallis occupying the bedroom that had once been Queen Victoria's and observed that she did not hesitate to give orders in the kitchen— much to the Duchess of York's disgust. David pointedly evaded spending any time with Bertie, not wanting to discuss Wallis or his plans to marry her. But all that was left unsaid hung in the air like a thick Scottish fog, and as the weeks went by the holiday became more and more strained.

Everyone, it seemed, was out of sorts or upset, the Duchess of York by the intrusive presence of Wallis, whom she did not want for a sister-in-law, Bertie by David's eva- siveness and by further political upheaval on the Continent, where a radical govern- ment had just taken power in France and civil war had broken out in Spain. David was haunted by a frightening incident that had taken place in July, at the Trooping the Colour ceremony, when an Irish assassin pointed a loaded gun at him and had to be subdued by the police. And Wallis was re- covering from a stomach ulcer that had given her a great deal of pain for several months.[14]

In the background of all their thoughts was the recent cruise David and Wallis had taken together, and the press sensation it had caused.

On August 10 the king and his constant companion had boarded the large white yacht *Nahlin*, owned by Lady Yule, at Sibernik in Yugoslavia. With a party of a dozen friends, they had spent the next four weeks cruising, going ashore at Corfu to visit the King of Greece, touring Athens, Istanbul, and the battlefields of Gallipoli which had become infamous in the Great War. Large unruly crowds gathered to greet the king at every port of call, and reporters were waiting to photograph David with his married mistress. He was not discreet, either on shore or at sea. His infantile antics on board the ship, his open displays of affection for Wallis, the slavish haste with which he did her bidding—she sent him to fetch her drinks, wraps, even a nail file—gave an unflatteringly candid glimpse of their intimate life, and foreshadowed disaster. David, it seemed, was completely in thrall to Wallis, and she savored her role as the woman he could not live without.

Queen Mary began calling Wallis "the adventuress" and repeating gossip that she was plotting to have David abolish the constitutional government in a German-backed coup. It would have surprised the queen no end to learn that Wallis, though she was consulting a divorce lawyer, was in fact having second thoughts about marrying her son, and tried to break off their relationship in September, 1936, intending to go back to her husband (who was at the time living with a mistress of his own, having reached an accommodation with David and removed himself from the entire situation). All the strain was making Wallis ill again, and she may have begun to prefer the dull but predictable life she had known with Ernest Simpson to the quixotic adventure with David.[15]

Throughout October and November Lilibet, who read *Punch* with its topical cartoons and had a vague understanding of political and dynastic affairs, sensed the deepening mood of crisis. She observed the frequent goings and comings of the portly Stanley Baldwin and was alert to the

fact that she and her sister were not allowed to accept invitations to tea at Fort
Belvedere. Lilibet and Margaret were learning to swim that fall, taking lessons at the
Bath Club. The new preoccupation was diverting, but did nothing to dissipate the
sensation that, as Crawfie wrote, "something was amiss." "The peace of the house
was broken," and Lilibet knew that it had
something to do with Uncle David, politics
and marriage.[16] When Margaret Rose
asked her sister what was going on, Lilibet
said, "I think Uncle David wants to marry
Mrs. Baldwin, and Mr. Baldwin doesn't
like it."[17]

Clear evidence that the family was in
emotional disarray was not hard to find. Lilibet's mother often took to her bed, exhausted and ill. Her grandmother, having
abandoned any hope that her stubborn
son's infatuation for the American would
wear off, wept privately and lost her appetite; in less than two months she lost
nearly thirty pounds, her old-fashioned long
gowns and narrow jackets hanging loosely
on her gaunt frame. But her father, the
nervous, chain-smoking, cocktail-drinking

Duke of York, was the most deeply affected of all.

Quite simply, he panicked.

He dreaded the outcome of his brother's dilemma; if David decided to marry Wallis, as he seemed bent on doing, would he be able to retain his throne? And if not—the alternative was all but unthinkable.

Slight, handsome Bertie, diffident and self-effacing, had never been looked on as anything but a sweet, bumbling cipher in the royal family. For a decade and more he had done little of a public nature, beyond inspecting factories and taking his one state tour of Australia and New Zealand. It was understood that his shyness and his stammer (which had diminished, but not disappeared) made him a liability, and so he had happily withdrawn into family life.

Even within the family, Bertie took a back seat to his wife, whose effortless charm and emollient personality enabled her tactfully to direct both household affairs and the Yorks' very modest calendar of social engagements. For this Bertie was grateful, but it meant that he was exceedingly out of practice presenting himself to the outside world. What fragile confidence he possessed collapsed at the thought of having to step into David's shoes.

The years of contented drift, it appeared were about to end. No longer would Bertie be able to enjoy his home life, have lunch with his family as well as breakfast and dinner, play hopscotch with his children or run with them (he was a very fast runner) in Hamilton Gardens or in the grounds of Royal Lodge. His hobbies, keeping detailed meteorological records, growing rhododendrons and azaleas, watching Marx Brothers movies, doing petit-point embroidery, would have to be abandoned. He felt sick, depressed, desperate to be released from what seemed a looming certainty. Others, watching him, thought that he might have a breakdown and felt compassion for his obvious suffering.[18] So frail did the duke seem that a rumor started, among the insiders who were aware of the king's probable abdication, that Bertie would refuse the crown; it would pass to Lilibet, with Queen Mary acting as regent for her.[19]

The object of these speculations was, most likely, ignorant of them, and of the implications of her uncle's plans and actions for her own future. She went on with her swimming lessons, prodding her sister to brave the deep water of the pool ("Don't be a limpet, Margaret"), while Wallis obtained her preliminary divorce decree (which meant that in late April, 1937, she would be divorced), while increasingly intense family and political discussions went on, with Bertie trembling and biting his lip and Baldwin taking an increasingly hard line against the marriage the king had equally firmly decided to make. Impassioned and noisy public reaction to the published news of the king's desire to marry Wallis—news withheld from the British press until early December—heightened the general excitement and anxiety. The Duchess of York likened the stress to "sitting on the edge of a volcano."

At last, on December 7, 1936, David told his brother that because of the political opposition to his intended marriage, he had decided to abdicate. "The awful and ghastly suspense of waiting was over," Bertie wrote in his journal.[20]

No one seems to have recorded Lilibet's reaction to the news that her father and mother were about to become the king and queen, and that she would become heir presumptive. Possibly she considered her status only temporary, not only hoping but expecting that her mother would have another baby, and that the baby would be a boy. Her father was only forty-one in 1936, a relatively young man. Even if she did succeed him, it would be a long way off, too long, by far, for even the most curious and imaginative ten-year-old to fully comprehend.

FIVE

"They're changing the guard at Buckingham Palace," chanted Lilibet and Margaret,
the A.A. Milne poem being their favorite.
Now they were going to live in the sprawling, drafty, musty-smelling palace with its
nearly seven hundred rooms and ten thousand windows. Mice scurried along the
endless chilly corridors, along with hundreds of servants, messengers, clerks and
secretaries. Housemaids vacuumed the
deep-pile red carpets and cleaned the crys-
tal chandeliers, dusted the gilt ornaments
and wiped down the walls of colored marble while footmen in scarlet livery trundled
food carts the half mile from the kitchen to

the dining rooms. All was distance, inconvenience, cold grandeur.

"People here need bicycles," Lilibet remarked. They needed sweaters too, or even
coats, for there was no central heating and
the bedrooms had only coal fires to keep off
the cold. The comforts of 145 Piccadilly
were gone forever, along with the relative
privacy of that home; at Buckingham Palace, not only officials but photographers
and press agents were a nuisance, and the
sturdy oak-timbered doors were not thick
enough to keep private conversations truly
private.

The guardsmen who patrolled the entrance to the palace were not the only
source of protection. Two detectives, Mr.
Cameron and Mr. Giles, now began to accompany the royal family everywhere, riding
in their car, hovering nearby if they went out
for a picnic, going along with them on holidays. Police too were on hand, in case the
everpresent onlookers tried to get too
close.

For Lilibet, a tall, long-legged ten-year-
old, the transition to the palace meant exchanging Hamilton Gardens for forty-five
acres of parkland, with gardens and ponds,

a summerhouse and a green hill overlooking Buckingham Palace Road. Lilibet liked watching the ducks in the lake. One afternoon there was a splash and a little scream. Lilibet rose out of the lake bed, covered in green slime.

"Oh, Crawfie, I fell in," she said, "looking for the duck's nest." Crawfie cleaned her up before Clara Knight—whom the princesses now called Allah—could see her and disapprove.[1]

If Lilibet had been a celebrity before, she was doubly so now that she was heir to the throne. Reporters and royal-watchers were on hand to observe and record her every venture outside the palace. If her grandmother took her to a concert, she felt she had to stay to the very end, no matter how restless or bored she became, otherwise the waiting spectators outside, expecting her to emerge when the concert was over and not before, would be cheated of their pleasure. If anything upset her, she couldn't show it, for she didn't want to read about her tears or her cross mood in the newspapers the following day. Queen Mary had taught Lilibet that "royalty never smile," but she had long since abandoned that maxim, and smiled and waved at her public whenever she went out.

Her abiding fascination with horses had developed further. "If I am ever queen," she told Crawfie, "I shall make a law that there must be no riding on Sundays. Horses should have a rest too. And I shan't let anyone dock his pony's tail." Riding her ponies Peggy, Comet and Snowball, reading books about horses, writing "long and confiding" letters to Santa Claus asking for horse gifts, even taking on the identity of a horse herself took up much of Lilibet's free time. She pranced, galloped, trotted. She sidled up to Crawfie and nosed in her pockets for sugar, the way Peggy did. She whinnied. Or she let Crawfie be the horse, harnessed with a pair of red reins with bells, and drove her along the palace corridors, delivering imaginary groceries and chatting at great length with imaginary customers.

"Crawfie," she whispered when the governess was calmly waiting, on all fours, for the game to proceed, "you must pretend to be impatient. Paw the ground a bit." On frosty mornings, when Crawfie's breath condensed in the air, Lilibet was delighted.

"Just like a proper horse," she said, and gave the governess a pat.[2]

Such juvenile games went on for years, though Lilibet had already reached the threshold of puberty and her developing figure was evident under the little-girl smocked silk dresses she and Margaret wore to palace garden parties, along with straw hats, flat shoes and white cotton socks.[3] Her adolescence was postponed as long as possible, the illusion of a prolonged childhood maintained, imperfectly, by the fact that she and her much younger sister were identically dressed.

Identically, that is, except on Coronation Day, May 12, 1937, when Lilibet's lace dress had a short train and Margaret's matching dress did not. The discovery of the difference some weeks earlier had caused a scene; Margaret had to be placated.

Lilibet, who had just passed her eleventh birthday, wrote an account of the coronation, dedicated, in red crayon, "To Mummy and Papa In Memory of Their Coronation From Lilibet By Herself."[4] In it she described being awakened at five in the morning by the playing of the Royal Marine band, the day being dark and drizzly, and crouching, with her maid Bobo, in the window looking out at the huge crowds that had continued to cheer and sing through most of the previous night.

"We did not eat very much as we were too excited," she recorded, and went on to describe how she and Margaret Rose were dressed and then went to show themselves to the visitors and housemaids, and to Crawfie, Lilibet lifting up her long dress to reveal silver sandals, cuffed ankle socks and scratched brown legs.

"Now I shall try to give you a description of our dresses. They were white silk with old cream lace and had little gold bows all the way down the middle. They had puffed sleeves with one little bow in the center. Then there were the robes of purple velvet with gold on the edge."

Lilibet gave a similarly detailed description of her parents' dress, then told how a page came to say it was time to go, "so we kissed Mummy, and wished her good luck and went down." Lilibet and Margaret Rose got into a carriage with their three aunts, Mary, Marina and Alice, and set off for the rainy ride to the abbey. ("At first it was very jolty but we soon got used to it.")

Lilibet had been concerned about how her sister would behave during the long ceremony. "I do hope she won't disgrace us all by falling asleep in the middle, Crawfie," she had said. "After all, she is VERY young for a coronation, isn't she?"[5] But Margaret, perhaps overawed, as Lilibet no doubt was, by the vast church with its congregation of nearly eight thousand, by the walk up the long red carpeted aisle, the girls following directly behind their father in his trailing ermine robe, played quietly in the pew with the prayer books ("I only had to nudge her once or twice") throughout the ceremony.

"I thought it all VERY, VERY wonderful," Lilibet wrote, "and I expect the abbey did, too. The arches and beams at the top were covered with a sort of haze of wonder as Papa was crowned, at least I thought so."

The music, the orchestra, the new organ, the singing, all the pageantry were splendid, the king and queen dignified and impressive, the sight of the glittering peeresses putting on their coronets in unison, "arms and coronets hovering in the air," magical.

Given the grandeur of the occasion, Lilibet supposed that no one who had gone through it could ever forget it. Yet when she asked her grandmother about her own coronation a quarter of a century earlier, Queen Mary said that her memories were vague. "What struck me as being rather odd," Lilibet wrote, "was that Grannie did not remember much of her own Coronation. I should have thought that it would have stayed in her mind for ever."

The service went on and on, and "got rather boring," the princess thought, "as it was all prayers." She looked through her program and was relieved to find the word "Finis" at the bottom of one page. She and Queen Mary smiled at one another and anticipated the end.

"When we got back to our dressing room we had some sandwiches, stuffed rolls, orangeade and lemonade," she wrote, leaving out few of the practical behind-the-scenes details. "Then we left for our long drive."

Rain poured down as the parade of gilded coaches processed along the Embankment, down Northumberland Avenue, and through Trafalgar Square, then via Piccadilly, Regent Street and Oxford Street ("with Selfridge's lovely figures") through

Marble Arch, Hyde Park, and so back to the palace.

"Then we all went onto the balcony," Lilibet concluded, "where MILLIONS of people were waiting below. After that we all went to be photographed in front of those awful lights."

The photography took an hour or more, and by then it was nearly six o'clock, seven hours after the royal party originally left for the ceremony.

"When I got into bed my legs ached terribly. As my head touched the pillow I was asleep and I did not wake up till nearly eight o'clock the next morning."

Lilibet's perspicacity, as well as her directness, her powers of imagination, and her lack of self-importance, were apparent in her coronation narrative. If, as she watched the solemnities, her mind leaped ahead to her own future coronation, she did not think to record these fantasies. Perhaps she continued to hope for a brother, for just at that time, some at court thought that her mother might be going to have another baby.[6]

Lilibet's old routine of morning lessons with Crawfie and afternoon music, dancing and drawing lessons had to be abandoned as she began to have more obligations, making official tours and meeting with other young people in a variety of settings. She opened bazaars, gave school and club prizes, went to horse shows and attended the inaugurations of buildings and organizations. Reporters wrote magazine articles about her, the newspapers reported her daily life in great detail. A biography was in preparation, and a portrait bust, requiring many sittings over two years, was well under way. At social events Lilibet met hundreds of people, often under trying circumstances, and managed a gracious few words to each. She was learning the art of what her great-great-grandmother would have called "circling," making the rounds of a large room or outdoor enclosure, passing with discreet haste from one person to the next, in an effort to say a little something to everyone.

In the course of fulfilling each of these obligations, Lilibet's sense of responsibility was deepening. She might still hope that the arrival of a brother would relieve her of the ultimate responsibility—that of becoming queen—but in the absence of such an event, her future was predetermined.

Concern over it made her anxious, her anxiety displaying itself in nail-biting and in excessive neatness and a compulsion to save wrapping paper, ribbons from chocolate boxes and bouquets, each carefully wrapped and folded and put away for reuse. Every square of colored paper was kept in a special box, every bit of silk or lace preserved lest it be needed.[7] All the horse books were arranged on shelves, dusted and straightened; all her toys were in their places. Even so, she worried. She lay in bed, unable to sleep, concerned about the possibility of disorder, until driven to get up, sometimes several times, and check to make certain her clothes were exactly in order and her shoes aligned.

Now such an obsession would be regarded as a mild pathology; in the 1930s other explanations were sought—and found, in her father's excessive worry and fussy overconcern with clothes and sartorial protocol. Bertie's worries were legion, and the outward signs of them (his persisting stammer, chain-smoking, heavy drinking, irritability) unmistakable. His daughter clearly took after him. And to the extent that she tidied her clothes too often, she was no doubt reflecting her father's compulsion to criticize others' dress (he complained if the pleats on a kilt were folded in the wrong direction) and to preoccupy himself with designing and redesigning uniforms.

A photograph of the Windsor troop of Girl Guides gathering wood for their campfire beside the lake at Frogmore shows Lilibet, tall and leggy, with seven other girls standing at the base of an immense tree. She is the prettiest of the girls; she stands tall and straight while the others slouch or stand awkwardly on one leg. It is, perhaps, a picture of the Kingfisher patrol, of which the princess was deputy commander.

The troop was formed, at Crawfie's instigation, in 1937 when Lilibet was eleven and Margaret seven. Margaret was too young to be a Girl Guide, but Lilibet did her best to get her admitted, arguing with the organization's representative, a Miss Synge, to make an exception. ("You don't think we could get her in somehow? She is very strong, you know. Pull up your skirts, Margaret, and show Miss Synge. You can't say those aren't a very fine pair of hiking legs,

Miss Synge. And she loves getting dirty, don't you, Margaret, and how she would love to cook sausages on sticks.")[8] Margaret was attached to the troop as a Brownie, along with a dozen other small girls.

In their blue uniforms, knee-length beige stockings and sturdy shoes, the Girl Guides and Brownies hiked and camped, learned the songs and markings of various species of birds, practiced tying bandages, sang campfire songs and carried out sentimental rituals of initiation and transition.

When a Guards sergeant called all three patrols to attention for squad drill they all fell into rank.

"Eyes right, right left!"

"Turn left!"

"About turn!"

They marched, wheeled, stood to attention in unison. At the sergeant's order the patrols began a mile-long march through the Windsor Grounds, following which they were dismissed to begin calisthenics and then games. Their weekly meetings were only mildly strenuous but quite invigorating, and for the princesses, instructive. They fulfilled Crawfie's objective of having the girls keep in touch with "what children of their own ages were doing."9

According to Patricia Mountbatten, who led the Kingfisher patrol and was a few years older than Lilibet, the princess was "nice, easy to deal with," competent and efficient. The other girls liked her, or appeared to, and she made friends. Friends were much in evidence, too, at Balmoral where the royal family spent their late-summer vacations.

"We went for a lunch picnic with the Hardings," Lilibet wrote to Crawfie, "and no grown-up. Winifred made buttered-up eggs and the rest of us did odd jobs. Libby and I fried potatoes and cooked sausages."10 Cousin Margaret Elphinstone, Patricia Mountbatten, and various other friends came and went for weekends and longer stays, and Lilibet, who was learning to take pictures, captured it all with her camera. Besides picnics of stuffed buns and venison pâté there was deerstalking—Lilibet was learning to shoot—fly-fishing for salmon with "Hairy Marys" and "Black Doctors," delicious teas of scones, baps and bannocks, and in the evening, before the nightly cinema showing, the ceremonial playing of the bagpipes by seven pipers in kilts and sporrans.

The world had changed much since Queen Victoria's time, but Balmoral, with its neo-Gothic towers, winding stairways and tiny ice-cold rooms, remained a monument to the old queen's outlandish taste. A life-size statue of her beloved husband Albert dominated the front hall, sentimental Land-seer paintings of stags, dogs and wildlife hung on the walls. Curtains, carpets, linens, even the linoleum were rendered in the hideous Balmoral tartan (designed by Albert) of lilac, red and black, while the silver wall sconces in each room were in the form of antlers, guns or game bags.

Another Victorian tradition was the annual Gillies Ball for the hunting staff and their families, a grand affair with hundreds of couples whirling and leaping in the immense torchlit ballroom. For the first time, at age twelve, Lilibet was allowed to join the adults and attend the Gillies Ball, in a little-girl party dress. She had learned to dance reels in the Girl Guides, and was proficient at them. Now she skipped, clapped and led the parade of couples in a real party, body atingle and eyes sparkling, while the wild music swelled and the dancers' excitement mounted.

She was growing up. At age eleven or twelve Lilibet was allowed to begin wearing silk stockings, and when she went with her mother to Clydebank to help launch the immense Cunard liner *Queen Elizabeth*, or accepted the presidency of the Children's League of the Princess Elizabeth of York Hospital, she was dressed as a miniature version of the queen in modest below-the-knee dresses, sensible hats and handbags.

But she was never happier than when wearing jodhpurs and tweed jacket, on her way to a riding lesson. In the summer of 1938, with political tensions once again on the rise following Hitler's annexation of Austria and demands for Czech territory, Lilibet and Margaret began riding lessons with Horace Smith, a knowledgeable stable owner and dealer and frequent judge at horse shows. Twice a week Smith went to the royal riding school at Buckingham Palace with his daughter Sybil and two ponies from his stable, and the princesses practiced their basic skills and mounted exercises, advancing eventually to jumping.

"Princess Elizabeth's progress was very

far above the average," Smith wrote in his book *A Horseman Through Six Reigns*. "She was very conscientious and anxious to improve her horsemanship, and her standard of riding, considering the small number of lessons that she had, soon became very high."[11]

Lilibet was just as interested in the care of the horses as she was in learning to ride well, and asked Smith questions about their feed and how they were trained, in addition to wanting to know how the stables were run and managed. In the fall of 1938 the riding lessons resumed, after the Balmoral break, Lilibet and Margaret jumping low barriers and learning to ride without their reins. Just as they had concentrated on learning to swim during the months leading up to the abdication crisis, they now focused on riding, with the king and queen and queen mother coming to watch the lessons on occasion.

Bertie laughed as he watched his daughters in the riding ring, telling Horace Smith that his own riding lessons had been a disaster, that "he had been run away with more times than he cared to remember."[12] He was proud of his older daughter with her firm seat and straight back, and told her so. He was also very concerned about her, for it seemed more and more likely that she would in time succeed him and she needed to be prepared for that eventuality.

The king talked to Lilibet, at age twelve and thirteen, Crawfie thought, "more seriously than most fathers do to so young a child," almost "as if he spoke to an equal."[13] There were limits to what she could be expected to understand, but he could tell that she was much more intelligent than he had been at her age, and not hampered, as he had been, by deep feelings of inadequacy. He saw that she was anxious—he referred to her "fretwork"—but he also saw her common sense and her flashes of dry wit, which she was fully able to turn on herself. He had confidence in her, and little by little, confided to her the precarious situation in Europe and his hopes and expectations for the future.

Just then, in the fall of 1938, Prime Minister Neville Chamberlain, whom Bertie liked (both men were diffident and reserved, and both had charismatic, overshadowing elder brothers), was making trips to Berchtesgaden, Bad Godesberg and Munich to meet with Hitler in an effort to avert war. Chamberlain's political prestige was immense, his popularity unrivaled. When he returned from Munich, having pledged not to interfere in the planned German occupation of the Sudetenland, he was met by a tremendous public outflowing of adulation and gratitude on the part of the public. War had indeed been averted, he declared. Hitler's aggression had been contained. An enthusiastic crowd collected to cheer the prime minister when he appeared on the balcony of Buckingham Palace with the king.

For the moment, the wave of euphoria drove off fears. But in the months to come, Chamberlain's triumph would be tarnished by Hitler's perfidy, and Bertie's serious talks with Lilibet would take on an ever more sober tone.

SIX

Lilibet bit her nails and stood at the window, gazing out down the mall toward Admiralty Arch, watching the people pass and the traffic flowing ceaselessly up and down. She was curious about the lives of all those others, their thoughts and activities; having nearly reached the age of thirteen, the outside world interested her more and more, despite the mood of apprehension that settled over Britain in the early months of 1939.[1]

The Munich terms so carefully negotiated by Chamberlain were never implemented. Hitler occupied Prague in March of 1939 and by summer Chamberlain's entire strategy was shattered. During that tense summer, as Britons dug trenches and tried on gas masks and generally prepared themselves for the war that now seemed inevitable, the royal family went on a weekend trip to the Royal Naval College at Dartmouth, aboard the yacht *Victoria and Albert*. Bertie was to hold an inspection of the cadets.

It was a brief respite from the past anxious months. The July weather was fine, the trip along the coast pleasant and uneventful. Lilibet and Margaret did their lessons on the deck of the yacht, in the sunshine, and later, learned to dance the Lambeth Walk and the Palais Glide from some of the young officers on board.[2]

When the red-brick college building came into view, high on its hill overlooking the River Dart, the scene was idyllic: the green hill, the sparkling blue water, dozens of small boats sailing up and down, manned by boys in white sweaters.

On Sunday morning, after church, the king and queen were taken on a tour but because two of the cadets had come down with mumps, Lilibet and Margaret were sent to the home of the College Commandant, along with Crawfie, so that they would not be exposed. They amused themselves with a train set, kneeling on the nursery floor and playing with the cars. After a while one of the cadets joined them.

He was, Crawfie recalled, "a fair-haired boy, rather like a Viking, with a sharp face and piercing blue eyes." He said "How do you do?" politely enough to Lilibet, but there was something in his manner, the governess thought, a careless ignoring of decorum, that all but gave offense. He was Philip of Greece, nephew of Louis Mountbatten, and in the summer of 1939 he had just turned eighteen.

Lilibet was fascinated by Philip, she "never took her eyes off him the whole time," Crawfie noticed. When he showed off on the soggy tennis court, jumping the net with athletic grace, she took note and admired his skill. When they all went on board the *Victoria and Albert* for lunch and Philip made everyone laugh, Lilibet watched—and laughed heartily. She noticed his good looks, his likes and dislikes in food, his formidable appetite (several platefuls of shrimp, a banana split, and more). She ignored the awkward qualities that others found tiresome—his barking laugh, his brash, edgy bluntness, verging on rudeness, his tendency to dominate.

She sat, "pink-faced, enjoying it all very much." And when, heedless of his safety, Philip followed the *Victoria and Albert* out of the harbor and into the rougher waters of the Channel in his small boat, Lilibet watched him through binoculars, rowing as hard as he could, until the boat was only a dot on the blue water.

Philip had made a strong impression, the impression of a forceful, energetic, entertaining young man who could leap nimbly over a tennis net with inches to spare, and who pursued his goals with a reckless determination. Their paths had crossed before, at the wedding of Lilibet's Uncle George and Philip's cousin Marina, at parties at Brook House, Lord Louis Mountbatten's huge penthouse in London, and at other official events. But this encounter, prolonged and at close quarters, went deep, on Lilibet's side. A shy, unworldly, impressionable thirteen-year-old, she had met many boys and young men but knew very few of them familiarly. And she had never before met anyone like Philip.

On Philip's side, the encounter cannot have had much emotional impact, though he realized it might be important for his future. His uncle Louis, George VI's aide-de-camp, had arranged for him to "amuse the girls," and what his uncle did, or suggested, Philip took very seriously.[3] One girl in particular was in Philip's thoughts in July of 1939, the American cover girl and model Cobina Wright, a stunning blond whose mother was a society columnist. Philip had tried to persuade Cobina to marry him, and was writing to her frequently.

He was open to love, bursting with vitality, greedy for admiration and, at bottom, for acceptance. Never having known a stable family life, he sought a substitute for it. To an extent he found a satisfying substitute in the concern and occasional hospitality of relatives, and in transitory social contacts. His good looks, attractiveness to women and royal family connections (Philip's Danish-born grandfather had been King of Greece; on his mother's side he was connected to the princely families of Germany) assured him invitations to parties at the homes of wealthy and titled socialites. At these parties he showed off, dancing with verve and energy, performing athletic feats (at one gathering he "swung from the pergola"), telling jokes and laughing loudly, and generally drawing attention to himself. His exuberance annoyed some and amused others, but left a definite impression on all, as did his lean figure and Nordic handsomeness.

Lilibet had recently begun seeing quite a few boys—at Eton, where she went twice a week with Crawfie to be tutored in what was called by the press "Constitutional History." Sir Henry Marten, Vice-Provost of the school and an authority in the field, taught her in his cluttered study, with the Eton boys in their silk top hats, white bow ties and striped trousers coming and going in the courtyard below, or occasionally interrupting the lesson with a message for Sir Henry.

"Crawfie, do you mean to tell me he has read them all?" Lilibet asked in amazement, looking around at the piles of books that covered the desk, the chairs, even the floor. She was overawed, but gradually began to enjoy her occasional hour with the avuncular, balding scholar, who always carried sugar lumps in his pocket and had an endearing habit of chewing on a corner of his handkerchief and staring up at the ceiling when he was thinking.[4] Lilibet thought history was "thrilling," and the lessons were no doubt limited to a few simple concepts. That Lilibet had any tutelage at all in the workings of government or political philosophy was the result of Queen Mary's urging. The queen mother remembered that George V, as a boy, had been tutored by J. R. M. Butler at Trinity College, Cambridge; she wanted her granddaughter to have the same sort of training—though the content of Prince George's lessons had been very limited in extent and he was hardly an apt pupil.[5]

Henry Marten remembered Lilibet at thirteen as "a somewhat shy girl" who when asked a question "would look for confidence and support to her beloved governess."[6] Another courtier thought her "shy to the point of gaucheness."[7] The American ambassador Joseph Kennedy, who first met Lilibet and Margaret in April of 1938, thought that Lilibet "handled herself beautifully," and recorded how she chatted with him at a Windsor lunch about movies (she liked *Snow White and the Seven Dwarfs*, "particularly the animals when Snow White talked to them"), about her favorite subject of study (geography), about horses and dogs and the garden she and Margaret had planted. A year later, in spring 1939, Kennedy again spent an afternoon with the royal family and noted in his diary how when a ladybug turned up at the table "Princess Elizabeth suggested it was good luck and sent it along to the prime minister." The bug, sitting on a gold spoon, was passed down the table from hand to hand until it was deposited on Chamberlain's shoulder.[8]

For Lilibet, the transition to being generally recognized as heir to the throne coincided with puberty. Nearly as tall as her mother, sensitive beneath her stiff-upper-lip exterior, always conscious of the demands of propriety and watched by the press as well as the everpresent detectives, Lilibet did her best to keep her composure. But life at Buckingham Palace was full of distractions and interruptions. Lessons were tucked into "spare moments" in the day, and even then were frequently abandoned because the princesses had to have fittings with dressmakers or join their parents for some important visit or ceremony.[9] Often they got to bed so late that they yawned through the following morning, unable to concentrate on anything.

This was especially true on the mornings after the formal courts at which debutantes were presented. Lilibet and Margaret, in their pink dressing gowns, looked through the windows at the arriving cars, admiring their occupants as they stepped out, the men in knee breeches, silk stockings, and tailcoats shining with medals, the women in long gowns with five-foot trains, brilliant jewelry, veils and ostrich feathers. They particularly admired Aunt Marina, glittering and beautiful in her court finery.

"Never mind, Margaret," Crawfie overheard Lilibet say, "one day you and I will be down there sharing all the fun. And I shall have a perfectly enormous train, yards long."[10]

The princesses were in Scotland when Britain declared war on Germany, September 3, 1939. King George and Queen Elizabeth soon left for London, but the girls stayed on, at Birkhall, under police protection.

"What dreadful things have been happening lately," Lilibet wrote to Crawfie, then on vacation. "More history for children to learn in a hundred years. Really the Germans are brutes the way they go on, torpedoing our ships and sending messages to the German people that they have taken Warsaw."[11]

She was worried about Hitler.

"Oh dear, Crawfie, I hope he won't come over here." Lilibet and Margaret both fretted over the safety of their parents, who called them every night from London, and followed the war news in the newspapers. When she read that the enemy had sunk the battleship *Royal Oak*, Lilibet "jumped horrified from her chair, her eyes blazing with anger. 'Crawfie, it can't be! All those nice sailors.'" She would still be grieving, and feeling compassion for the bereaved parents of the sailors, four months later.[12]

Remote as the Highlands were from the actual arena of conflict, signs of the war were everywhere, windows covered with blackout curtains, busy train stations with young men leaving for training camps, hundreds of evacuees from Glasgow sent north for safety. The princesses became involved in war work, volunteering with the Red Cross, serving tea and cake to evacuees, helping out with refreshments at the weekly sewing parties Crawfie organized for the local women. In the afternoons there was dancing class, now and then in the evenings an old Charlie Chaplin or Laurel and Hardy movie put on by a man in the village who owned a projector.

At Christmas the family gathered at Sandringham, conscious of the risk they took, for the Norfolk estate was very near the coast and a German invasion was a possibility. The king was not intimidated, either by invasion rumors or anything else. Wearing his uniform, practicing shooting his revolver and even learning to use a tommy gun, keeping a sten gun on hand when he went out in his car, George VI was prepared to fight—as was the queen, who also began taking target practice in the Buckingham Palace grounds. The king abandoned his needlepoint for machine tools, installing a lathe at Windsor Castle and making parts for antitank guns. He took rationing seriously, observed the limitations on food and clothing and marked a number of the bathtubs at Windsor and Buckingham Palace with a black line to indicate how little water was to be used.[13]

He had more than enough to occupy him, and was late sending out his Christmas cards, as Lilibet learned to her dismay. In mid-January no card had yet been sent to Philip, who was serving on the *Ramillies*. Lilibet and Philip were corresponding, and early in 1940 Philip remarked to the captain that his uncle Dickie Mountbatten "had plans" for him. "He thinks I should marry Princess Elizabeth," Philip said, indiscreetly.

"Are you fond of her?" the captain asked.

"Oh yes. I write to her every week."[14] Of course, he was also writing to Cobina Wright, and perhaps to others.

In the early months of 1940 the family stayed at Windsor, spending weekends at Royal Lodge. London was full of war preparations, with people carrying gas masks, digging defensive works and storing away provisions against the likelihood of a German onslaught, but at Windsor, and especially at Royal Lodge, the war seemed unreal. Lisa Sheridan visited the family there in the spring, and was surprised by the lack of obvious security arrangements. There were no soldiers or police anywhere in sight, no sandbags, no visible precautions against air raids. Lilibet and Margaret went riding, cultivated vegetables and, with Crawfie, collected scrap iron for the war effort, walking through Windsor Great Park with a garden cart and picking up old railings, pots and pans, nails, anything usable.

Birds sang in the garden, and in the silver birch copse adjacent to it, tranquillity prevailed. "The setting was enchanting," Sheridan thought, "with the dappled light falling through the trees, where nature grows untended in the loveliness of semi-disorder; . . . the shafts of slanting mist dancing with sunbeams, and the sight of a tiny rabbit which popped up just at our feet to give the excited dogs a good chase."[15]

The dogs drew the family's attention, growling, eating the queen's nosegay of jasmine off her jacket, starting after hares, demanding attention. Dookie had been joined by another corgi, Jane, Jane's offspring Carol and Crackers, Spark, Flash, Scruffy, Mimsey, Stiffy and the Tibetan lion-dog Ching. Lilibet had just acquired two new ponies, Pussyfoot, which had once belonged to her cousin Gerald Lascelles, and a small gray Welsh pony supplied by Horace Smith to pull a "governess cart." In addition they had Jock, George V's old pony, Hans, a Norwegian, and Snowball, Comet, Grey Light and Harmony.[16]

The few months of illusory calm ended abruptly in April, 1940, when the German army invaded Denmark and Norway and soon afterward, moved into Belgium and the Netherlands. France came under attack, and soon surrendered. It was only a matter of time before the German juggernaut encompassed Britain as well.

"The decisive struggle is now upon us," King George said in a broadcast at the end of May. "Against our honesty is set dishonor, against our faithfulness is set treachery, against our justice, brute force." In the last days of May and into early June, nearly 350,000 British and Allied troops, cut off from retreat on land by the advancing German army, were evacuated from Dunkirk by British craft, while British fighter aircraft provided cover. Losses in the evacuation were high, and many civilian volunteers who ferried troops across the Channel in small boats died in the attempt—a foretaste of large-scale civilian casualties to come.

For the royal family, an important decision had to be made: would they, like the ousted rulers of Denmark and Norway and the Netherlands, prudently exit to Canada, or at least send the children to safety there? Hesitation was dangerous. Hitler had shown himself eager to capture not only countries but their rulers, and in the case of Britain, he had a special incentive. With King George and his children out of the way, the Duke of Windsor could be reinstalled as King Edward VIII, a monarch in sympathy with the Führer's philosophy and aims.[17]

The princesses had been moved into the strong fortress of Windsor Castle on May 12 for their protection, guarded, as their parents were at Buckingham Palace, by an elite bodyguard of soldiers and a small fleet of armored cars. At the first news of German landings on the coast, they were to be taken to a secure country house (several were made ready), and from there presumably to Canada.

Windsor, squat and massive on its hill, had withstood the centuries. Nothing, it seemed, could penetrate the immensely thick medieval walls and no invader since the time of William the Conqueror had managed to capture it. Cold winds blew along the drafty corridors and the thick stonework kept out the light; blackout curtains covered the windows and only an occasional dim lightbulb shone, the chandeliers having all been taken down as a precaution against flying glass. "We seemed to live in a sort of underworld," Crawfie thought, a twilit environment reminiscent of the past. In the old castle dungeon, made into an air raid shelter with reinforced walls and temporary beds, the atmosphere was even gloomier, with beetles scuttling along the walls and the fearsome drone of planes overhead.

For Lilibet, who had just turned fourteen, the war was very real, and very troubling. She lay awake at night, listening to the dull thud of explosions—which sometimes made the old castle walls shake—and the rattle of antiaircraft fire, the tinkle of broken glass and the roar of bombers. Gradually she and Margaret began to be able to distinguish between the German planes and the British, and would call out "ours" or "theirs" when the drone of engines was heard. She wore her gas mask for a time every day, in order to get used to it, and kept the eyepiece clean with Vaseline.

Reflecting her father's admiration for Chamberlain and support for his policies, Lilibet wept when the prime minister made his farewell broadcast on May 11, and slowly adapted to the idea of Churchill as head of the cabinet. She associated Churchill with a fascinating story she and Margaret had heard the previous fall, from Sir Richard Molyneux, a veteran of the Battle of Omdurman, Kitchener's final assault against the Mahdist state in the Sudan in 1898.[18] Sir Richard described how he and young Churchill had taken part in the famous charge of Omdurman, and how, when he was wounded, the surgeon took a piece of skin from Churchill's thigh and grafted it onto Sir Richard's hand. He showed the girls his hand proudly.

Fears of invasion became more and more acute as the hot summer of 1940 went on. Rumors proliferated: the Germans were coming by August 1; they were going to land in Ireland; the thousands of resident aliens in Britain would rise up en masse and help the invaders. To destroy morale, intense bombing raids began, first along the coastal areas and then, from the middle of August, on London, Coventry, Plymouth,

Liverpool, Hull, Swansea and other major ports and urban areas. Night after night waves of Messerschmitt Me 109s, the best fighter aircraft then made, dropped bombs on British airfields, factories and residential areas. Pinpoint accuracy was impossible, and destruction was widespread. Thousands of civilians were killed or injured, and thousands more were made homeless.

A fresh invasion scare spread on September 1, and many people moved out of London, as far away as they could get, even though it meant living in tents or camping in the open. Through September the onslaught worsened, until some ten thousand civilians had been hurt and thousands of buildings flattened. But Londoners, inspired by Churchill, were on the whole stalwart (though a few were overheard to remark that "it might not be such a bad thing" if Hitler prevailed), and bore their losses resolutely.[19]

The king and queen were never far away from the suffering, touring the bombed neighborhoods, walking amid the rubble of bricks and upturned earth and broken pavement, offering support and comfort. By his presence King George put heart into his subjects, showing his concern by the hours he spent talking with the bombing victims and hearing their stories; the queen, sympathetic and motherly, was another beacon of hope. Everywhere the royals went, crowds formed and called out "Good luck," "God bless you" and "Thank Your Majesties for coming to see us." The sense of camaraderie was genuine, for Londoners knew that the king and queen were not mere spectators of the war, living in gilded safety; they had been through the bombing themselves.

There had been a harbinger of disaster on September 9, when a bomb exploded just below George VI's study at Buckingham Palace, breaking all the windows and shaking the walls and floor violently. The king's shattered nerves and ever-delicate stomach had hardly recovered when, three days later, the zoom of an aircraft was heard and, as the king and queen watched in horror, two bombs fell in the quadrangle only thirty yards from where they were sitting. Four more struck the forecourt, the chapel and the garden.

"We all wondered why we weren't dead," Bertie wrote afterward. "Two great craters had appeared in the courtyard . . . the fire hydrant had burst and water was pouring through the broken windows in the passage."[20] They could have taken shelter— another attack was likely, the German bombers coming, as a rule, in three waves, but instead the king and queen rushed to see what harm had been done elsewhere on the palace grounds and to see what they could do to help. They found the chapel destroyed and the basement full of hundreds of servants and staff, all fortunately unharmed, and "quite calm through it all."

"There is no doubt it was a direct attack on Buckingham Palace," the king wrote. "It was a ghastly experience and I don't want it to be repeated. It certainly teaches one to 'take cover' on all future occasions, but one must be careful not to become 'dugout minded.' "

Badly upset by the near miss, Bertie was unable to settle down to work for days afterward, and kept looking out the window, watching for further attacks. He was convinced, though no proof was ever to be found, that the attack was intended to kill him so that David could be brought in to replace him; he suspected that the pilot had been given a plan of the palace by Bertie's Nazi cousin Charles, Duke of Coburg.[21]

Knowing that her parents might have been killed, Lilibet worried. She was very close to both her mother and father, the father-daughter bond in particular was deepening as she grew older. He took her hunting, they walked together along the windy paths at Sandringham, they had serious talks about the war. Probably the king confided some of his own worries to his sympathetic daughter.

Had King George been killed, Lilibet, at fourteen, would have become queen. Unthinkable though it might have seemed, she knew that it was so—and that the possibility of a sudden accession was now ever-present. Her father did not spare himself, indeed did not adequately protect himself. Bombs were falling on London every day as well as every night, and he spent hours each day in the war-torn heart of the capital, where the danger was greatest—or traveling to other bombed-out cities. There was the added danger of assassination by a foreign agent, or of his being kidnapped.

All these things Lilibet knew, and largely kept to herself, as September, 1940, passed and October began. The Luftwaffe was taking large losses daily, as the Hurricanes and Spitfires of the British Fighter Command proved a formidable obstacle to the swift conquest the Germans had expected. The Hawker and Vickers factories were turning out hundreds of new planes every month, and the two air forces, which had been at a rough parity in numbers in August, became unbalanced, with the British stronger.[22] The numbers of German pilots steadily declined, while new recruits enlarged the British ranks.[23] Though the population at large did not yet know it, the tide of the war had turned, and the unbroken succession of German victories had ended.

Britain was standing firm.

After much rehearsing, in mid-October Lilibet prepared to deliver her first radio broadcast, on the BBC *Children's Hour*. She spoke simply and naturally, in the high, bell-like voice of an upper-class English girl. The address had been written for her, but she added some phrases of her own, and practiced her delivery in front of her parents who, having been bombed out of Buckingham Palace, were temporarily spending more time at Windsor. When the time came for the broadcast, a BBC official arrived to set up the equipment. Then Lilibet sat before the large microphone, composed herself, and began.

"Thousands of you in this country have had to leave your homes to be separated from your father and mother. My sister Margaret Rose and I feel so much for you, as we know from experience what it means to be away from those we love most of all." She concluded on a note of optimism. "We know, every one of us, that in the end all will be well."

Hundreds of thousands were listening, many adults as well as children. They would write to the palace in the coming days to say so, and to tell the princess how moved they were by her words. They did not know where she was, of course; the newspapers said only that the princesses were at a "country house." But they knew, from the strength of her clear, unwavering voice that she was safe, and that as long as she was safe, the monarchy would go on. In that lone, touching voice, amid the ongoing catastrophe of war, lay the hope of Britain.

SEVEN

In 1941 a young officer was posted to
Windsor Castle, a gentle, poetic man with a
charming sense of humor. He had been
wounded and was being given light duty
until he recovered. He fitted in very well with
the household, joining the princesses, as
the other officers did, for meals and being
available for dances and impromptu parties.
Lilibet had a crush on him.[1]

Eventually the poetic young officer left,
and if the princess regretted losing him, her
governess did not detect it. Other officers
were always near at hand, especially the
aristocratic Hugh Euston, whom the king
liked and thought of as a future husband for

Lilibet. She met eligible men—wellborn, likable—at parties and teas, and while singing in the madrigal group Crawfie established. With her girl cousins, and the other Girl Guides, she laughed over their "flirts" and boyfriends. But the temporary attachments made at Windsor were brittle, the social atmosphere strained, for the men arrived only to leave again on short notice, and the war overshadowed all. Each day brought its share of welcome or alarming news, its air raids, its grim battle statistics. There was no escaping the fact that all the young men in uniform stood in mortal danger, and a number of them did not survive the war. Lilibet's cousin Patrick was killed in action in 1941, and another cousin, Andrew Elphinstone, was taken prisoner by the Germans, his future uncertain.

Having been emotionally sheltered all her life, Lilibet was thrust, as an adolescent, into an emotional forcing-house, an artificial wartime environment in which time was short in every encounter and lives were constantly at risk. Her exceptional sensitivity was heightened, her responsiveness quickened. The stratagems of sophisticated flirtation eluded her, and were in any case contrary to her open nature and directness. Nothing in her experience prepared her to cope with or understand the mysterious workings of sexual power and magnetism. When she felt it, she succumbed to it, and did not question its source.

Philip visited Windsor, on leave from his battleship, in October of 1941. Lilibet was fifteen, Philip twenty. He was slim, exceedingly handsome in his uniform, athletic, amusing, and a war hero. He took center stage, as he had during their encounter two years earlier, but this time his elders were fascinated rather than annoyed, for his war stories were exciting. On board the battleship *Valiant* in the Mediterranean, his squadron had intercepted part of the Italian fleet and helped to sink two vessels, scattering the others. For this action he received the Greek War Cross. Shortly afterward the *Valiant* came under fire off Crete, a powerful bomb striking the ship and causing many deaths. Unscathed, Philip went on with his duties and helped to bring the battered vessel into port. The stories were hair-raising; Philip had survived an ordeal. Many of his shipmates had been killed, other ships in his squadron sunk with great loss of life.[2]

Lilibet listened, enthralled. It was clear to others that she idolized Philip. (Queen Mary would later say that she thought the two fell in love during this visit.) The stories were familiar of course. Lilibet already knew what Philip had been through aboard the *Valiant*, from his infrequent letters—letters he wrote, as he told his cousin Alexandra, because "perhaps I am going to marry her."[3]

Philip had been living with this suggestion for some time. Both his Uncle Dickie (Lord Mountbatten) and his father's family favored the idea, and he himself was not averse to it, though he was still enthusiastically playing the field. When on shore leave the following year he caroused with his fellow officer Mike Parker and his cousin David Milford Haven at Scapa Flow, Rosyth and London. Amorous encounters in wartime were often brief, steamy and occasionally anonymous; it may be presumed that Philip, who was much admired and in demand, enjoyed his share of such encounters. He went out with attractive women, and visited brothels. Among his girlfriends was one whose father sold cars. He also visited and kept in touch with a childhood friend, Helene Foufanis Cordet, a divorcée.[4]

The reserved, demure Lilibet showed that she had hidden fire in the elaborate pantomimes staged at the castle during Christmas, 1941, and 1942. She acted, sang and danced well, and was, Horace Smith thought, "full of confidence and vigor." On the stage, outside the cocoon of family, she blossomed. An earthy, suggestive sensuality came forth, an unexpected charisma, even a touch of glamour. She sang a number of solos, and led the chorus in other songs. As a performer, she was funny, sexy, a natural actress. "When she took the arms of the two sailors and sang 'Mind Your Sisters,' " Lisa Sheridan wrote, "she brought the house down. . . . She is marvelous."[5] The audience of four hundred Guardsmen, transport workers, servants and friends was brought to its feet, clapping and shouting for more.

At the Christmas pantomime in 1943, "Aladdin," Lilibet played the title role and swaggered across the stage, joking and taking pratfalls, exchanging silly vaudeville dialogue with Margaret ("Where's your grammer?" "She's gone to the pictures"), and crooning "Shall I Never Have a Girl in My Arms?" In one scene she put on a white wig and a costume made from pieces of old velvet and brocade found in the castle storerooms and, emulating Marie Antoinette, sang "Sur le Pont d'Avignon." In another she tap-danced in shorts and a skimpy top. In still another she wrestled with the machinery in a laundry (a topical scene, the inefficient cleaning of the castle laundry being a colossal nuisance) while a telephone rang incessantly. In the grand finale she led the forty-voice chorus in "A Red-White-and-Blue Christmas" as flags unfurled and a Guards band played.[6]

At all three performances Lilibet seemed to sing to the front row, where Philip sat, enjoying himself and clapping loudly. Most likely he and Lilibet had been seeing one another, without the restricting presence of Lilibet's parents, for the previous two years. Philip had been spending his leaves at Coppins, the Buckinghamshire country home of Lilibet's widowed Aunt Marina (her uncle George having died in a plane crash in Scotland in August of 1942). Lilibet was thought to have joined Philip at Coppins, though how often she joined him, and who else may have visited him there, is impossible to say.

By the close of 1943 Lilibet was convinced, as she told Crawfie, that Philip was, as she put it, "the one." No one else attracted her, and she happily devoted herself to Philip during his Christmas leave. They danced to gramophone records, and to the radio, for four straight nights, rolling back the carpet and jitterbugging. Philip's cousin David Milford Haven came one night and, as Margaret told Crawfie, "he and Philip went mad." With Margaret and other friends they played charades, hide and seek, and then "danced and danced and danced." It was all too much for Lilibet, who came down with a cold.[7]

Between Philip's leaves there was plenty to occupy her. Her studies, their purely academic content always neglected, took on the character of a finishing school with a Belgian tutor, Madame de Bellaigue, coming to the castle to improve the princesses' French. She read to them from the classics, and conversed with them, in an effort to give them at least a patina of cultivation—a touch of cosmopolitanism to counteract their rather narrow provincial outlook. But Madame de Bellaigue's efforts, and Crawfie's, were constantly being undermined by the girls' other obligations and preoccupations. The meetings of the Girl Guides, the preparation of the annual pantomimes (which took at least six weeks of effort each year) and other benefit performances they gave, the walks through Windsor Great Park with the elderly Lady Mountbatten, Philip's grandmother, who lived at Windsor, the war work—collecting scrap metal, picking chestnuts and acorns and damsons in the fall to aid a short-handed jam factory ("very backbreaking work but quite fun," Lilibet commented), the unexpected meetings with distinguished guests at the castle, all made keeping a strict study schedule impossible.

Besides, Lilibet's principal interest had now taken center stage: the care and breeding of horses.

Her gift for managing horses had now combined with her eager intellect to make her a burgeoning expert on racing. It was her absorbing hobby, her chief object of study, her delight. On her own, she had acquired a broad knowledge of the horses in the royal stud and the leading two- and three-year-olds belonging to other owners. Visits to Beckhampton Stables on the Wiltshire Downs and to the royal stables at Hampton Court enlarged her knowledge, and she continued her riding lessons with Horace Smith, who judged her to be "a memorable pupil in every way." She soaked up everything Smith could teach her, applying herself and taking challenges in stride. The better rider she became, the more difficult horses Smith gave her to ride. But she rode them all, even the temperamental ones, her innate ability to communicate well with the animals evident to Smith and to others who saw her ride.[8] She learned to ride side-saddle and also began driving a pony-cart, a skill she mastered sufficiently to win first prize in the Royal Windsor Horse Show in 1943 and again in 1944.

At sixteen, Lilibet, eager to do her part, signed up at the Windsor Labour Exchange. Volunteering characterized the royal family. Lilibet's cousin Lady Mary Cambridge joined the Voluntary Aid Detachment working in bombed-out neighborhoods. Lilian Bowes-Lyon, the queen's cousin, collected furniture for families in the East End of London who had been displaced when their homes were destroyed. Louis Mountbatten's wife Edwina volunteered as a driver in the St. John's Ambulance Brigade (which she financed) and toured air raid shelters at night, bringing needed supplies.

"I ought to do as other girls of my age do," the princess announced, expecting to be given a volunteer assignment. But her parents held her back, allowing her to do no more than cultivate a vegetable garden at the castle and grow strawberry plants, continue to collect scrap iron and carry out small acts of private charity. During the war, children evacuated from London attended the Royal School in Windsor Great Park along with the children of palace servants. Lilibet and Margaret got to know some of them because they took part in the Christmas pantomimes, and they occasionally brought out Lilibet's strong caretaking instincts. One of the girls, she discovered, needed sturdy shoes; she went into a shop in the town and bought the child "a good strong pair of brogues," the kind she herself wore, and paid for them out of her pocket money. Another time one of the children left the palace dancing class because her mother could not afford ballet slippers. Lilibet supplied the need.[9]

The Girl Guides, camped out in the castle

grounds in the summer of 1944, had built a fire and were cooking sausages when they heard the high-pitched mechanical screech of a flying bomb. Crawfie and the Guides captain shouted for everyone to lie down, and the governess pulled Margaret to the ground and flung herself across her. They watched the sky as the terrifying sound grew louder and louder. Presently they saw the bomb, fire shooting from its tail, streak past overhead, and a moment later, become absolutely still. This was the most frightening moment, when the engine ceased; the explosion inevitably came within seconds. Suddenly there was a terrific bang, making the ground shake. The bomb had struck the Windsor Race Course several miles away.[10]

Flying bombs, pilotless devices that struck the capital and nearby areas by the thousands, escalated the level of fear among the civilian population. Many dozens of bombs fell in Windsor Great Park, which was pitted with craters. Buckingham Palace was bombed, once again while the king and queen were together in their sitting room (they had ignored the warning to take cover in the bomb shelter and had a narrow escape), and walls fell down. A flying bomb hit the Guards' Chapel in Wellington Barracks, only a short distance from the palace, on a Sunday morning, killing more than a hundred people.[11] The queen's perpetual sangfroid was shattered, she was visibly unnerved, and lost her usual look of gentle amiability, the lines of her mouth becoming grimmer and more firmly set.[12]

Windsor, Crawfie thought, was in a state of chaos. There were frequent red warnings, sending everyone scrambling into the dungeons. Alarms rang, the drone of planes and the shrill whine of the infernal flying bombs seemed incessant. The exhausted king ranted, lashing out and shouting, and the queen, trembling, applied her usual remedy: she held his wrist and began to count—"tick, tick, tick"—which eventually made him laugh and defused his wrath.

Everyone was under strain, tired of having to dive under tables or take refuge in corners, away from the windows. For Lilibet the strain intensified when the bad news arrived that her beloved Scottish grandfather had died at the age of eighty-nine.

She came into Crawfie's room, her face pale, her eyes wide with dismay and sorrow.

"Oh, Crawfie," she said, "Grandfather Strathmore is dead," and bursting into tears, she walked into her governess's outstretched arms.[13]

In 1944 Margaret was a lively, infectiously high-spirited, thoroughly spoiled fourteen-year-old, her sister a reserved, usually self-contained eighteen. The contrast between the two sisters was heightened by the expectations placed on Lilibet as heir to the throne, but even without that distinction they struck casual observers as very different. Margaret was precociously flirtatious, irrepressible, funny, a temperamental extrovert. Lilibet was unsophisticated, gentle in manner, unassertive and shy, conscientious to a fault, temperamentally placid. The king reinforced the differences between his daughters by making an adult companion of Lilibet and treating her with serious regard but indulging and pampering Margaret and encouraging her eccentricities. When Margaret sat at the piano and played and sang popular songs, King George drank in every note, an adoring fan. Her musical gift overawed him; because of it, and because of her charm, he overlooked her willful, disobedient headstrong side—the side of her that Crawfie had trouble managing. (Margaret had become such a temperamental student that she would only learn while reclining.)[14]

On the surface at least, Lilibet was conventional, obedient, diffident, unassertive, her emotions held tightly in check. Every piece of furniture in her neat pink and fawn bedroom (the colors chosen because they were her mother's favorites) was neatly in place, every novel on her bedside table symmetrically arranged. When she went with her mother to attend a ceremony or make a formal visit, she was dressed like a very youthful matron in a drab shapeless dress and coat, unbecoming gray hat and sensible black shoes with ties.

Yet just beneath the surface lay her other persona, bold, audacious, saucy. It was much in evidence in the last wartime pantomime, "Old Mother Red Riding Boots," which featured a Victorian Bathing Ballet. Lilibet promenaded and flirted in a pink satin gown with a froth of white lace, the gown flattering her pretty face and full figure, her straw hat tilted at a rakish angle. The part brought out all her burgeoning sensuality, the sensuality and radiant happiness that were apparent when she was photographed with Philip.

She had been seeing more of him than ever. He was often on leave, or on standby, waiting months for a new ship to be ready. For a time in 1944 he lived in a small hotel in London, at other times he was at his uncle Louis Mountbatten's country house or in Mountbatten's London penthouse. Family members thought that the princess and her handsome distant cousin were in love, and in the spring of 1944, Philip put out a tentative and cautious query, through his uncle George of Greece, to ask if a proposal from him might meet with approval from the royal family. The response was not an outright no, but a "wait." ("Philip had better not think any more about it at present," was the king's response to George of Greece.)[15]

Whether Lilibet herself knew of this rather bold query is unknown, as is so much about their courtship. Apart from mutual attraction, very great on her side, unguessable on his, they had a good deal in common. He was very funny and she loved to laugh, and had her own droll wit. They were both gifted mimics. While neither had been well educated, both Lilibet and Philip had genuine intellectual curiosity and good, if undeveloped, minds. They complemented one another emotionally; Philip was greedy to be accepted and admired, and Lilibet admired him intensely, apparently blindly, and without limit.

On Philip's side, there were other forces at work. He had been poor all his life, a poverty all the more cruel in that it was experienced amid surroundings of privilege. The prospect of enjoying the security, comforts and material satisfactions of life amid the Windsor establishment was very appealing. His uncle, who had improved his own circumstances immensely by marrying an extremely wealthy woman, was doing everything he could to ensure that Philip married Lilibet, attempting to use his influence to expedite Philip's becoming a British citizen (which, in fact, he was already although no one realized it), talking up the probability of a marriage, pushing Philip to advance his suit.[16]

Lilibet's choice of Philip had more than a little to do with her desire to break free of the claustrophobic overprotectiveness of her parents. Her father and mother were all that was safe, loving, unworldly and sweet—but they were stifling her. Philip, on the other hand, was dangerous, bracing, sophisticated and edgy. He invited her across an intriguing threshold beyond which stretched the unknown. She longed to cross that threshold, not only for the few brief hours or days she spent in his exciting, unpredictable company, but for the rest of her life.

EIGHT

In the back of the chauffeur-driven limousine, Princess Elizabeth and her lady-in-waiting Jean Gibbs sang "People Will Say We're in Love" and "The Surrey with the Fringe on Top," tapping their feet on the thick carpet in time to the music. Lilibet was nineteen, the war was over at last and in her exuberance she often burst into song, playing the radio loudly at the palace and upsetting her mother.

"Don't be old-fashioned, mummy," she chided when the queen complained that Mrs. Gibbs, "a rather bohemian young person," Crawfie thought, arrived at the palace hatless and on a bicycle.[1] The informality

suited the mood of the young in the postwar world: loose, devil-may-care, impatient
of the deadweight of the past. Lilibet, ex-
pansive and more confident than ever before, incarnated it.

She seemed always to be going to parties, dances, or to the theater, and she
came home humming the tunes of the new
American musicals. The queen arranged
the entertainments, eager for her daughter
to meet eligible young men, ensigns from
the Household Brigade, officers on leave,
aristocrats who would one day inherit great
fortunes. Philip was away, on duty in the Far
East; both the king and queen hoped that,
in his absence, Lilibet's affections would
become engaged elsewhere. American reporters, following the princess's social life in
the summer and fall of 1945 with avid interest, were convinced that she was in
love with Prince Charles of Belgium. She
danced, sometimes until five in the morning, with a variety of men, but Philip continued to be the one she wanted. His photo
was on her mantelpiece. She looked forward to his letters. He was, and would remain "the one," and the members of the
palace staff were sure of it. They whispered,

gossip spread, and before long the newspaper stories about Charles of Belgium
ceased to appear.

There was a newfound self-assuredness
about Lilibet in the early postwar months. In
part, it came from her recent training in the
Auxiliary Territorial Service, in which she
learned to drive and maintain staff cars and
vans. Her course had not been long, but it
had greatly increased her belief in herself;
driving Red Cross vans through London in
heavy traffic, and knowing how to repair
them, was empowering. "I've never worked
so hard in my life," she told a friend. Looking up from under the hood of a car, her
face smudged, a wrench in her hand, she
was delighted and proud to be making a
contribution. She passed her driving tests,
was certified as an expert driver and vehicle
maintenance specialist, and completed the
course successfully, becoming a junior officer. Though the war was almost over, she
had a few weeks of actual service, and
made the most of them.[2]

What was more, she made acquaintances among the other eleven women in
her course at the training center in Surrey.
At first she had been kept at a distance

from the other trainees, flanked by sergeants assigned to protect her during lectures and whisked away to the castle immediately after each day's training session ended. Before long, however, she managed to break free of these restrictions, and began to mingle with the other trainees—all of whom were carefully selected to be of the "right sort," sergeants and corporals, all of them instructors themselves, politely sitting through the specially tailored, abbreviated introductory course for the princess's benefit.[3]

Lilibet was curious about the others, eager to learn about their lives; they in turn were curious about her, impressed by how attractive she was, by the fact that she wore lipstick (quite daring in 1945, and all but unheard-of in the royal family), and by how rapidly she opened up and was "not a bit shy."[4] She ate with her classmates in the officers' mess, where the fare was pilchards in tomato sauce, horsemeat and soggy greens. As a special concession, she alone was served with a small jug of condensed milk—a great treat.[5] She did not, of course, bunk with the others in their temporary huts, but she was exposed to their swearing, their knowing, worldly manner and their smoking.

When she completed the course Lilibet told her new acquaintances how sorry she was that it had come to an end and how much she looked forward to her appointment as a junior officer.

Lilibet's contact with the other trainees, like her friendship with her unconventional lady-in-waiting Mrs. Gibbs, made the queen nervous. She wanted to know their names, and inspected them quite critically when she came, with the king, to visit her daughter in the training camp. She had, as Crawfie had once noticed with a chill, "a long cool stare," and a shrewd appraising eye.

The queen's appraising eye had been trained for many years on everyone in Lilibet's small circle of friends and associates, and most recently, on Philip. Quietly but firmly, she had decided to oppose the idea of Lilibet's marriage to him.

Like everyone else, the queen looked on Philip as a Mountbatten protégé. And the Mountbattens she considered to be the most unsavory of her royal in-laws, those she least wanted near her daughter.

They were, to their credit, descended

from Queen Victoria, Lord Louis Mountbatten's elderly mother Victoria being the daughter of the great queen's daughter Alice. But the Mountbattens were also the product of a scandal—an old scandal, to be sure, but one that had reverberated in the Hesse and Windsor families for generations.

Prince Alexander, son of Grand Duke Louis II of Hesse, had fallen in love with a lowborn Polish woman, Julie Hauke, a maid of honor at the Russian court. Alexander had eloped with the pregnant Julie and the grand duke had been forced, much to his embarrassment, to accept their indiscretion. He had given Julie the title Princess of Battenberg.

The outrage to mid-Victorian propriety had been very great—nearly as great as that other contemporary outrage, the dalliance of Queen Victoria's son Edward, Prince of Wales, with the Irish actress Nellie Clifden. Edward's moral lapse had broken his father Prince Albert's heart and hastened Albert's premature death.

There had been scandal in every generation since, always surrounding a handsome, ambitious, rebellious son. Alexander and

Julie's son Louis had left home to join the British Royal Navy, and rose to its highest ranks, only to be reviled and driven out of the service during World War I, rumored (unjustly) to be a spy for his German relations. Lord Louis Mountbatten had attracted so much gossip for his own and his wife's promiscuity and alleged bisexuality that Queen Mary excluded them from court in the early 1930s, and Mountbatten was verbally reprimanded.[6] Now Philip, it seemed, had inherited the role of the good-looking, scandal-attracting, defiantly unconventional family scion, raised primarily by his unsavory, decadent uncle George Milford Haven and his exotic aunt Nadejda, whose lesbian liaisons were notorious.

Notoriety—and of the worst sort: that was what both the queen and king feared. Even if Philip was innocent of all the slanders that attached themselves to him, the stories themselves were damaging, and would damage whomever he married.

And beyond that, there was the deeply uncomfortable fact of his Nazi relations.

All of Philip's three surviving older sisters (his fourth sister, Cecile, had died in 1937) were married to German officers; his sister

Margarita's husband was a corps commander, Theodora's husband helped to lead the German assault against France before being severely wounded in a machine gun attack, and Sophie's husband, Christopher of Hesse, was head of Hermann Göring's research office—a sinister intelligence-gathering agency—and a colonel in the SS.[7] Christopher's brother Philip was a close confidant of Göring's and an envoy for Hitler, who gave him an honorary generalship in the SA, and was accused of war crimes. This much was widely known, and the king was aware of more damning information from boxes of documents relating to the British royal family captured in Philip of Hesse's castle, Schloss Kronberg, soon after the war ended.[8]

Had Philip been a well educated, well-spoken, well dressed Old Etonian he might have overcome the liabilities of being a Mountbatten protégé and having many close relatives who had fought for Hitler. But he was not well educated; he had attended the respected Old Tabor school at Cheam but went on to the rigid, Nazified Salem (where he was "flagrantly irreverent") and to Gordonstoun, an innovative but experimental school looked on with skepticism by the British upper class. And while he excelled at cricket and hockey and the high jump, he did not exert himself academically, and was judged "reckless and wild" by the school's founder, Kurt Hahn.

Instead of being well-spoken, Philip was outspoken. He was unsparing in his criticisms, not only tactless but bruising. No one escaped his acerb, often arrogant remarks, not the staff of the royal household, not even the prime minister. In situations that called for emollient attitudes, Philip was like sandpaper, scraping sensitive nerves raw and multiplying wounds. Disdainful, foul-mouthed, a bully when crossed, he grated on others with his loud raucous laugh.

Far from being well-dressed, Philip was a sartorial disgrace. When out of uniform, he was reduced to wearing the out-of-date clothes of his late father, or to borrowing dinner jackets and tuxedos from his uncle Mountbatten, who was a much larger man. He possessed only a single suit, and appeared in public with badly-tied ties, conspicuously darned socks and shoes in need of a polish.

In short, he was no gentleman. And at a

time when the royal family needed to project an image of civility, decency and wholesomeness, of devoted consideration for one another and solid domestic virtue, they could not afford to risk letting an ill-mannered, risqué, volatile and irreverent adventurer into their ranks. A court official who was in the confidence of both the king and queen summed up their view. They felt, he said, that Philip was "rough, ill-tempered, uneducated and would probably not be faithful."[9]

Quite suddenly, in the fall of 1945, Clara Knight died. She had been Lilibet and Margaret's nursemaid all their lives, stern and correct, fiercely protective of them, old-fashioned and unchanging through all the vicissitudes of war, social transformation and family turmoil. Her death was a break with the past, the loss of a link to childhood. Lilibet regretted her, and sent a wreath of violets to be laid on her coffin with the message "In Loving and Thankful Memory."[10]

Lilibet was outwardly self-possessed that fall during the family's long stay at Balmoral. Borrowing a pair of her father's tweed plus-fours, she went out stalking stags with the head keeper, following him up and down the heather-covered hills, scrambling over boulders and along the banks of streams. Shooting became her new passion, the art of stalking her newest accomplishment. Each evening she came back to the castle full of talk about antlers and points, the stags she had shot and those that had managed to evade her. She wrote out her game book and discussed the following day's hunt with her father; together, that fall, they brought down stags and roe deer, grouse and pheasant, hares and wood-cocks and wild ducks. Between battues there were rural idylls, trips into the moun-tains and afternoons of salmon and trout fishing, pony rides and picnics on the moor. They loaded up George V's elderly pony Jock and set out along the hill paths, their destination a deserted schoolhouse with a kitchen where they cooked onions and meat and dined on stuffed rolls, plum cake and ginger cookies.[11]

The days drew in, and the evenings be-gan to become chilly. Rain swept down across the moors in thick sheets, and dense fog obscured the mountains. Un-daunted by the weather, Lilibet continued to stalk and shoot, and to ride, more recklessly than usual, across the muddy hill tracks. One day she took a fence, cleared it, but then was thrown from her horse. She hit a tree, and bruised both legs badly.[12]

Like Allah's death, the fall was a jarring interruption, an unexpected break in an otherwise positive, self-assured advance. An unwelcome reminder that there were other obstacles in her path, chief among them her parents' opposition to her hoped-for marriage to Philip.

Philip came roaring up to the gates of Buckingham Palace in his black MG in January of 1946. He was back from Tokyo, finished with sea duty for the time being. His new assignment, at a training school for cadets in north Wales, was undemanding and allowed him to come to London often, which he did for a time.

But once in the capital, he behaved, not like a lovesick would-be husband, but like a wild schoolboy, staying out very late at nightclubs with his cousin David Milford Haven, running up and down the corridors of Kensington Palace, where he stayed with his grandmother, dashing off to Buckingham Palace where he played ball in the former nursery with Lilibet and Margaret, the three of them "racing about like a bunch of high-spirited children."[13] Palace servants would hear the sound of a loud car engine and know that it was Philip; they heard Lilibet playing "People Will Say We're in Love" over and over, and saw that she brightened up when Philip was nearby, and concluded that an engagement announcement would be issued shortly.

But no announcement was made, even though Philip had begun to arrive for an informal dinner almost every night with boisterous games to follow. Stories speculating about the likelihood of an engagement appeared in the newspapers, and when Lilibet went out to open a new library or present prizes at a school there were questions from the watching crowd: "Where's Philip?"[14] Lilibet blushed and cringed.

Then, suddenly, Philip was gone. He was in Paris, visiting Helene Cordet. He stayed on there week after week, spending time with Helene and playing with her two children, enjoying the multiple pleasures of the Parisian spring, missing Lilibet's twentieth birthday party in April 1946, and triggering the repetition of old rumors that he was the father of at least one of Helene's children.

Whether or not these rumors had reached Lilibet is unknown; certainly they had reached her parents. But nothing was said. Her life went forward in its customary pattern, with early morning visits to her parents' bedroom, breakfast with Margaret, meetings with one of her ladies-in-waiting—she now had two—to answer letters, and appointments with the dressmaker. She had begun to sit in on meetings of the royal council, and to spend time with her father each day talking over current issues and events. There was always a full schedule of afternoon appearances, military inspections, factory or hospital visits, bazaars to open and receptions to attend. In addition, she tried to find time to ride, and to spend time in the garden with the corgis, whose care and feeding were given priority.

Swarms of mosquitoes rose in clouds out of the damp earth at Balmoral in the fall of 1946, their numbers greater than usual. The royal family and their guests could hardly stir out of the castle without slapping at their necks, hands and ankles—any exposed patch of skin—where the flying pests landed and stung. Everyone itched, everyone scratched. It was an uncomfortable fall.

Philip had been invited to join the family for an extended stay, but instead of feeling honored to be included he was annoyed. According to protocol, he was informed by letter what clothes he was expected to bring, and acquainted with the rules of the Balmoral establishment. Instead of regarding these stipulations as quaint but unavoidable, and borrowing money from his uncle to fill out his inadequate wardrobe so that he could comply with them, Philip bristled; he did not like to be told what to do, authority invariably brought out all his defiance, his "flagrant irreverence." He arrived at Balmoral without the requisite wardrobe, and proceeded to cause offense.

To Philip, accustomed to speed, efficiency and the immediate gratification of all his physical needs, the stately pace and antiquated accommodations at Balmoral were irritating. He liked sleek modernity, and the old castle was a shrine to Victorian kitsch. He liked warmth and comfort, and Balmoral was cold, drafty and Spartan, the plumbing inadequate, the stinking water brought to his cramped bedroom dark with sediment. He liked admiration and approval, and almost as soon as he arrived, the servants, and soon the other guests, began to register in small ways their disapprobation—indeed their faint repugnance—of who he was and what he represented. As sharp as the cold wind off the moor, Philip felt the chill of snobbery, and it brought out all his mocking insolence and irascibility.

"What infernal cheek!" he exclaimed when he discovered that it had been the king's equerry and close personal assistant Peter Townsend who suggested that he, Philip, be invited to join the family vacation in Scotland. What Townsend had meant by the suggestion was that Philip should be offered a sort of trial run, a chance to prove himself. That he should have to submit to such scrutiny, and at the hands of an equerry, was insulting to Philip, ever sensitive to hierarchies and social status and acutely aware that his own precarious niche in the hierarchy of the wellborn was ambiguous.

Philip began to collide with protocol, offend staff and other guests and outrage members of the royal family almost immediately. He sneered at Townsend, ate greedily, smoked constantly, drank too many "pinks"—pink gins, his favorite—and dominated every conversation he entered with his restless energy and bluntly phrased opinions. The servants assigned to look after him complained that he made extra work for them by throwing his clothes on the floor and demanding special services. On shooting days, he appeared in flannels instead of tweeds (deliberately defying the clothing regulations), and caused inconvenience by not having brought along a gun of his own—another breach of decorum. His loud, barking laugh could be heard not only in the rooms where the family and guests gathered but in the corridors outside—and sometimes the rest of the company joined in, for he could be very entertaining. But no one laughed when, having put on a kilt to conform to palace custom, he curtsied to the king—and King George was affronted.

Through it all, Lilibet observed the predictable reactions of her parents and the others who came and went during the month that Philip stayed on. She knew that they thought him boorish and rough, that they concluded he didn't fit in. Whatever hopes she may have had that he would adapt, or that the others would, for her sake, embrace him, unconventional behavior and all, did not come to fruition. Embarrassed and somewhat heartsore, she went on picnics with her beloved, or out driving, or took long strolls through the gardens—always with chaperones hovering.

"The general opinion was that both Lilibet and Philip had had rather a bad break, and the summer could not have been much fun for them," Crawfie wrote. The household was sympathetic to her, but disapproving of him.[15] Behind his back they called him "the Hun," or "the Kraut," and talked privately of the unfortunate restoration of the autocratic Greek monarchy and of Philip's regrettably close ties with the Greek royal family.

All Lilibet's confidence and buoyancy seemed to have vanished. She grew quiet and withdrawn. According to Philip, they talked about getting married, but whether or not they actually pledged themselves to one another during those tense autumn days, as they fought off the savage mosquitoes and tried to shrug off the atmosphere of disapproval, is unknown. Early in September, 1946, a formal announcement was made that rumors of an engagement between Princess Elizabeth and Philip of

Greece were untrue, and that the princess was about to embark with her parents on a lengthy tour of South Africa—a tour that would separate her, for many long months, from the man she loved.

NINE

There had been a quarrel. Not a bitter, abuse-hurling, bruising battle but a battle of wills, firm and outspoken and at times harsh. Lilibet adored her father but she fought with him, challenged his authority and triggered his hot temper. She wanted to be engaged to Philip, her father said no. She was stubborn, but in the end, he won.

Just what was said between father and daughter at Balmoral in that autumn of 1946 will never be known, but one may safely surmise that on the king's side, much was left unsaid. King George would not have been likely to tell his audacious but sheltered daughter about the salacious rumors circulating about Philip's past and present erotic liaisons; these were things men told one another in club rooms, or in discreet after-dinner conversations from which ladies were excluded. He would not have tried, in his stammering fashion, to educate her in worldliness. He would not have explained that what worried him was not so much that Philip had, as sailors do, visited brothels, or that his preferred companion, his cousin David Milford Haven, collected pornography and was said to seek out low company and decadent sexual thrills. He would not have said that: for what worried him most was that Philip's adventurism had an unhealthily reckless edge. He seemed to be in search of not only pleasure but risky pleasure.

And there was another nagging concern. Beneath Philip's cocksure facade there was a note of ruthlessness, of amoral self-seeking that could not have been more at odds with the gentle, warm, and close family bond linking the king and queen and their daughters. They cared deeply for one another, while Philip, the king feared, cared deeply only for himself.

George VI was in a pessimistic mood. His

kingdom was in rapid and precipitate decline. Large expanses of her cities lay in ruins, her debts were immense, her finances
in disarray. She could no longer afford her
far-flung empire, which was in any case
shrinking as colonies became independent
nations. The end of the war seemed, to the
king and many others born to wealth and
privilege, to mark the onset of a melancholy
Götterdämmerung, a fading of the old order.
Monarchy was in retreat and aristocracy in
financial decline, all over Europe, while pro-
letarian forces advanced. In Britain, a Labour government had come to power and
was rapidly dismantling the prewar economy, nationalizing the coal, electricity and
gas industries along with the Bank of England and a host of other institutions, creating a National Health Service and a national
insurance system, raising old age pensions
and building state-subsidized housing—all
at great cost in increased taxes. No one
could foresee how far Britain's political
swing to the left might go; some thought
the monarchy itself would be eliminated.

The beleaguered king faced labor agitation close to home, when the underpaid
boilermen at Buckingham Palace organized

the rest of the staff to insist on higher wages. A strike threat resulted in not only long overdue wage increases but greatly improved living conditions, an oversight in need of correction for decades, as some palace servants had been living in dark, beetle-infested basements since the days of the late Queen Victoria.[1]

The strike threat, like the broader shift in public sentiment toward social reform, left the king shocked and distressed. His own very conservative views were under assault, leaving him with a sense that, in every sphere of life, the pillars of civilization were crumbling, the barbarians were at the gates. Philip, with his ungentlemanly habits and self-absorbed hedonism, was one barbarian he was not going to allow in.

Nor was King George the only one who felt as he did about his daughter's preferred candidate to be her husband. Queen Mary, sensible and shrewd in her judgments of people, was dubious about Philip, while Queen Elizabeth's brother David Bowes-Lyon was strenuously opposed to allowing Lilibet to marry him. The queen herself, who valued unpretentiousness, wholesomeness and altruism above all, was much put off by

Philip's flash, rumored dissipation and self-aggrandizement. No doubt she could perceive his devastating sexual allure, and understand why Lilibet was irresistibly drawn to him—but at the same time the thought of her guileless daughter married to her much more sophisticated cousin must have made the queen shudder. Others weighed in with negative opinions: Old Etonians were skeptical, Conservative politicians (many of whom were Old Etonians) adverse. Closing ranks, they stood with the king in opposition to what the princess so ardently wanted.

And, equally important, what Lord Louis Mountbatten wanted—for in the fall of 1946, Mountbatten was working urgently to prepare the way for his nephew to marry the princess. While the royal family tried to block Philip's naturalization process—he would have to renounce his Greek citizenship and become a British subject before a marriage could take place—Mountbatten facilitated it, through his close ties with the Labour government. He also facilitated Philip's name change, from the German Philip of Schleswig-Holstein-Sonderburg-Glücksburg to Philip Mountbatten. Lord

Louis himself was in high political favor, about to be appointed to be Viceroy of India, and given the delicate task of overseeing the transfer of power from British to Indian rule.

Despite family opposition, Mountbatten proceeded with his campaign to promote the Lilibet-Philip wedding.[2] He had already made inquiries about the title of Prince Consort, the title by which Prince Albert had been known. He asked his sister Alice, Philip's mother, who lived in Greece but was currently in residence at Kensington Palace, to research how the issue of Albert's rank had been handled in Victoria's time. And he made use of the newspapers, informing reporters hungry for information about Philip that despite his Greek birth and European upbringing, his nephew was British to the core, with the speech, thoughts and habits of life of a serving officer in the Royal Navy.

Evidently Philip himself was convinced that Lord Louis was doing all in his power to bring about the marriage. He wrote to his uncle in January of 1947, alluding to Mountbatten's "liking the idea of being the General Manager of this little show"—i.e., the behind-the-scenes maneuvering to further an engagement—and expressing some doubt about Lilibet's "taking to the idea quite as docilely" as he did. "It is true that I know what is good for me," Philip went on, "but don't forget that she has not had you as uncle loco parentis, counsellor and friend as long as I have."[3]

What Lilibet thought about Lord Louis's promotion of her engagement is undiscoverable, but it was clear she was unhappy about the frustration of her hopes. A four-month exile to South Africa loomed, and until the tour was over, no progress could be expected on the matter of her engagement. Meanwhile, speculation about it continued to appear in the newspapers, along with articles covering every facet of her daily life. Having been a celebrity since earliest childhood, Lilibet now found herself the object of redoubled publicity, easily eclipsing that surrounding her parents who, as they aged, were moving out of the center of public awareness. The fresh-faced, blue-eyed princess was very attractive; pictures of her, and stories about her, sold newspapers and magazines—and not only in Britain, but especially in America, *Time* magazine (which had had the princess on

its cover when she was a very little girl) portrayed her as a swing-dancing, nightclub-
going member of the postwar generation
who just happened to be heiress to the
British throne.

The South African tour proved to be exhausting. Heaving seas caused the ship in
which the royals sailed, the *Vanguard*, to
lurch and pitch until nearly everyone was
seasick. ("I for one would willingly have
died, I was so miserable," Lilibet wrote to
Crawfie.) The weather in Cape Town was
scorching, the schedule of travel and royal
appearances "absolutely staggering."

"I hope we shall survive, that's all!" wrote
Lilibet, and survive they did, but not comfortably. They were often ill, and always
tired; sometimes Margaret fell asleep just
as they had to attend a ceremony or make
a formal presentation. Lilibet confided to
her father's sympathetic equerry Peter
Townsend that she didn't sleep much during the trip. A special train carried the family
to Basutoland, Natal, the Transvaal and
Northern Rhodesia. In Maseru Park, Lilibet
insisted on being taken to greet a busload
of leper girls, all of them Girl Guides as she
herself had been, who had been deliber-

ately kept out of sight because of their disease. In the Witwatersrand, the gold miners were on strike and violently opposed to the government. Nor was this the only dangerous situation. Extra security had to be provided in many regions because Indian nationalists and extremist Afrikaners made death threats against the royal family.

Week after week, the cavalcade wound its way from town to town, the family having to present themselves, freshly groomed and beaming with good will, at every stop. The terrible heat, the unfamiliar food that disagreed with them, the dust-clouds that rose out of the earth and deposited layers of dirt and ash over them again and again, the immense chanting crowds that surged forward, threatening to engulf the king and his party at every stop, gradually wore them down. Lilibet and her father lost weight, the king looked particularly pale and tired and complained of shortness of breath and severe pains in his legs. By the end of April, with the long journey nearly over, the royals could barely endure the final nights of banqueting and parties in Cape Town— events held to celebrate Lilibet's twenty-first birthday.

"I am six thousand miles from the country where I was born," she said in the eloquent birthday speech Sir Alan Lascelles wrote for her, "but I am certainly not six thousand miles from home." She spoke movingly of the shift from Britain's empire to the emerging Commonwealth (from which the Republic of South Africa would secede in the following year), of the need to make "of this ancient Commonwealth which we all love so dearly an even grander thing," and of her own dedication to devoting her whole life to the service of her people and "the great imperial family."

Her sincerity was affecting, but futile, and most of those who heard her speech knew it. The dictatorship of Jan Smuts was in its final months, and would soon be replaced by a Nationalist government that instituted apartheid and, in so doing, set South Africa at odds with world opinion.

A thinner and paler Lilibet stepped off the ship at Portsmouth in May, 1947, having been away for the better part of half a year. Her lady-in-waiting Margaret Egerton saw the princess "dance a little jig of sheer delight" at being home again, and soon she was reunited with Philip.[4] Over the following two months a last assault was launched by opponents of the engagement, but the resistance was crumbling. Early in July Philip gave Lilibet an engagement ring set with some of his mother's diamonds, reset in a design he and Lilibet had chosen together. The official announcement of the engagement soon followed, celebrated at a garden party where the princess proudly showed off her new ring.

There remained an undercurrent of flinty resistance to Lilibet's fiancé on the part of the senior courtiers, resulting in tension and at times in friction. Many Britons reacted unfavorably to the news that their future queen was about to marry a foreigner—and a German foreigner no less. Parliament, with its blunt-spoken Labour majority, and conscious that millions were out of work and that the American loans that had been keeping the government afloat financially were about to run out, resisted voting funds for wedding decorations or for repairs to Clarence House, the dilapidated, bomb-damaged London residence the king had given his daughter and Philip as an engagement present. In the end the sums were supplied, along with an increase in the Civil

List for Lilibet and an allowance for Philip. But resentments smoldered, and came to center on Sunninghill, a twenty-five-room grace and favor house near Windsor that the king had designated to become the couple's country home.

Squatters had moved into an abandoned army camp on the vast seven-hundred-acre Sunninghill grounds, waiting for the local council to implement its decree that the house be converted into apartments to provide housing for some of the many homeless families in the area. The king's decision to give the house to his daughter meant that these plans would have to be given up, and the squatters evicted. The idea that the princess, whose parents lived in a seven-hundred-room palace and who had already been given another mansion for herself, needed Sunninghill when others needed it far more seemed contrary to reason and justice; when a large part of Sunninghill's south wing burned in August, 1947, many suspected arson.

Wounded by the incident, though she was reluctant to believe the fire had been deliberately set, Lilibet refused to take the loss of Sunninghill as an omen, and went on planning her wedding, choosing music, the order of service, designating attendants and deciding on the guest list. Innumerable decisions had to be made, from the ordering of the gigantic wedding cake (which was to take a full four months to make) to the commissioning of the wedding ring from the West End jeweler Bertollé, made from the same nugget of rare Welsh gold that had yielded the queen's wedding ring nearly a quarter of a century before. The Archbishop of Canterbury was to perform the service, the Archbishop of York to deliver the address. The bridal march was not to be the traditional Mendelssohn wedding march but a march by Sir Hubert Parry, from his incidental music to *The Birds*. Two of the bride's favorite hymns would be sung, "Praise My Soul the King of Heaven" and the Scottish metrical tune to "The Lord's My Shepherd."

During the war years, British brides had been married in suits or heirloom gowns handed down from their mothers or grandmothers or improvised dresses made of old curtains or parachute silk. Strict clothing rationing, still very much in effect in 1947, made new wedding gowns an impossibility.

But the restrictions were lifted for Lilibet, who was allowed a generous extra measure of ration coupons to subsidize her wedding gown and trousseau. The couturier Norman Hartnell, who had been dressing the queen for many years, submitted twelve designs from which the final choice was made, and dozens of seamstresses went to work in Hartnell's atelier embroidering the elaborate gown and veil with thousands of pearls and crystals in intricate patterns of roses and wheat sheaves, star flowers and orange blossoms.

Very late one rainy night the telephone rang at the palace. A frightened equerry awakened the king with the news that Lieutenant Philip Mountbatten, on his way home from a night out with friends, had lost control of his MG. The car had skidded on the wet road and overturned in a ditch. He was alive, indeed he was lucky to be alive, but he was injured. No one else was hurt.

Lilibet was awakened and given the alarming news. In distress, she talked to Philip on the telephone herself. He was badly shaken up, bruised all over, and had twisted his knee in the crash. But otherwise he was all right. The main thing was, he had survived.

He had survived—but for how long? He drove much too fast, recklessly, deliberately inviting disaster. He drove when he was in no condition to drive, when he had had too little sleep, when he had been drinking. It was remarkable that he hadn't had an accident before. And since Lilibet often went driving with him, it was remarkable that he hadn't injured her.

In the aftermath of the accident, a frisson of fear swept through the palace. Staff members, many of whom had known and cared for Lilibet since she was a child, and were deeply concerned for her welfare, didn't want her to ride with Philip any more. The palace chauffeurs didn't want Philip driving their beautifully maintained cars; how much more concerned should everyone be about safeguarding the heir to the throne?

Philip was making the most of his waning number of bachelor days. Living with louche cousin David, going out nearly every night, sneaking back into Kensington Palace in the early hours of the morning by climbing over the roof. Much more in the public eye than ever before, Philip was the object of renewed speculation and gossip. His accident made headlines, and reporters dug deep for other stories, reviving tales of his rumored liaison with Helene Cordet. The reports and gossip angered him and set him on edge, increasing his volatility.

Clearly he was nervous about the role he was about to take on as husband of the future queen, and his nervousness went beyond ordinary pre-wedding jitters. He must have known, or sensed, the deepgoing hostility he aroused. During the family vacation at Balmoral, he was subtly snubbed by the other guests, and referred to behind his back as "Charlie Kraut." His valet John Dean was meanwhile revealing to the public embarrassing details about Philip's poverty, leading to more speculation that he was a fortune-hunter. According to Dean, Philip had only six pounds in the bank, and his navy pay was a mere eleven pounds a week. He had in his closet only one shabby uniform and three suits, one of which had been his father's. His underwear drawer needed filling and he was relying on his mother to supply him with new shirts, made

up from lengths of silk supplied by the mer-
chants of Athens.[5]

What the newspapers did not report was
that Lilibet's husband-to-be was seeking
relief from all his stress in the company of a
group of genial hedonists who belonged to
the Thursday Club, a collection of artists,
writers and actors who gathered each
Thursday at Wheeler's Restaurant in Soho
for a long afternoon of carousing. They
drank, dined, told funny, filthy jokes and
generally forgot their inhibitions—sometimes to the extent of making a night of it at
private parties with similarly uninhibited female companions.[6] Indulgent observers
dismissed the Thursday Club and its activities as unbuttoned fun, but there were hardened voluptuaries in the club's circles, and
some of the goings-on, especially at parties
given by photographer Baron Henry Stirling
Nahum, known simply as "Baron," were reportedly sordid. For Philip to risk his own
and the royal family's reputations by taking
a chance that his involvement with the
group would not come to light was both ir-
responsible and a foolish challenge to fate.
Either way he was guilty, not only of a serious error of judgment, but of inviting disas-

ter, just as he did when he drove too fast on rain-slick roads.

The date fixed for the wedding, November 20, 1947, was fast approaching. Philip was once again out driving, this time with Lilibet in the car beside him.[7] He had hardly left the precincts of Buckingham Palace when he collided with a taxi at Hyde Park Corner. No one was hurt, but Philip and the taxi driver got into a heated argument. The press was informed, and once again tongues wagged and heads shook.

"Oh, Crawfie," Lilibet cried in exasperation when she got back to the palace, "how am I to make Mummie and Papa realize that this time it REALLY wasn't Philip's fault. It was the taxi. They will never believe it."

TEN

They were a golden couple. She with her lovely skin and eyes, her bright smile, her curvaceous figure, he tall and straight and so good-looking in his navy uniform, his medals gleaming, his grandfather's sword strapped to his waist. Her gown fell away from her slender waist in rich satin folds, twinkling with tiny flashing beads, her long veil floating about her in a cascade of gauze. They were like perfect figures atop a wedding cake come to life, and on their wedding day, even the harshest critics of the monarchy had to admit that Princess Elizabeth and her new husband were much-needed symbols of radiant vitality in a season of scarcity and chill.

> *When hope is dim and luck is out of*
>   *joint . . .*
> *Where a Crown shines . . .*
> *There a land's spirit finds a rallying-*
>   *point.*

So sang John Masefield, the Poet Laureate, in his Prayer for the Royal Marriage printed in the wedding program.[1] The thousands who lined the streets to catch a glimpse of the couple, shivering in the biting November cold, needed a spirit-rallying lift. Their meager meat ration had just been cut in half, sugar, butter, potatoes, bread and other staples were in very short supply and butchers were offering horseflesh and whale meat ("rich and tasty") as alternatives to bacon and beef.

For months, talk of the wedding had been a welcome diversion from dreary conversations about inadequate food, clothes, fuel and housing—or even more disturbing talk of the advance of communism in Eastern Europe and the alarming threat of atomic weapons. Londoners had lined up by the thousands to view the royal wedding gifts, more than two thousand of them, most of them laid out on display in St. James's Palace. To optimists, such lavish bounty was heartening, it undergirded their hope that in time, Britain would be prosperous once again. To pessimists, recalling the grim winter just past, the display of gifts was a reminder of all that they lacked, and might never have again.

The plight of the realm had indeed been dire in the early months of 1947. To begin with, the cold was unlike anything experienced within living memory, a cold so deep and so penetrating that it swept the entire realm into its harsh, frozen grip. Sheep froze stiff in the fields. Water froze in the pipes. Trucks and cars were snowbound, the roads impassable. And when supplies of coal ran out, as they soon did, there was no heat for houses and entire towns were without electricity.

Nor was the government able to alleviate the catastrophe. The Prime Minister ordered many industries shut down and others radically curtailed, to save precious coal. But for nine weeks the population suffered, desperately short of food, until the icebound roads became usable again and snow melted from the railroad tracks, allowing trucks and trains filled with food and coal to make their deliveries.

Surveying the long tables where the royal wedding gifts were displayed, tables overflowing with handknitted blankets and Shetland shawls, thick rugs and warm fur-trimmed coats, assortments of cheese and cans of food, Londoners must have thought of the bleak times they had been through. Many of the gifts, especially those sent from America and Canada, were meant to compensate for shortages. Two thousand pounds of food, hundreds of pairs of nylon stockings, table linens and handkerchiefs in abundance, all were intended to fill a well-publicized deficit. Other gifts were more traditional, such as the silver gilt dressing table set given to Lilibet by the heads of the London diplomatic missions and the picnic set from Princess Margaret. Bobo Macdonald, Lilibet's dresser and confidante, gave the no-nonsense gift of a wastebasket.

But it was, above all, the beautiful gifts of jewels that the spectators at St. James's Palace waited in long lines to see, the sacks of rubies from Burma, the immense uncut pink diamond that weighed fifty-four carats, the antique diamond earrings and the priceless sapphire and diamond necklace that was a wedding present from the king and queen. Queen Mary had given her granddaughter a treasure chest of gems, among them ruby earrings, Indian bangles heavy with diamonds—a relic of the great Delhi Durbar of 1911—and the "marguerite tiara," a diamond tiara presented to Mary on her own wedding day half a century before, a gift from all her subjects named Mary.

Some of the gifts could not be laid out on tables: the grand piano the Royal Air Force gave the couple, the Arabian horse sent to Lilibet by the Aga Khan, the hunting lodge in Kenya, Sagana Lodge, presented by the Kenyan people, and the movie theater being constructed in Lilibet and Philip's rented weekend country home, Windlesham Moor, the cost of construction a gift from the Mountbattens.

Pale but composed during the wedding ceremony itself, Lilibet's color returned at the large lunch party afterward, where family and guests dined on filet of sole Mountbatten and bombe glacée Princess Elizabeth and were served from the twelve wedding cakes, the principal one nine feet high. After the toasts were drunk the bride disappeared, then came back wearing her pale blue crepe going-away dress, her hat a blue beret with a feather. Family and guests threw rose leaves (rice being scarce) over the bride and groom as they went out, hand in hand, into the wet forecourt of the palace where an open landau waited to take them to Waterloo Station. Lilibet looked "so happy," Crawfie thought, as she climbed into the carriage, a blanket over her lap and her corgi Susan beside her.

Lord Louis Mountbatten's six-thousand-acre Hampshire estate, Broadlands, was the honeymoon destination, and in an attempt to keep annoying curious spectators at bay, police and gamekeepers patrolled the grounds. Privacy proved to be impossible. Large crowds, eager to catch a glimpse of the royal couple, invaded the estate, reporters and photographers pressing past the gates and even hanging from the trees. Fleeing the onlookers, Philip, in a bright blue jeep, raced through the nearby town of Romsey one day, with Lilibet beside him, hair flying, both singing at the top of their lungs.[2]

They were happy, but beleaguered. Seeking peace they left Broadlands and went to Birkhall, where the snow lay deep on the hillside and the old house, chilly even in summer, was icy. Philip caught a bad cold, and Lilibet amused herself by acquiring another dog, a puppy.[3]

There was to be no stability for the princess and her new husband during the first year and more of their married life. No permanent home was yet ready to receive them, and so they stayed, first, at Clock House, home of Lilibet's great-uncle the Earl of Athlone, on the grounds of Kensington Palace, and then moved to Lilibet's old suite at Buckingham Palace—an arrangement Philip found stifling. The bride, who by February of 1948 was contentedly pregnant, found this arrangement cozy; it allowed her to consult her mother about everything, which she did, constantly, and was convenient for keeping the full schedule of public appearances she made, despite morning sickness and fatigue, in the first five months of her pregnancy.

At Windlesham Moor, Lilibet and Philip contended over how the rooms should be decorated, he asserting a strong preference for bare, sleek modernity while she chose Victorian antiques and attendant clutter; her tastes prevailed. Philip had to content himself with ordering the conversion of the tennis courts to a cricket pitch where he could organize the six resident servants into a cricket team and play against opponents from Windsor.

While she nested, he fumed, restless in his new desk job at the Admiralty, missing his seagoing life, unable to settle graciously into the background of his wife's highly regimented, tightly scheduled royal routine and resenting having to be her unobtrusive, decorative escort at receptions and official functions. His lack of status grated on him, as did the thicket of Buckingham Palace regulations and formalities. He disliked the rigid timetables that governed palace activities, with even the feeding of the royal corgis following an unalterable pattern. Every afternoon at four-thirty a footman brought a tray for the dogs, with plates of meat, vegetables and gravy, to be served out with silver spoons.

Philip wanted to advance himself, and soon exchanged his Admiralty job for an officer training course at the Royal Naval College at Greenwich, his goal being command of his own ship. But his class attendance was interrupted time and again when he was summoned to accompany his wife to this event or that—a reminder that his primary job was, after all, to support Lilibet whenever needed.

Philip's irritation reached an extreme when the couple made an official visit to Paris in May of 1948. The princess was able to overcome her morning nausea and bravely withstand the heat, the crowds, the long parades and tedious speechmaking, giving five speeches herself in her excellent French. She enjoyed herself and the French loved her, calling her "little mouse" and declaring her to be "entirely Parisian." But Philip grew more and more impatient as the days of relentless appearances and scheduled events continued. He had been ill from the outset, suffering an attack of food poisoning on the boat from England. The noisy crowds and swarms of photographers brought out his bad temper, and he lashed out at them in anger. Paris held no enchantment for him, rather the reverse; the one appealing outing the royal couple made, to dinner at the Tour d'Argent followed by a visit to a fashionable nightclub in the rue Pierre Charron, was marred by spying reporters and by the fact that the nearly nude dancers were under instructions to cover up with extra feathers and gold leaf.

For relief from the straitjacket of obligations Philip turned to his friends at the Thursday Club, and to his yachting companions. Among the wedding gifts was a Dragon class yacht, *Bluebottle*, which Philip sailed competitively, with a raffish companion, the boat-builder Uffa Fox, in his crew. Philip and Uffa were mildly outrageous together, drinking and carrying on, but Philip and his newly appointed Private Secretary, his old partner in debauchery Mike Parker, went further in their silliness and ultimately, in their indiscretions.

Adopting the joke nicknames "Murgatroyd" and "Winterbottom," from the wartime radio show *ITMA* ("It's That Man Again"), Philip and Parker went out together often, announcing airily that "Murgatroyd and Winterbottom will be home late tonight." They stayed out very late, meeting friends, going nightclubbing, keeping questionable company. Both were now married men, but acted like footloose bachelors, racing around in Philip's Humber (he had given his MG to Parker), flirting, dancing, drinking and generally carrying on.[4]

The kind of loud ragging, joking and telling of offcolor stories Philip liked to engage in with his male friends helped him to let off steam harmlessly while reminding him of his days at sea. He had a taste for pranks, calling randomly chosen phone numbers in the middle of the night, or deliberately tripping duchesses at parties, or suddenly deciding to play cricket indoors, to the peril of the furniture.[5]

But as usual, he dared too much, went too far. On a trip to the South of France with David Milford Haven in the spring of 1948, Philip talked recklessly and at length about his married life, complaining that his wife was constantly pestering him for sex. He repeated the same story in a number of sitting rooms where English visitors were vacationing, telling a variety of people. That his comments were ungentlemanly, and cruel to his pregnant wife, was the least that could be said about them. Titled Britons who heard his remarks thought Philip "disgusting" and foresaw damage to the monarchy.[6] The ill-chosen words revealed an ugly undercurrent of resentment in Philip, a desire to strike back. He felt trapped, and if he could not free himself at least he could lash out and wound.

An incident that led to much more damaging notoriety concerned Philip and an actress, Pat Kirkwood, then starring in a musical at the Hippodrome in the fall of 1948. The Thursday Club lunch having extended late into the evening, Philip and Baron, who was enamored of the stunning Pat, went to the theater after the show and took Pat with them to Les Ambassadeurs and another nightclub. When Philip and Pat—he very recognizable, she exceptionally conspicuous in a dress of glowing fluorescent orange—began dancing together, laughing and flirting, heads turned and phone calls were quickly made. They danced on and on, waltzes, sambas (Lilibet's favorite, as Philip well knew), foxtrots, for several hours, while the nightclub filled up with gawkers and evening turned into early morning. Baron drove Philip and Pat back to his apartment, and neither got home until nearly seven in the morning.

What had happened between Philip and Pat Kirkwood in Baron's apartment? Had

Philip been unfaithful? Gossip said yes, Pat herself, many years later, said no.[7] Had Philip embarrassed and hurt his wife, who was then in the eighth month of her pregnancy? Undeniably. The king lectured him, and the courtiers who already disapproved of him redoubled their censure. Worst of all, the night of indiscretion underscored existing rumors about Philip and Helene Cordet, making it impossible for him to restore any claim to fidelity. He was forever tainted in the public mind, and associated with sordid and disloyal behavior to his wife.

What Lilibet thought of the hubbub surrounding her husband and the actress is unknown. Perhaps she ignored it, perhaps he reassured her that she had nothing to worry about, and she wanted to believe him. Perhaps, like her mother, she had adopted the habit of turning aside from unpleasantness, especially emotional unpleasantness, and chose to overlook the entire episode.

She had been getting ready for her child's birth, expected in mid-November, occupying herself with setting up the nursery—her old schoolroom in Buckingham Palace—and choosing furnishings. There

was the cot she herself had slept in, and a
baby basket—like the cot, an heirloom—
now re-lined in yellow silk trimmed with
lace. For the nursery at Clarence House she
ordered a renovation, a bathroom built to a
child's scale, with a miniature tub, small
towels, and a low sink, recalling the "Little
House" she and Margaret had spent so
much time playing in as children. The
layette, sewn by twenty-five retired dressmakers from the Cottage Homes for the
Aged, was adequate but not lavish, and
was supplemented by baby clothes, knitted
blankets and bootees sent from all over the
world. From these gifts layettes were made
up for needy mothers.

Letters of advice and good wishes reaching the palace increased in volume as the
expected delivery approached. Experienced mothers sent the princess suggestions on how to improve her health, admo-
nitions about diet, rest and maintaining a
positive frame of mind. Time-honored
methods of determining the child's sex
were spelled out, along with recommendations for the delivery itself. German mothers
wrote to say that they shared in Lilibet's
happiness, and to confess that, throughout

the war, they had always secretly admired the British royal family. It was a surprising and moving admission, and one the princess no doubt took to heart.

Nothing, in these waning days of her pregnancy, seemed to disturb her or dampen her spirits, not her husband's escapades, not her father's evident illness, not the betting on the baby's exact birthdate by the growing crowd of bystanders on the steps of the Victoria Memorial opposite the entrance to Buckingham Palace waiting for news that the princess had gone into labor. Though heavily pregnant, Lilibet was seen "doing a brisk sprint" down a palace corridor, and running with the corgis in the garden. If her obstetrician, William Gilliat, or the three nurses and midwife who were on hand to assist him objected to her vigorous activity, no one recorded it. She was in vibrant good health, she trusted Gilliat implicitly and was if anything eager to deliver her baby. As she told Crawfie, who was now married herself, having finally wed the man she had been in love with for at least nine years, "After all, it is what we're made for."[8]

By midafternoon on November 13, 1948, Lilibet was feeling uncomfortable, and spent a restless night.[9] On the afternoon of the fourteenth her labor intensified and she was wheeled to the Buhl room, converted to an operating theater, where Dr. Gilliat and three colleagues were waiting. The baby was born at nine-fourteen that evening.

An hour later, just after ten o'clock, a footman came out of the palace gates and approached the waiting crowd. "The Princess Elizabeth, Duchess of Edinburgh was safely delivered of a prince," he announced. "Her Royal Highness and her son are both doing well." The cacophony of cheers, singing and shouting reached the new mother and kept her awake for hours, as did the pealing of bells from all the churches of London.

Lilibet thought that baby Charles Philip Arthur George looked like his father, though others thought he resembled her. He was a strong, healthy child with a well-shaped head, an oval face and beautiful hands with long fingers. To his mother he was "quite adorable." "I still can't believe he is really mine," she wrote to a friend, "but perhaps that happens to new parents. Anyway, this particular boy's parents couldn't be more proud of him. It's wonderful to think, isn't it, that his arrival could give a bit of happiness to so many people, besides ourselves, at this time?"[10]

Noisy rejoicing filled the capital for days, celebrating the arrival of the boy who would one day, in the natural course of events, be King Charles III. Bursts of artillery fire shook the ground and rattled the remains of bombed-out buildings, of which there were many. Blue dye was put into the fountains, blue rosettes graced buttonholes, blue ribbons and streamers decorated shopwindows. Baby Charles inspired works of art, poems, musical compositions. At night bonfires were lit, and Londoners gathered around them to warm their hands against the November chill and sing. At the palace, the usual stream of mail and telegrams widened to a flood, and a special office with a dozen typists had to be set up to respond to all the messages of good will.

Not all the extra mail was occasioned by the baby's birth, however. George VI's subjects were anxious about him, having read in the papers that he was canceling all his engagements and would not be able to make his planned tour of Australia early in the new year. He needed rest, the doctors said. The arteries in his leg were obstructed. He would not be going anywhere for some time. Get well messages poured in by the thousands.

If Lilibet was flourishing, her father was in a state of sharp decline. His thin, lined face had an unhealthy pallor, his voice, to which the awkward stammer had returned, was tired and lifeless. "What's the matter with my blasted legs?" he kept asking his equerry Peter Townsend. "They won't work properly." He complained of fatigue and continued to imperil his weakened health by chain-smoking and drinking too much.

On some level, Lilibet must have known, in the fall of 1948, that her accession could not be long delayed. This knowledge, and the anticipatory grief she may have felt at the prospect of losing her adored father, must have sobered and subdued her as she took up her increasing responsibilities in the months following Charles's birth. She was taking her father's place more and more, going on official tours to Lancashire, Wales, Belfast and, in July, 1949, to the Channel Islands where despite severe seasickness, she managed to overcome her nausea and carry out every one of her engagements. ("Of course I'm going," she said when her entourage tried to persuade her to cancel the tour of the island of Sark and stay in her sickbed on board ship. "I won't disappoint those poor people.") Looking fresh and attractive in a lemon-colored dress, she managed to get into a motor launch and to endure the violent chop of the waves, hanging on for dear life, until after three tries the boat was able to be secured to the quay.

Jock Colville, her Private Secretary, was tutoring Lilibet for her future role, taking her to watch parliamentary debates, bringing her state papers to read, introducing her to the desk work of the monarch. She needed no tutelage, however, to guide her in her relations with her future subjects. Though shy and reserved, she possessed the common touch and genuinely cared about people. The same protective, practical instincts that had led her to buy shoes for the shoeless evacuee children during the war guided her to respond to people's yearning to make a personal connection with her.

Just before her tour of Wales she got a letter from a woman in Barmouth who said that when the royal car passed through her town, she would be waving a big red white and blue rosette; would the princess please be on the watch for it? Lilibet wrote back that she would. Sure enough, once arrived in Barmouth she spotted the signal, had the driver stop, and got out of the car to chat with the woman for a few minutes, taking her grandson in her arms and murmuring "What a fine baby he is."[11] Nor was this an isolated incident. Such personal acknowledgments were to become a feature of Lilibet's tours.

She was learning her craft, defining herself as she matured. And if, at first, she seemed overly concerned with protocol and decorum, chastising the Grenadier Guards, for example, for making too much noise and behaving badly in her presence at their annual dinner, and making a surprisingly curmudgeonly speech at a Mother's Union rally against "the age of growing self-indulgence, of hardening materialism and of falling moral standards," she defended her position eloquently.

"I believe there is a great fear in our generation of being labelled priggish," she told the women at the rally. "In consequence people are sometimes afraid to show disapproval of what they know to be wrong, and thus they end by seeming to condone what in their hearts they dislike."[12] She was speaking against divorce, which was still, in 1949, socially stigmatized and mentioned, when mentioned at all, in whispers.

Just how much her own marriage meant to her was about to be demonstrated. When the king gave Philip permission to resume his naval career and he flew to Malta to take up his duties as First Lieutenant aboard HMS *Chequers*, Lilibet joined him as soon as she could, leaving baby Charles with his grandparents. For the next year and a half and more she was to divide her time between Malta, where she kept Philip company when he was on leave, and London, where she kept up her round of official obligations.

It was a fissured life, a month or more at a time spent at the Mountbattens' rented villa, then a few months at Clarence House and Windlesham Moor, then back to Malta for another month or two. Lilibet's new routine had hardly been established when a second pregnancy complicated it. Though Philip was with her when she gave birth to Princess Anne on August 15, 1950, Lilibet was on her own for most of that year, returning to Malta only in November. This time, on her return to the island, she took with her forty trunks filled with clothes and household goods, clearly intending to stay a long time. Once again, Charles and the infant Anne were left with their royal grandparents.

But there was a shadow over this sojourn. Both Lilibet and Philip had gotten used to living on their own, pursuing different interests—Philip yacht-racing in his new boat, the *Coweslip*, and playing polo; Lilibet horseracing, now with her own horses in addition to those in the royal stud. He enjoyed being unfettered, she seemed somewhat adrift. The fact that she had put on twenty pounds, and was continuing to overeat, irritated her husband, and he criticized her choice of clothes. "You're not going to wear that thing," he snapped when she put on a new dress. "Take it off at once."[13] Her waistline had broadened, her dresses, chosen on the advice of her mother and Bobo Macdonald, were distinctly unfashionable. The smart, tailored Christian Dior "new look" had recently come into fashion, skirts were long and flowing, waists cinched, hats small and elegant. Lilibet had stayed with the rather dowdy old look, and her image suffered. She was criticized in print, and contrasted unflatteringly with Margaret, who at twenty had come into her own as a beautiful, chic and stylish, if somewhat wayward, young leader of fashion.

Margaret had her own set of friends, worldly, artistic and sophisticated. With her bright fuschia nails and her long jeweled cigarette holders, she made very good copy for journalists—a sparkling, outgoing royal girl with a risqué edge, so unlike her shyer older sister with her passion for horses and her premature matronliness.

But Lilibet was not to be eclipsed for long. With the aid of diet pills she lost weight, and, as her ill and troubled father retreated more and more from the everyday work with which he was burdened, she undertook to accomplish what he was unable to do.

It was a tonic for her. Though proud of her children, motherhood had failed to define Lilibet, and marriage was presenting unforeseen challenges. Deputizing for her father gave the princess a much-needed focus, she seemed to gather maturity and strength as George VI failed. Under the pressure of her own imminent rule, she was reassembling herself.

By the end of 1951, George VI, bright-eyed but gaunt, with a constant cough, was succumbing to lung cancer. An operation in September of that year had not been successful, a further operation would not be possible. Lilibet had worried about him throughout her strenuous tour of Canada that fall, and was preparing to make another long trip, this time to Australia and New Zealand by way of Africa, in the new year of 1952.

The larger life that she knew lay ahead, the life she would have as queen, was already unfolding, as her frail father, his thin chest shivering under an electrically heated waistcoat, hobbled toward his recessional.

ELEVEN

Deep in the Aberdare Game Reserve, half a mile from the nearest road and even farther from any settlement, one by one the animals were coming down to the pool to drink.

The tropical night was warm, and full of the high whirring buzzing of cicadas and the cries of jackals and the screeching of baboons. The rank scent of decay mingled with the sweetness of wild jasmine and the rich earthy stench of massed beasts. Earlier in the day, locusts had risen in thick swarms, their wings red with dust, but with nightfall they had gone, and the air was clear, the stars glittering, an occasional meteor flashing red or blue across the black sky.

Lilibet sat on a platform high in an immense fig tree, watching elephants and rhino drink from the gleaming water, illuminated by searchlights that augmented the light from the half moon. She had not meant to stay up past midnight, for she and Philip were leaving the following day for Mombasa and they needed their rest. But she was so delighted by the steady parade of animals that she sat where she was nearly all night, a cardigan around her shoulders, binoculars around her neck, her camera beside her.

She threw sweet potatoes to the baboons, watched the grunting and snuffling of the warthogs and the timid approach of the deer. A small herd of waterbuck came down to the pool and two of the males began a fierce battle, goring one another with their curved horns and splashing the reddened water. One of the bucks fell, badly injured, and lay in the reeds at the edge of the pool.

The few days the princess and her husband had spent in Kenya had been full of marvels, Lilibet's encounter with a lion feeding on a wildebeest only ten feet from her (it looked at her, began to come toward her, then yawned and retreated), herds of elephants covered in red dust ("Philip! They are pink! Pink elephants! I don't believe it"), journeys along unpaved roads past small villages and across expanses of tall grass, thorn trees and scrubland, thick jungle and the enervating, inescapable equatorial heat.

"How father would love this," the princess remarked, wishing she could share it all with him. He had come to the airport in London to see them off, waving goodbye jauntily. On the first several days in Nairobi Lilibet had called her mother and father at the palace each day, but there were no phones here in the game reserve, no direct contact with the outside world; the ramshackle hotel built high in the fig tree was little more than a crude shelter, it had few amenities.

Tired but exhilarated, the princess continued to watch the animals until a faint pearl-gray light showed above the trees. The crowds of beasts had thinned out. The wounded waterbuck hadn't moved, and out of concern, Lilibet sent one of the staff to examine it as soon as the sky was light. The buck was dead.

Later that morning, having gone to nearby Sagana Lodge for a rest, Lilibet and Philip went fishing in a stream and then had lunch. They planned to go to Nanyuki, to preside at a formal inspection of three battalions of the King's African Rifles, before traveling to Mombasa.

They were in the large paneled sitting room of Sagana Lodge when Philip noticed Lilibet's private secretary Martin Charteris beckoning to him from beyond the bay window. He went out, met Charteris in the garden, and received the news from London, confirmed through Reuters, that King George had died earlier in the day.

Mastering his own shock, Philip went in to tell Lilibet.

There are conflicting accounts of what happened next, but several of those who were present remember seeing Lilibet and Philip walking together in the garden, or by the nearby river, talking earnestly. Philip's private secretary Mike Parker recalls seeing the princess "weeping desperately for the loss of her father," but not for long—soon she "straightened up," went back into the lodge, to the desk where she had been writing letters earlier in the day, and began to compose telegrams to her mother and sister, and to the officials in Australia and New Zealand, explaining that the tour would have to be canceled because of her father's death.

To her lady-in-waiting Pamela Mountbatten Hicks she said, "Oh, I'm so sorry, it means we've all got to go home, I'm afraid."[1]

Going home took some time and much staff maneuvering, made more difficult by the remoteness of their location. It was late in the afternoon before the royal party left Sagana Lodge, Lilibet remembering to give each lodge employee a signed photograph of herself and a gift before leaving. She hadn't slept, not even a nap. Between her grief, her shock, and the flurry of hastily made decisions—among them the decision, she told Charteris, that her regnal name would be Elizabeth II—and the packing of her things, there must have been an air of the surreal. Whether, as yet, she had begun to adjust to the fact that she was now queen her actions did not reveal; she was her usual efficient, empathetic self, a weary-looking young, pretty woman in a beige cotton dress (she had not wanted to change into mourning black as yet) in the midst of an immense trackless forest on an African mountainside.

All along the road into Nanyuki there were clusters of Kenyans, aware, for the news had traveled very fast, that the British royal lady who had come among them had suffered a bereavement. "*Shauri mbaya kabisa*," they whispered to one another. "The very worst has happened."

Lilibet may have remembered, in those first few hours of her queenship, what her father had once told her, that she must always keep in mind that whatever she said or did to anyone, they would never forget it.[2] She maintained her composure, watched by thousands of eyes, among them the eyes of reporters who had followed her throughout the trip, and who now, out of respect, did not photograph her, though they continued to observe all she did.

Long after dark the party arrived at Nanyuki airport. On the short flight to Entebbe a telegram was received on the plane. THE CABINET IN ALL THINGS AWAITS YOUR MAJESTY'S COMMAND, Churchill wrote.

A swift-moving tropical storm blotted out

the stars by the time the royal party arrived at Entebbe, high winds began lashing at the jacaranda trees, blowing their purple-blue blossoms to the ground, and rain began to pour down, churning to thick mud the waste ground beside the runway. There was no going on, they had to wait out the storm.

For hours the tired Lilibet sat in the small airport, surrounded by local officials, everyone stiff and awkward, until at last the storm abated and the waiting plane could take off.

On the twenty-four-hour flight to London Lilibet was "forlorn," Mike Parker thought. "Really bowled over" by the loss of her father and her grief. Pamela Hicks remembered that as the long flight finally came to an end and the plane landed at London Airport, Lilibet looked out the window and saw the entourage that awaited her.

"Oh God!" she cried. "They've sent the hearses!" The heavy black palace limousines were drawn up along the tarmac, a funereal display. To the lady-in-waiting it seemed that the moment held a revelation, Lilibet's realization that "the end of her private life had come." For the foreseeable future she would belong to her public role.

"And as she is by nature rather a private person," Pamela Hicks added, "it was quite a blow."[3]

Almost from the moment she stepped out of the plane and received the formal greetings of her prime minister and his cabinet, Lilibet was put to work. No sooner had she arrived at Clarence House than Alan Lascelles brought her the red dispatch boxes full of state papers she had to read and sign. Then there were the hundreds of letters of condolence to be read and answered, and the first of many audiences with dignitaries—the Prime Minister of New Zealand, the Crown Prince of Norway and the King and Queen of Sweden, among others. On the day after her arrival she met the many privy councillors, and in a high, unwavering voice read her Declaration of Sovereignty to them.

One task after another fell to her, and she accomplished each, methodically and conscientiously, surprising her advisers by how swiftly she read documents, twice as fast as her late father had, and how retentive and accurate her memory was. She kept strict working hours, disciplining herself to get done all that needed doing, and never indulging herself or shirking, as her uncle Edward VIII had so notoriously done. She corrected inaccuracies and typing errors in the documents submitted to her, and made sensible marginal comments on the state papers she read. And while all this went on, in the first days of her reign, she made time to sit for hours while her likeness was sketched for use on newly issued stamps and coins. She had her photograph taken and her portrait painted. Through it all she showed remarkable stamina, and a strong constitution.

Far from causing her strain, the deluge of work seemed to buoy her up, even as she grieved for her father and adjusted to the demands of her new life. She liked being queen, it fulfilled her. To an extent that her father and uncle never had, Lilibet subsumed herself in her role, and found satisfaction.

"Extraordinary thing," the new queen said to a friend soon after her accession, "I no longer feel anxious or worried. I don't know what it is—but I have lost all my timidity."[4] The vigor and self-assurance she had once found on the stage playing leads in pantomimes now came to the fore on a much vaster stage.

"I didn't have the apprenticeship," she would say many years later, looking back on the early part of her reign. "My father died much too young, and so it was all a very sudden kind of taking-on and making the best job you can. Here you are, it's your fate."[5]

She grasped her fate, firmly, and moved forward.

A journalist watched the queen brace herself to meet her public, and recorded her impressions. The occasion was a banquet to celebrate the opening of a new wing of the Baltic Exchange, the London shipping and grain market. Nearly a thousand guests, staff and reporters were assembled in the banqueting hall, waiting for her to arrive. Her limousine pulled up at the entrance, and the journalist watched the queen enter the foyer, wearing a gown of apricot lace and the marguerite tiara that had been her grandmother's wedding gift.

She paused just outside the entrance to the banqueting hall, where a few dignitaries whom she knew well were waiting for her. She laughed and joked with them "in a completely relaxed way," the observer thought, then moved toward the doorway. "There was a little pause before she entered the room, and the queen took a deep breath and stiffened for one instant—then, a composed and relaxed figure, she moved forward among those hundreds of eyes."[6]

The moment of transition between the queen's private and public selves which the journalist noticed, the pause, the bracing of herself to meet her public, then the confident stepping forward: Lilibet was to cross this psychological threshold again and again, and the crossing was invariably, to outward appearances, a smooth one. Not for her an anguishing confusion of public and private selves, or an inappropriate merging of the two, as had been the case with a number of her predecessors as sovereign. Despite what she perceived as a lack of apprenticeship, Lilibet had a clear grasp of the behavioral demands of monarchy, and was, from the outset, mistress of herself as queen.

The air of gravity that Lilibet was able to assume at will was all the more affecting given her relative youth and diminutive stature. Elder statesmen were moved to tears at the sight of her. Churchill, always an emotional and romantic man, and easily overwrought in the aftermath of a stroke, "used to look at [the queen] and the tears would pour down," the Liberal politician Jeremy Thorpe remembered, "rather like Lord Melbourne with Queen Victoria."[7] To the middle-aged and elderly politicians, the young queen was like a pure and unspoilt daughter, and the more sentimental of them took her to their hearts. There was an innocence about her, an ingenuous quality, that brought forth all their gentlemanly protectiveness. She was a wife and the mother of two very young children, and might well be expected to have more children before long—indeed the press was already speculating that she might be pregnant. Those closest to her were under the impression that, before her father's death, she had wanted another child, but her accession, with all its attendant demands, had interrupted her plans.

George VI's death caused an unanticipated disjuncture in the family. With mourning came confusion, a loss of cohesion; Lilibet was too young to step into her father's shoes as head of the family, and her mother, overwhelmed by the emotional impact of her loss and uncomfortably marginalized by her daughter's becoming queen, retreated into isolation.

"Oh, Betty, this is so awful for mummy and Margaret," Lilibet wrote to a family friend, Elizabeth Cecil, soon after she became queen. "I have Philip and the children and the future, but what are they to do?"[8]

Margaret, as it happened, had found an emotional anchor in her late father's handsome, sensitive equerry Peter Townsend, though even Townsend's sympathetic comfort could not help her over her initial shock on learning of her father's death and she needed sedatives. The queen mother, as she now became, turned to a medium, Lilian Bailey, in an effort to communicate with her late husband. With Margaret, Lilibet and Philip, Marina of Kent, widow of the late king's brother George, and Marina's sixteen-year-old daughter Alexandra, the queen mother met with Mrs. Bailey. Later she visited the medium alone.[9]

Rather than stand by her daughter and help her adjust to her exceedingly demanding new role, the queen mother recoiled from the awkwardness and pain of the new

family configuration. She now had to curtsey to Lilibet when meeting her, as did
Margaret. She felt—and was—superfluous.
Overnight the customarily warm, sympathetic and gracious queen became the
snappish, short-tempered, unapproachable
queen mother, clinging to her tenure of
Buckingham Palace and resenting—so
some thought—the need to vacate the royal
residence. Privately, she suffered a prolonged and oppressive mourning, depressed and wretched, her deep unhappi-
ness made more acute by her sudden
demotion in status.

Lilibet, sensitive to her mother's difficulty
in making the necessary transition, was
content to wait, and did not press her own
rights, as sovereign, to dislodge her mother
from the palace. But her staff did press her
rights—on her behalf. After many months
the queen mother moved into Clarence
House, vacated by Lilibet and Philip, and
later bought herself a rural retreat, the isolated castle of Barrogill (she renamed it the
Castle of Mey) on the Scottish coast, which
she visited frequently.

And as the queen mother retreated, Lord
Louis Mountbatten appeared to advance.

He was the only strong male figure in the royal family, some patriarchal role seemed to descend on him by default. He had extensive executive experience, a wide acquaintance, close ties to the recent Labour government. And a nephew whose wife had become queen.

Lilibet, who had gotten to know Mountbatten better, and to like him more, during her stays in Malta, did not share her close advisers' disdain for Lord Louis; his charm and sense of fun drew her, she basked in his evident admiration. As for Mountbatten, he declared himself fond of her, indeed enchanted by her. "I've lost whatever of my heart is left to spare entirely to her," he told his daughter Patricia. "She dances quite divinely and always wants a samba when we dance together and has said some very nice remarks about my dancing."[10] Others feared that the queen's warm feelings toward Lord Louis would lead to dependence, that he calculated on becoming the eminence grise of the new reign. Philip, they feared, would share his wife's power in some form, perhaps as prince consort. He would then become the conduit through which Mountbatten would dominate the queen.

And Mountbatten, with his leftist political views, seemed more dangerous than ever in the spring of 1952, with Britain receding as a world power and communism on the rise. Any left-leaning political influence around the throne was alarming in the context of the Cold War. British soldiers were fighting alongside those of a dozen other states against communist forces in Korea. Government officials were on the alert for spies; the previous year, Guy Burgess and Donald Maclean of the Foreign Office had defected to Russia, taking valuable secrets with them. The threat of an atomic bomb attack by the Soviet Union underlay all strategic planning, and Britain carried out its own initial test explosion of an atomic device in the year of the queen's accession.

It was amid this tense political climate that Queen Elizabeth II began her public role, advised by the same tightly knit, meticulously self-regulating group of senior household officials that had advised her father. Under the stern and unforgiving supervision of Sir Alan Lascelles, a decorated veteran of World War I noted for his cleverness, his complete discretion and his subdued suits of old-fashioned cut, the household served the queen according to an elaborate canon of regulations. Some of the rules had been customary in Queen Victoria's time, others had taken form under Edward VII and George V. All were unbending—and Lilibet made no effort to change them. The weight of tradition hung heavy over Buckingham Palace, but rather than bend under that weight, the new queen appeared to find strength in it, adapting her habits to the rigid timetables, time-honored routines and somewhat archaic procedures of the longstanding palace establishment.

She chose to adopt as well her parents' conception of the daily tasks of monarchy, a conception formed under the extraordinary conditions of wartime. Visits to hospitals and schools, attendance at major sporting events, the laying of foundation stones and the opening of bazaars augmented a full schedule of evening receptions in the state apartments, audiences given to diplomats and ceremonies granting honors or awarding medals. In her first year as queen Lilibet kept the astonishing total of some five hundred such engagements, a staggering workload when it is recalled that these appearances were only a part of her overall obligations.[11] Probably it never occurred to her to adopt any other style of reign, to revert to the domestic queenship of Victoria, for example; Lilibet had been bred to a life of service, and to revere self-sacrifice when it came to her time and her energies. To redesign her days along less strenuous lines would have seemed a betrayal of her royal mandate—though in fact she was under no constitutional obligation to make so many appearances or mingle with her subjects to such an extent.

She sought continuity—in those who served her, in her own routines, in the image of monarchy. She would reign as her father had. In so doing she would not only honor his memory, but promote stability, and project gravitas.

"She is a true daughter of her father—and with that we are well content," announced the *Daily Mail* in the early days of the new reign. The judgment was gratifying to the queen, it was the effect she intended to give. Among her first discoveries, as she took thought about the ceremonies over which she would be presiding as queen, was that she could economize by wearing her father's robes. The shoulders would require some alteration, and the old velvet and fur would have to be carefully cleaned. But the used robes would do very well, she thought, and the cost of new ones would be saved. Uniting practicality with sentiment, she gave orders for the alterations to be made.

TWELVE

Rain poured down on London on the morning of Coronation Day, June 2, 1953, flooding the streets, the water spreading in deep pools beside clogged gutters. Red, white and blue streamers hung dripping along Fleet Street, their colors running, and the large golden coronets atop the giant arches along the Mall gleamed wetly under dark skies. Fresh flowers newly planted in beds, hanging baskets and flowerboxes were flattened under the constant rain, flags drooped, even the tall bearskins worn by guardsmen lining the procession route grew soggy and heavy. Water poured in rivulets down the glass of Selfridge's windows where a lifesize statue of the queen on horseback was on display. Liberty's windows too were streaked and all but occluded by rain, their exhibit of royal costumes unregarded.

But the cold, wet spectators who had camped out for two days on the sidewalks and along the Mall were prepared for the bad weather. They had on their winter coats and their fur boots, they sat under wide umbrellas eating sodden sandwiches, their good humor undampened. Traffic had been halted the previous afternoon, the roads closed and sealed off. Here and there groups of waiting bystanders burst into song—"Singin' in the Rain"—and there were impromptu reels danced up and down the Mall. Cheers went up when the announcement came over the radio that New Zealander Edmund Hillary and his Nepalese guide Sherpa Norgay Tenzing had summitted the highest mountain in the world, the mountain the Nepalese called Chumolungma and known to the British as Mount Everest. It seemed a British triumph, and it matched the ebullient mood of the hundreds of thousands in the enormous crowd.

For London, on that wet morning, was

caught up in coronation fever. The chaos among the millions of spectators, the cold, the noisy street parties that had gone on all night were entered into with great good humor for the sake of what the headlines were calling "the Liz Biz," the most important spectacle since the royal wedding six years earlier. For months seats in the stands erected along the procession route had been sold out, and scalpers were demanding as much as thirty-five hundred pounds for a balcony view along the procession route. For most of those in the immense crowd, periscopes had to suffice; hundreds of thousands of periscopes were sold, and many more homemade, but they were constructed of cardboard and they melted to shapeless lumps of doughy paste in the constant rain.

Excitement mingled with reverence as the hour approached when the queen's great golden State Coach was expected to leave the palace and make its way toward the abbey. The parade of dignitaries began, the Lord Mayor of London passing in his coach, the prime minister, foreign monarchs and other celebrated visitors, the queen's relatives, the carriages and cars interspersed with bands, honor guards and troops of soldiers. The crowd greeted each passing notable with a low hum of recognition, adding a long chorus of cheers for Churchill and the queen mother and the ebullient, exotic Queen Salote of Tonga. But they kept their acclamations muted, waiting for the climactic moment, the long awaited arrival of the queen.

Taut with anticipation, the object of all this mounting excitement came out into the courtyard of Buckingham Palace and, with Philip, stepped into the golden State Coach. If she was aware of the degree of her subjects' near-boundless adulation, her reserved demeanor did not reveal it. She knew that thousands of telegrams of congratulations had arrived at the palace, that the American magazine *Time* had named her Woman of the Year for 1952, that some two million people, so it had been estimated, would be crammed into the seven miles of road between the palace and the abbey, eager for a glimpse of her. She may even have known that, according to one British newspaper survey, two-thirds of those questioned believed that she was a direct descendant of the Almighty himself.

But her attention was elsewhere—on the details of dress, liturgy and protocol she had to remember if she was to perform the long, intricate ceremony of coronation correctly.

She had been preparing for months, anxious that her coronation should come as close as possible to being a repetition of her father's, and that it should be perfect in every detail.[1] There had been the coronation gown to decide on, from a dozen sketches worked up over many weeks by Norman Hartnell and discussed at every stage with the queen. The gowns of the Maids of Honor and the peeresses too had to be discussed, and the style of the coronation chairs selected, and the color and depth of the new carpet for the abbey decided on. (The depth of the carpet pile was an important matter; it had to be deep enough to look luxurious, yet not so deep that, as at previous coronations, the long robes and trains and the high heels of the women would get caught in it.) No doubt Lilibet remembered the tedium of George VI's long ceremony, how she had worried about Margaret's fidgeting, how she had sat beside her grandmother Queen Mary and waited through the interminable liturgy until seeing the welcome word "Finis" at the back of her printed program.

There were so many small particulars to be determined: how many seamstresses would be needed to sew spots on the ermine of the robes, what food would be served at the many coronation banquets and parties, what extra cooks and kitchen assistants would be hired, which printers would be asked to print the many invitations, which regiments would be asked to march in the procession, which assigned to fire the cannon during the ceremony, and so on down a long list of vital minutiae.

Philip was no help. Lilibet had appointed him chairman of the committee to oversee the planning of the coronation but he regarded the entire grand production as a relic of the past—which of course it was—and therefore as something outworn and largely unnecessary. He was cavalier in his attitude toward rehearsals for the rite, in which he was to have only a very minor part. He would be the first of the peers to pay homage to the queen after the crowning, and would kneel and recite an oath of fealty. In rehearsing this oath he flippantly rushed through it and then, with a kiss tossed to his wife, prepared to leave the rehearsal room.

"Don't be silly, Philip. Come back and do that again, properly." The royal words were heeded, Philip came back, knelt, and repeated his oath more slowly.

Philip had taken up flying, and crisscrossed the country often in his small plane. Lilibet worried about him. If the phone rang at the palace when she knew he was out flying, she tensed, and could not relax until reassured that the call was not about him.[2] No doubt she could not forget the frightening call she had received in the middle of the night shortly before their wedding, the call that had informed her he had had an accident and was in the hospital. He drove larger and safer cars now, to be sure, among them a Rolls-Royce, a Phantom Four. But he drove no less recklessly than he had in the months before their wedding, just as he rode his polo ponies recklessly, suffering frequent collisions. And he flew recklessly—or so it was presumed.

The queen's advisers had wanted to underscore Philip's subordinate status during the coronation festivities by having him ride to the abbey in a separate coach, or ride on horseback alongside the State Coach. There was no historical precedent to look to. Mary Tudor, her half-sister Elizabeth I and Queen Victoria had all been unmarried at the time of their coronations. Queen Anne, who was married when she was crowned, did not ride to her coronation in a coach but was carried into the abbey in a sedan chair, because of her excessive weight and her gout. So no decision had had to be made about whether she should ride alone or with her husband George of Denmark. In the end Lilibet decided that Philip would ride beside her in the Golden Coach.

A much more important decision was whether or not to televise the coronation. The queen and her advisers were opposed to it, but eventually succumbed to the overwhelming weight of public pressure and agreed.[3] Sales of television sets soared in the weeks preceding the royal ceremony; more than twenty million Britons, over half the adult population, were watching when the queen was crowned—marking a new and, for many, a surprisingly intimate bond between sovereign and people.

By coronation morning, Lilibet was ready. She had memorized long passages from the liturgy, and knew the order of the service well. She had practiced walking up and down the length of the palace ballroom with a sixty-foot-long train (made of sheets fastened together), timing her steps and gauging distances. She had put on the heavy St. Edward's crown, which weighed more than five pounds, and had worn it for long periods of time in order to strengthen her neck muscles. And she had changed her diet, eating lots of hard-boiled eggs to induce constipation and lots of salt to retain water—she would be without a nearby bathroom for many hours.

It was just after ten-thirty when the Golden Coach left the palace and began its slow progress toward the abbey. One journalist swore afterward that the sun broke through the dark clouds just at that moment, glinting on the gilded leaves and cupids, the plumed helmets and carved crown surmounting the flamboyantly decorated carriage. Through the wide side windows Lilibet could be seen, diamonds sparkling in her diadem and at her throat, an ermine-trimmed cloak around her shoulders. She was smiling and animated, and Philip, in his admiral's uniform and dark cocked hat, was equally affable.

"She looked indescribably beautiful," wrote one observer. "So delicate and frail."[4] At the sight of her, a tremendous roar went up from thousands of throats, drowning out the clopping of the eight high-stepping Windsor Greys, the music of the bands, the crisp tramping of the guardsmen's boots. Louder and louder grew the noise and shouting, until it became a continuous, thunderous clamor, following the coach down Northumberland Avenue and along Victoria Embankment to the abbey.

Once inside the cathedral the orchestra, military trumpeters, organ and four-hundred-voice chorus saluted the queen, as the seventy-five hundred spectators watched her walk, pale but composed, in her robes of crimson velvet down the long aisle, her Maids of Honor holding the immense length of train that spilled down from her shoulders for twenty yards. The metal fringe of her gown snagged on the carpet, making forward motion difficult. She appealed to the Archbishop of Canterbury to push her forward ("Get me started!"), giving her momentum, and he complied.[5]

Despite the momentary awkwardness she moved down the aisle with "firm and measured step," wrote Stanley Clark, a journalist who was present and has left a detailed record of the coronation.[6]

The grandeur of the scene, the vast echoing chamber with its soaring vaulted ceiling, the galleries hung with garlands and tapestries in blue and gold with the queen's monogram, the huge candelabra and the burnished gold plate in the facade of the royal gallery, the flashing and twinkling of many jewels, the masses of crimson uniforms, white gowns and long white gloves, all contributed to the air of transcendent splendor. On its golden dais stood the throne, surrounded by a golden carpet, and before the high altar was St. Edward's chair, on its gilded lions, holding the Stone of Destiny, the chair on which many kings and queens had been crowned.

An ancient rite was being reenacted in an ancient edifice, and the young woman at its center was linked by blood to the first ruler, the Saxon King Edgar the Peaceful, to be so crowned at Bath in the tenth century, and to Edward the Confessor who had built Westminster Abbey a century later.

Her pallor evident throughout, the queen was officially recognized and spoke the words of her oath, then took communion as the chorus sang the initial fortissimo phrases of Handel's anthem "Zadok the Priest," the Old Testament words having been repeated at coronations for a thousand years. Mystery followed high drama. Lilibet entered an enshrouding canopy where her royal robes and jewels were removed and a plain white gown was put on for her anointing. Using an oil made up specially for this crowning—the traditional holy oil having been destroyed during the war—the Archbishop of Canterbury made the sign of the cross on the queen's hands, chest and head and daubed her with the liquid. This solemn procedure having been accomplished, she was revested in magnificent golden robes and seated in St. Edward's chair. Having received the orb, scepter, cross and rod, and with a ring placed on her finger, Queen Elizabeth II was ready to be crowned.

Cecil Beaton thought that she had an expression of "intense expectancy" as the archbishop took the great St. Edward's crown from the altar and held it over her head, its diamonds, emeralds, and rubies blazing in the reflected light of the candles and the bright television lights.

"Oh God," the archbishop prayed, "the crown of the faithful, bless, we beseech Thee, this crown, and so sanctify Thy servant Elizabeth, upon whose head this day Thou dost place it for a sign of royal majesty, that she may be filled by Thine abundant grace with all princely virtues."

A hush fell over the chamber as the attendant bishops gathered around St. Edward's chair. Then the crown was swiftly lowered, and amid a violent cacophony of blaring trumpets, organ chords and the booming of artillery from the Tower guns, the onlookers shouted "God save the Queen!" "God save the Queen!" again and again. It was the blood-stirring, heart-stopping climax of the ceremony. Bells pealed wildly, guns continued to boom their salutes and from the streets outside the cheering of the crowds could be heard. For a few in the abbey, the moment of pure exultation was too much. Several people fainted, tears flowed freely.

The queen got up and went to her throne, to be lifted into it by the clergy and peers.

Now Philip came forward, the first of the peers to offer homage. "I, Philip, Duke of Edinburgh, do become your liege man of life and limb, and of earthly worship," he said as he knelt, measuring his words appropriately. His oath complete, he kissed his wife on the cheek, and stepped back to allow the others to make their professions of loyalty. The crown weighing more heavily by the minute, Lilibet sat, pink-cheeked, hands folded, her demeanor "simple and humble," while one by one the many peers recited their oaths. Resplendent in her crown and golden garments, she was an icon of good rulership, a symbol of historical and political continuity, a beautifully dressed, magnificently appointed sanctified doll.

And at the same time, she was a daughter, wife and mother. Four-year-old Charles was present, sitting in the front row of the royal gallery and wearing a coronation medal pinned to his shirt. The queen was seen to glance in his direction during the proceedings. Charles alternately watched his mother and turned to his grandmother or his aunt to ask questions, "vigorously nodding his head at the answers," Stanley Clark noticed.[7] The queen mother, a gleaming figure in a diamond-encrusted gown, sat on one side of the prince and his Aunt Margot, stunning and radiant and much scrutinized by the press, on the other. Queen Mary, who had sat next to Lilibet at the previous coronation and answered her questions, was conspicuously, and sadly, absent; she had died ten weeks earlier. Nor was Lilibet's errant Uncle David, Duke of Windsor, among the royals. He had come to England for his mother's funeral, but had not been invited to stay for the coronation. The oldest of the queen's relations, eighty-one-year-old Princess Marie Louise, daughter of Queen Victoria's daughter Helena, stayed in her place for the entire ceremony but was observed to be restless, angry with the lady-in-waiting who had tangled the long train of her gown when she made her entrance into the abbey.

The oaths of homage went on and on, while the chorus sang five anthems. The Maids of Honor, wilting under the hot television lights and having been kept standing for hours, were led away briefly by a prelate who offered them a flask of brandy to share. Others fortified themselves with smelling-salts. With extraordinary patience the group of blind guests, seated behind pillars in the West Gallery, waited through the long sequence of oaths while sighted companions whispered to them a running commentary. The peers, having concealed supplies of sandwiches, fruit and candy (and even the morning newspapers) in the pockets of their robes, endured the tedium with aplomb. Hours later, when the abbey was empty, cleaners had to sweep away the mess of fruit peelings, candy wrappers and uneaten sandwiches they left behind in the South Transept.

When after further acclamations, and the queen's receiving communion, the chorus began singing the *Te Deum Laudamus*, those in the abbey realized that the liturgy was at an end. Lilibet went into St. Edward's chapel to change her clothes and take a welcome rest. She ate a sandwich and drank a glass of wine, then put on her violet velvet robes and the lighter imperial state crown. Carrying the orb and scepter, and looking tired, the weight of the crown seeming to "press her down," one spectator thought, the queen processed once more down the long center aisle of the abbey while those assembled sang "God save our gracious queen" again and again.

On the return journey to Buckingham Palace the coach went along Whitehall and Pall Mall to Piccadilly, through Hyde Park to Marble Arch, then down Oxford Street and Regent Street and Haymarket then back down the Mall. The afternoon was nearly spent when all was over and the queen and her husband alighted in the palace courtyard. The eight Windsor Greys were unhitched and returned to their stalls in the royal mews, the postilions took off their liveries and relaxed. But for the queen, there were more obligations to be performed. She posed, still wearing her robes, for Cecil Beaton, while Philip, "making wry jokes, and definitely adopting a rather ragging attitude towards the proceedings," paced impatiently in the background.[8] She broadcast a speech to the waiting spectators. Time and again she went out on the balcony with Philip, Charles and Anne, the queen mother and Margaret to receive the acclaim of her subjects.

She was "cool, smiling, sovereign of the

situation," Beaton thought, but very tired. She boasted about her stamina ("I'm strong as a horse," she liked to say), but the taxing day had taken all the stamina she could muster. When at last the floodlights were turned off, leaving the balcony in darkness, and the damp crowds, hoarse from cheering, began to disperse, the queen must have collapsed gratefully into the nearest chair, relieved and exhausted.

And pleased, as she had been all day, by the news that had come to her just before she left for the abbey in the morning. She had gotten a call from her horse trainer, Cecil Boyd-Rochfort, to say that her promising three-year-old Aureole had gone very well in his morning workout. In four days Aureole would run in the Derby, and Lilibet, who was not only a queen but a horsewoman, was now confident that he would win.

THIRTEEN

Aureole. The rich chestnut colt with the blaze of white on his nose and three white fetlocks. High-strung, difficult, temperamental, swift Aureole. He was the leading horse in Lilibet's growing stable. He had the breeding, the wind, the essential fire to be a great winner. His sire, Hyperion, had won the Derby and his dam, the bay mare Angelola, had won the Lingfield Oaks, the Yorkshire Oaks and the Newmarket Oaks. Aureole himself had won impressively earlier that year, in the spring, at the Lingfield Derby Trial, though he had been beaten in the Two Thousand Guineas at Newmarket. Lilibet had watched the latter race, her gaze intent, mentally running every inch of the course with the colt and his experienced jockey Harry Carr. Aureole had been beaten in the Two Thousand Guineas by Nearula, but had surprised everyone by running so well and showing such stamina. He had greatness in him, Lilibet was sure of it.

But his jockey was nervous. Aureole "had a mind of his own," as Harry Carr said. He didn't always start well. He was obstreperous, jittery. He wouldn't settle down. At times he shied away from other horses and would not respond to his jockey's commands. The trouble was inbred; all Hyperion's colts, if they ran well, were easily alarmed and slow to come to hand. If they were placid, they lacked the winning edge.

Lilibet herself had seen the waywardness in him almost from birth, when she had fed him from a bottle at the Hampton Court stud. Later, during his training, he had once lashed out at her when she offered him an apple. All her life Lilibet had had the ability to calm excitable animals. She knew the power of a soft voice and a light, steadying touch. Yet she could not tame this colt. His jockey Carr appeared to have great ability with his mounts. But Aureole remained a challenge.

On the day of the Coronation Derby, crowd sentiment was with the queen. Many of the spectators at Epsom Downs had watched the coronation earlier in the week, and would have liked to see the queen's horse triumph in Britain's premier race. They cheered Lilibet when she appeared in the royal box. Yet they bet heavily, not on Aureole, but on two other horses in the field of twenty-seven: Premonition, which had won the Ascot Gold Cup and the Great Northern Stakes at York, and the big colt Pinza, which had won the Newmarket Stakes.

When the race began, Aureole started well and kept up with the leaders going up the hill. At Tattenham Corner he was sixth, and as Lilibet watched eagerly, he made good time on the middle of the course and moved up to third, where he remained. Though Aureole strained and galloped hard in the final stretch, he could not catch the lead horse, Pinza, and came in second.

Pinza's trainer Norman Bertie went up to the royal box.

"Congratulations, Bertie, on winning the Derby," the queen said with a smile.

"May I congratulate you, Your Majesty, on winning the world," was the gallant reply, which was met with silence. Eventually Lilibet found words.

"Thank you very much, Bertie."[1]

She was a gracious loser, and was becoming a very prominent owner and breeder. She had inherited some twenty mares from her father's stable, and maintained the Royal Studs. She loved the horses, visited them, talked to them, watched them exercise, discussed their feed, behavior and care with her trainer Cecil Boyd-Rochfort. She decided which stallions would cover the mares, and which colts and fillies showed most promise as yearlings. Every race interested her, not only the oldest and most prestigious races—the Derby, the St. Leger, the Oaks, Thousand and Two Thousand Guineas—but the smaller races run on lesser courses. She loved to watch the strategies and skilled maneuvering of the jockeys, the bravery and power of the horses, their remarkable bursts of speed, all the random elements that entered a race and determined its outcome.

Nothing gave Lilibet more pleasure than making the rounds of evening stables, inspecting the legs and feet of each of her horses, checking each one's feed, watching for signs of fatigue, illness, apathy. And, with Aureole, watching his disposition.

Aureole's good performance in the Derby gave her hope that he might win the St. Leger. To steady him and prepare him for the longer and more arduous race (the Derby being a mile and a half, the St. Leger a mile and three-quarters), she decided, after consulting with Boyd-Rochfort, to bring in a London neurologist who had had success in treating nervous humans—and animals—by his soothing touch. Dr. Brook had successfully calmed several excitable horses that had taken part in the coronation. In June and July he came to Newmarket twice a week to visit Aureole.

There was mystery in Dr. Brook's ministrations. On his arrival Aureole would be pawing and fidgeting, tossing his head uneasily; within moments the horse would be standing quietly, head lowered, muscles relaxed. The doctor would put his hands flat on Aureole's withers and stomach, lay his head on the colt's shoulder and then communicate with him, wordlessly, the effort taking all the physician's strength. After twenty minutes Aureole would be calm, Dr. Brook pale and exhausted. Over the weeks there seemed to be some long-term improvement in Aureole's temperament, and the treatments were continued.

But as the St. Leger approached, the colt regressed. Boyd-Rochfort informed Lilibet that he was refusing to train, resisting his rider's commands and flinching from other horses. Some days he simply wouldn't move, and only endless coaxing would lure him out of his stall. When surrounded by other horses he shied away.

With far less hope than she had held on the day of the Coronation Derby, Lilibet came down from Balmoral to Doncaster in September, 1953, to see Aureole race in the St. Leger. In the paddock he seemed relatively calm, but when the race began he became unsettled, could not find his rhythm and fought his jockey for control. He swerved, running wide of the pack and falling behind; at the finish he was far behind. Premonition took the prize.

Aureole's failure to win seemed emblematic of a variety of knotty issues, public and personal, that descended on the queen in the immediate aftermath of the coronation. With her in the royal box at Doncaster was the prime minister, noticeably enfeebled, moving with difficulty. It was a closely guarded secret that Churchill had suffered a massive stroke only three weeks after the coronation and that, even though he had astounded his colleagues and his doctors— and Lilibet herself—by making a swift recovery there was strong feeling that he ought to resign.

There was no need for the queen to wait for Churchill to make the decision on his own; among her constitutional prerogatives was that of encouraging an unfit prime minister to step aside. It was a delicate matter, made more delicate by the bond of affection between Lilibet and her prime minister, and by Churchill's enormous, nearly iconic stature among Britons. The urgent reality facing her was that the elderly prime minister, having come so near death, might well die at any time, and in the meantime, was not really able to continue in office with anything like full competence.[2] She was about to undertake a lengthy world tour, and expected to be out of the realm for six months.

What would she do if he were to die, or if he suffered an incapacitating stroke, while she was thousands of miles away?

She had several options. She could do nothing, and let the situation deteriorate—for deteriorate it would—at its own natural pace. She could dismiss Churchill and appoint a successor, either the unofficial but obvious heir designate, Anthony Eden, who was himself seriously ill, or R.A. Butler. Or she could follow the advice of her courtiers, who pressed her to appoint an interim government headed by the experienced, trustworthy acting Foreign Secretary Lord Salisbury, who had been among those closest to her father; Salisbury would preside until Eden was strong enough to take over. The latter suggestion was creative and not unreasonable, but there was no constitutional precedent for it, and no one could say when, or even if, Eden would be restored to health.

In the end Lilibet chose not to act. Churchill stayed on, an embarrassment to his colleagues, a liability to the cabinet. Whatever her reasons, and they are veiled from her biographers, she resisted the strong suggestions of her courtiers and took the risk that the prime minister would not succumb to further strokes and would function adequately, at least until her return in spring 1954.

In another, more personal sphere she acted along much the same lines.

When Margaret, who was twenty-two at the time of the coronation, told her sister that she wanted to marry the thirty-eight-year-old Peter Townsend, Lilibet neither gave nor refused her consent. She waited, letting events unfold.

Margaret's strong attachment to Townsend seemed, on the surface at least, to represent a surprising change of direction in her life. Stunningly attractive, notoriously flirtatious, a frequenter of both stylish and déclassé nightclubs, the princess had had a number of boyfriends, among them aristocrats, entertainers and even, so it was said, palace servants. A long relationship with the married comedian Danny Kaye had threatened to erupt into scandal in Margaret's late teens. But in falling in love with the sensitive, introspective Townsend, Margaret seemed to be reaching, not only for a different kind of man, but for a different kind of life. He was the opposite of flamboyant, not the kind of man to seek the pleasures of nightlife. He talked about serious things. He quoted the Bible. Evidently he touched something deep in Margaret, and she responded eagerly.

Townsend had served the royal family for many years, his handsome, gentle, somewhat overwrought presence had become habitual. He was self-conscious, with a stammer, like that of the late George VI, though not as pronounced. As an RAF pilot he had been a hero, though he had paid a heavy price for his bravery, suffering several nervous collapses. Some found him long-winded (despite his slight stammer) and overly self-absorbed, but nearly everyone, with the exception of Philip, liked him, Margaret most of all.

But Townsend was a commoner of middle-class background, he lacked the social status to marry a princess. To be sure, King George had been very fond of him, almost, it was said, looking on him as a son. But even the late king's fondness could not remove the stigma that clung to Townsend as a divorced man. Just as in 1936, when King Edward VIII caused scandal by contemplating marriage with the divorced Wallis Simpson, so in 1953 Margaret's hope of marrying Townsend, who had only recently divorced his wife, threatened to shatter the carefully nurtured image of the royal family as a bastion of social rectitude, where marriage and family life were cherished and treated as inviolate.

Even though views of divorce had begun to alter in postwar Britain, being divorced continued to put a man or woman in a socially dubious position. The queen did not allow divorced people to join her household, even if, like Townsend, the court had judged them to be the innocent party in the suit. The Church of England taught that no marriage could be dissolved; as head of the church, the queen had to uphold its teachings.

Officially, the palace could not give Margaret permission to marry Townsend—and without the queen's permission, she could not legally marry until she reached the age of twenty-five, and even then she had to notify Parliament and wait for approval. If Parliament did not approve, then following her marriage she would be removed from the succession and stripped of her royal rank, with all the privileges that went with it.

So the austere, scrupulous Alan Lascelles explained to Margaret and Townsend— without conveying how impossible their situation was, or what potential political damage could be caused if they persisted in contemplating marrying. Lascelles was chilling, he seemed to embody an archaic tradition that, in its rigidity and inhumanity, was needlessly cruel. Yet he spoke for the throne, indeed for Lilibet, who did not give her sister and Townsend any explicit reason to hope that the law would be altered for their sakes.

The queen was not unsympathetic. She loved her sister, and knew from her own experience how wrenching it was to meet with opposition in matters of the heart. Only by persistence, argument and strength of will had she managed to triumph over family and courtiers' determined resistance to her choice of husband. Yet she stood back from involving herself in Margaret's dilemma, allowing Lascelles to speak for her and hoping that, if Margaret and her beloved were separated for long enough, their love might cool or they might lose heart; both were emotionally fragile, and might wilt if thwarted. Townsend was sent to Belgium as British air attaché, with the understanding that he and Margaret would wait a year before raising the question of their marriage again.[3]

But if the queen remained detached on the question of Margaret's marriage, the public did not. Informed by the press that the princess wanted to marry a good-looking war hero who had won the Distinguished Flying Cross, but was being prevented by the fact of his divorce, Britons were overwhelmingly on the side of the lovers. Why should the palace stand in the way, even if Margaret was third in line of succession to the throne? At the time of Edward VIII's abdication the public had been on the side of love, and against what they saw as an outmoded social prejudice. Now, nearly a generation later, and with many prewar attitudes softening, people were even less tolerant of old-fashioned rules.

In the Conservative cabinet, however, there was resistance, despite the fact that some members were themselves divorced. Salisbury announced to his colleagues that he would resign if the princess married Townsend. He came to the palace to consult with the queen early in July, barely a month after the coronation, and no doubt he made his views clear to her.

As with the question of whether or not to act where the prime minister was concerned, on the issue of her sister's marriage Lilibet could have intervened to enable the couple to overcome the obstacles they faced. She could have given them permission to marry. Salisbury might have resigned, the authority of the church would have been challenged. But the monarchy would have aligned itself with change, advancement, the overturning of old ways, outworn restrictions. The New Elizabethan era much spoken of by journalists would have seemed validated. Instead the queen let the opportunity pass.

In one other vital area Lilibet was inactive: that of the increasing strain in her marriage.

Though correct in his public duties as the queen's husband, in private Philip had become remote, angry, and resentful. He chafed under the restrictions placed on him by the queen's flinty courtiers, whose long-standing aversion to him remained undiminished. Philip's friend, the harmonica virtuoso Larry Adler, has told interviewers that

Philip was bitter in his resentment at being humiliatingly subordinated to his wife, having to walk behind her and having to call her "Your Royal Highness" when appropriate.[4] Hostile members of the queen's household treated him with indurate indifference, and saw to it that he was excluded from taking any active role. They minimized his ill-defined sphere of influence—and with good reason, for when unshackled he was rude and offensive. Now that his wife was queen, such behavior could do widespread harm.

Unlike the ingratiating, softspoken Peter Townsend, who had been quick to learn the subtle codes and manners of the palace, Philip was loath to adopt the ways of the queen's principal courtiers—a behavioral style he considered fundamentally dishonest and inauthentic. He refused to be anything but himself—and the result was that he was almost invariably provocative, loud and self-assertive at times, even with politicians and diplomats, officials and officeholders.

It was a damaging cycle: the more resentful Philip grew, and the more dangerously outspoken he was, the more he was denied official scope for his abilities, and the more limited he was, the more obstreperously he rebelled—leading to further curtailment of his official activities.

When in April of 1952 Lilibet announced that the family name would not be "Mountbatten" but would remain "Windsor," Philip reacted with fury. Neither he nor his uncle, who had spent years compiling an elaborate book on the Mountbatten lineage, expected the dynastic name to change, of course, but they did imagine that the queen and the children would be Mountbattens. Lilibet's explicit rejection of the name seemed to Philip one more in a series of humiliations.

He became depressed, complained that he had no job, and soon fell ill with jaundice. For weeks he lay in a dark room, his face yellow, his diet severely restricted. The enforced inactivity was as galling to him as the illness. His recovery was slow.

The queen's accession caused an unanticipated shift in the couple's relationship. Lilibet's elevation in status was too sudden, and too extreme, to permit a smooth adjustment. And the barriers her cliquish, protective courtiers threw up around her were too steep for Philip to hurdle. His ego, his vanity, his male self-respect were severely wounded. Societal expectations in the fifties were that the husband be the senior partner in a marriage, the father the head of the family. But in the queen's family, the husband had little or no role to play, he was marginal. Aggrieved and defiant, he took out his resentment in ways that caused further strain.

In the summer and fall of 1953, with Margaret's romance the principal topic of public interest, rumors once again began to spread concerning Philip's alleged infidelity. Stories of sex parties, of organized debauchery, of Philip escorting models and actresses to parties circulated and, as they were repeated, inevitably became elaborated until whatever incidents gave rise to them were hopelessly obscured.[5] According to Adler, "everyone knew that he had girlfriends all over the place."[6] Philip's biographer John Parker refers to Philip's "period of exuberant misjudgment," in which he descended for "brief interludes" into a sordid world of sexual adventurism and fleeting erotic liaisons. Adler was under the impression that Lilibet blamed Baron, the society photographer, for getting "Philip into trouble" and "helping him find girlfriends."[7] With his companion Mike Parker, also, Philip could be "completely at home," certain that Parker would not betray his transgressions to the press.[8]

The rumors were shadowy, vague, never backed up by hard evidence. Women's names were bruited about as the object of the royal consort's lust, but none of the women themselves came forward to tell all—or even to tell a little. Still, the accretion of rumor led to a presumption that the queen was having to share her husband with others, an unflattering presumption that gathered force the longer it went un- challenged. And even if Philip's flirtations were innocent, they were disparaging, even humiliating, to his wife—hardly the behavior of a loving and considerate husband.

Journalists took note of Philip's public undemonstrativeness toward Lilibet. When she delivered a speech, he was seen to look anywhere but at her—perhaps a sign of distaste or indifference. When it was re- ported that the queen had installed an un- comfortable horsehair mattress in her Windsor bedroom, the change was seen to suggest that Philip was not welcome in her bed. (In actuality the mattress was good back therapy, and the castle had plenty of other, more comfortable mattresses.[9] Moreover, upper-class British couples usually had separate bedrooms.)

It was hard to escape the conclusion that the royal marriage had soured.[10] Philip, like Aureole, was wayward and needed gentling and taming—or, failing that, he needed to be contained.

But if the alchemy between the queen and her husband had altered, it still bound them together. They made each other laugh. She liked his practical jokes (the false teeth he brought to the breakfast table, the bread rolls he offered that squealed when she touched them), his lapses into immature silliness, his reminding her of old jokes. He invigorated her, her face visibly brightened when he entered a room (unless he had stayed out too late with his "funny friends," as she called them, the night before, when her face visibly darkened). His ill-judged flirtations, and the rumors of sexual escapades angered her at times, and may have caused her much heartache, but outwardly at least, she did not remain angry, and concealed her heartache from those around her.

She still needed Philip. She relied on him to put her at ease, especially in public.[11] That reliance diminished somewhat after her accession, when she discovered that she had "lost all her timidity," but it never entirely went away. Philip was her rock, the arm she leaned on. He was so much better than she was at coping when things went wrong, when the timetable at a public event was upset. He could improvise, maneuver, if necessary bully his way through an impasse, while she could not.

"There is a little-girl quality about her devotion to [Philip] which is perhaps old-fashioned but endearingly feminine," writes journalist Ann Morrow.[12] Something of the awe the thirteen-year-old Lilibet felt for the devastatingly good-looking, athletic, exuberant eighteen-year-old Philip remained, despite the shift in their relationship.

They were efficient working partners. They undertook the modernization of Windsor Castle, planning the installation of wall lights and electric fires. They rearranged furniture, lifting heavy antiques and moving chairs and tables. On the queen's long world tour in 1953–54, she watched her husband play deck hockey and he laughed when she, wearing an evening gown, mimicked (in private) the Fijian dancers they had seen, grunting and waving her arms. After the ceremony of crossing the equator, they were both pushed into the ship's pool, where they splashed each other like children.

Their partnership was enduring, symbolized by Philip's reliable presence at his wife's side when she made foreign visits or entertained ambassadors or attended the opening of a factory or presided over a meeting of the Royal Engineering Society. But by 1954, Philip was spending less time with his wife, attending fewer public functions with her and even traveling by himself. He had coped with his frustrating sense of uselessness by taking on a host of official responsibilities, sponsoring the Duke of Edinburgh's Commonwealth Study Conferences, giving some eighty speeches a year, giving interviews, running the royal estates, plus answering hundreds of letters a year on everything from African horse sickness to the national shortage of mathematics teachers to endangered ants to publishing problems for would-be writers. He raced his yachts, flew his plane and played polo at Cowdray in Sussex where teenage girls, responding to his handsomeness and sex appeal, swarmed the playing field trying to get closer to him.[13]

Philip's increasing amounts of time away received an official explanation. It was announced from the palace that because the queen was in such demand, she had decided to delegate some of her journeys and appearances to her husband. But the separations and times apart were to grow longer, and Philip's negativity, hardened into an aggrieved detachment, was to become more marked.

They had begun to diverge.

Mercurial, hyperactive, elusive, Philip had begun to disengage himself and carve out a separate life of his own. And Lilibet, knowing him as she did, must have realized that she had no choice but to let him go his own way. The fissure was just beginning to reveal itself; it would widen in the following years. What inner or outer turmoil it caused, with what heartache or relief she greeted it, no outsider to the marriage can say.

Rather than attempt to force changes,

she chose to stand back and let her husband's nature drive him where it would, adjusting as best she could to the result.

It was rainy and dark on the day the King George VI and Queen Elizabeth Stakes were run at Ascot in July of 1954. Lilibet watched as the horses entered in the race were walked up and down in front of the stands, Aureole among them. He was stronger and tougher as a four-year-old than he had been the previous year, more confident at the gate and more trusting of his trainer and jockey. Earlier in the season he had won twice, the Coronation Cup and the Hardwicke Stakes, but the queen hadn't been there to watch either race. She had talked at length about Aureole's future with her racing manager, however, and they had decided that the King George VI and Queen Elizabeth Stakes would be his last race.

The course was wet, the going was certain to be difficult. And Aureole was not fully recovered from an injury to his eye suffered a month earlier while in his box. His sight was limited on one side. He was to run in a field of seventeen horses, among them Premonition, the rival who had beaten him in the St. Leger the previous year.

Walking up and down, Aureole began to snort and toss his head, and his jockey, Eph Smith, decided to lead him to the starting gate early. Suddenly he shied; something had startled him. He threw Smith off his back. The jockey fell to the muddy ground. A gasp went up from the crowd, intent and on edge.

Lilibet too was tense and excited, her face set in a rictus of concentration. She saw Smith get up, brush himself off and re-capture the riderless Aureole by holding a handful of grass out to him. To her relief, Smith managed to remount and lead the horse into the gate.

At the start of the race Aureole fell behind but managed to recover, so that at the halfway point he was among the leaders.

"Aureole! Aureole!" went up the cry from many throats. "That's it boy! Pull strong for the finish!" They had bet heavily on him. They wanted him to finish well. "Good old Liz!" some were heard to shout. "Aureole and Lizzie!"

He went out in front, and managed to stay ahead despite late challenges from two tenacious contenders, Darius and Vamos. In the final furlong, smarting under his jockey's whip, Aureole shot ahead, straining and gasping. He won the race by three-quarters of a length.

Then came an uproar of cheers, the crowd was jubilant. Lilibet, nearly running, hurried to the unsaddling enclosure where Eph Smith led in the lathered chestnut colt. Something like rapture lit her face as she petted the horse and praised him, stroking his nose, telling him again and again how well he had done, how brave he had been. Pride and pleasure made her radiant. The applause of the racing fans was long and loud. The queen's horse had won the richest prize in British racing. He was a true champion, and could retire with honor.

Lilibet's happiness was enduring. Difficulties might arise, people and situations might prove volatile, even ungovernable. But like Aureole, the queen had grown stronger and tougher in the past year, able to stay the course. With enough patience, she too might have a winning season.

Meanwhile she would send Aureole to stand at stud at Wolferton Stud in Norfolk, where she would visit him when she was in residence at Sandringham. She looked forward to seeing the fillies and colts he would sire, year after year, long-legged, high-spirited and swift, winners and potential winners all.

FOURTEEN

The queen was in the Duke of Richmond's box at Goodwood, watching the racing, when a special dispatch reached her from the palace on August 2, 1956. It was the text of a proclamation calling out the army reserve. A privy council session had been called for the following day, at which she would be expected to sign the document. There was no doubt in anyone's mind, least of all Lilibet's, that the drawing up of the proclamation was a preamble to war.

Scarcely a week had passed since Colonel Gamal Abdul Nasser, Egypt's forceful, dynamic president, had declared that the Suez Canal belonged to Egypt, and not to the International Suez Canal Company that had operated it for nearly a century. Nasser had waited until the last British troops had left the Canal Zone for Cyprus, until the days of dancing in the streets and shooting off of guns and fireworks to celebrate the departure of the British had run their course. Then he had acted, swiftly and decisively, to seize the canal. British and world opinion had been sent reeling ever since.

The prime minister, Churchill's successor Anthony Eden, reacted with indignant fury. That Egypt, which had long been virtually a client state of Britain, should assert her sovereignty in a way that threatened the economic wellbeing of Europe, and of Britain in particular, seemed monstrous. The canal was the great global waterway through which more than a million barrels of oil passed daily, most of it en route to Western Europe; the majority of the ships passing through the canal were British ships, carrying British goods to markets around the world. Since the 1880s British troops had protected the vital hundred-mile-long trench through the desert, now it was under the control of a hotheaded, left-leaning dictator who had recently come under strong communist influence.

For the shadow of the Cold War fell across the canal. In July the United States and Britain had both announced that they would not, as previously promised, provide funding for Nasser's great engineering project, the Aswan High Dam, and the Soviet Union had moved in to oblige the Egyptian president with the money he needed. The soviet funds, plus the revenues from the canal, would be a great boon to Egypt's economy.

All this Lilibet knew as she signed the proclamation calling up the troops at Arundel Castle on August 3. She was well aware of government attitudes toward Nasser—and toward Egypt generally. Churchill had held a dark view of the Egyptian people, referring to rioting mobs in Cairo as "degraded savages," and Eden, who for months had been saying that Nasser "must be got rid of," was on a hair trigger. "It's either him or us, don't forget that," he had said in March, four months before the seizure of the canal.[1]

Lilibet found Eden to be difficult, her weekly meetings with him were quite unlike the cozy chats she had enjoyed with Churchill, who was amusing and with whom she could talk about a variety of things, including their mutual interest in horseracing. (One of Churchill's mares was bred to Aureole.)[2]

Eden's customarily suave, elegant manner, his youthful buoyancy seemed to have all but deserted him under the strain of his anger at the Egyptian president in the summer of 1956. He had become agitated and restless, he paced and fumed.[3]

Both the queen and her prime minister knew that there was much at stake in how the situation in the Middle East was handled: Britain's repute in the world hung in the balance. If Nasser's challenge went unanswered, Britain's stature would seem to diminish. Yet to take military action against Egypt would be to invite the dangerous complication of provoking the USSR. In the background of all thinking, military and diplomatic, was the looming peril of nuclear conflict.

Of one thing Eden was certain. Nasser, the prime minister told his cabinet, "must not be allowed to get away with it." The Mediterranean Fleet was at Malta, ready to be deployed. The troops were ready, the reserves being summoned. The British public, or at least a voluble, volatile segment of it, was demanding a military response.

But war had not been declared, and indeed cooler heads around Eden pointed out that the Egyptian president was not in fact in breach of any international agreement in taking control of the canal. The Americans, who like the British had a large stake in keeping ship traffic flowing through the disputed waterway, cautioned the prime minister that unless Nasser actually blocked the canal, interrupting navigation, there could be no grounds for sending in troops.

The queen was in the deeply uncomfortable position of being at the center of events, yet all but powerless to influence them, other than by asking a question here or making an impartial comment there. Constitutionally, she had to remain uninvolved, she could not let her personal opinion be known. Yet she had strong views, and was apprehensive, not only about the government's mood, but about Eden's agitated state. She listened to him when he came to the palace, observing his pacing and his edginess, aware that his health was poor and that the great stress he and those around him were under was putting it even more at risk.

Ever since an unsuccessful operation for gallstones had left him weak and subject to fevers and jaundice, Eden had relied heavily on medicinal drugs and stimulants to keep himself functional.[4] He took a large arsenal of pills with him everywhere, had to have injections at times, and joked that he had a "largely artificial inside." As the urgency of the Middle East situation intensified in the coming weeks, Eden had more and more recourse to his pill chest.[5]

If Eden was upset, it was with good cause. As both he and the queen were well aware, Nasser's bold move in nationalizing the canal was part of a broader, alarmingly destabilizing strategy. Even before the canal became an issue, Palestinian fedayeen, Arab commando groups, armed and supported by the Egyptian president, had begun blowing up roads and buildings and assassinating officials in Israel. And while British Foreign Office and Conservative Party sentiment had traditionally been pro-Arab—and Britain was dependent on Arab oil—the continued existence of the seven-year-old state of Israel was strongly to be desired. War between Israel and Egypt would be a disaster.

And it now appeared to be inevitable.

After three months of tense meetings, of strategies prepared and abandoned, on October 29 news came that Israeli forces had crossed the border into Egypt and attacked fedayeen bases. It was the provocation the British and French governments had been looking for. The Israeli aggression, and the certainty of Egyptian retaliation, put the safety of the canal in jeopardy, which provided justification for intervention.

Two days later, on October 31, 1956, with no declaration of war, British and French planes flew over Cairo and bombed oil pipelines and storage tanks and annihilated two hundred planes of the Egyptian air force. Just off Malta, an immense flotilla of ships was ready to invade Egypt, its commanders having been told to prepare for an assault on November 8.

The eruption of emotion in Britain was immediate, and intense. People responded with outrage, shock, patriotic fervor, horror—all of it strongly felt. Arguments broke out, tempers flared. No one, it seemed, was neutral; everyone had a view, and needed to express it and defend it.

Lilibet was in the crossfire of heated debate. Her own private opinion, in the view of her courtiers, was that the invasion was foolhardy, but she was careful not to voice that opinion.[6] Instead she took care to retain a consistent appearance of neutrality, while being buffeted by others' strongly held judgments (Mountbatten vehemently opposed to the government's actions, as were her assistant private secretary Martin Charteris and his deputy, and most of the Commonwealth governments, her private secretary Michael Adeane and others fervently in favor).

"I'm having the most awful time," she said to a friend. "My lady-in-waiting thinks one thing, one private secretary thinks another, another thinks something else."[7] She always resorted to Malvern water when unwell or under stress. One imagines that orders from the palace for Malvern water must have increased in the first week of November.[8]

One strident voice at the palace was not heard amid the cacophony. Philip was absent. For months he had been preparing to leave on a long tour, occasioned by an invitation he received to attend the Olympic Games in Melbourne. With his close friend Mike Parker he was to sail on the *Britannia*, with its crew of nearly three hundred officers and ratings, to Australia and back, visiting New Zealand, Papua New Guinea, the Falkland Islands, Antarctica and Africa. The voyage was expected to take five months.

Lilibet told one of her attendants that it was just as well Philip was not around to embroil himself in arguments about the wisdom of Britain's military actions in the Middle East. He would have been "impossible to live with."[9] He had left on October 15 for Mombasa, the leavetaking not without strain. Lilibet was uneasy about Philip's being away for so long, and with Parker, his companion in late-night revelry. (His other would-be companion, the notorious debauchee and party-giver Baron, had died six weeks before the scheduled departure.) When she kissed her husband goodbye at the airport, her apprehension was apparent on her face; observers noted that she barely managed to smile.[10]

Though intense, the Suez crisis was not

prolonged. The military phase lasted barely a week. The national backlash, the large and noisy demonstrations against what was in effect an undeclared war, the growing suspicion that Britain and France had incited—or at least encouraged—Israel to cross the Egyptian border to further their own purposes, the American threat of withdrawal of aid to Britain, and above all, the very real possibility of financial collapse because of falling confidence in the pound all left Eden no recourse but to accede to a United Nations cease-fire and withdraw British troops. The French too withdrew, as did Israel, leaving Nasser not only master of the canal, but much enhanced in international stature, at Britain's expense. Eden's aggression had proved to be a fiasco, gravely damaging to Britain's prestige. He resigned early in January, 1957, citing failing health, and the queen sent him a gracious letter of thanks and regret.

But the damage had been done, and it was not just military and political. Suez had seared Britain's soul.

And amid the maelstrom of soul-searching there came the first in a series of tidal waves that battered the palace walls.

The press, hungry for scandal, had been paying close attention to Philip on his cruise. The reporters had learned, during the course of the drawn-out rocky courtship between Princess Margaret and Peter Townsend, just how insatiable was the public's appetite for personal drama in the royal family. So much gossip clung to Philip, stories appearing in the foreign papers about apartments he shared with other men— among them Mike Parker—where he enjoyed assignations with a variety of women, a rich broth of hearsay. Much of the tale-bearing had to do with Parker, who was said to be living a double life, as a husband and family man and also as a free-wheeling playboy; it was assumed that Philip, being very close to Parker, indulged in a similar lifestyle.[11]

Philip was clearly enjoying himself at sea, calling in at exotic ports to shoot crocodiles, carousing with Parker and his other companion, the artist Edward Seago, enjoying the company of two attractive typists brought on board in Singapore. Free from the constricting protocols of the palace, he flourished. He grew a beard, wore whatever he liked while at sea, kept his own hours and answered to no one. On November 20 he wired a bouquet of white roses to Lilibet—it was their ninth wedding anniversary—and took a photograph of two large iguanas embracing—a quirky, amusing, rather ambivalent tribute to his marriage.[12]

With Philip in Australia the rumors grew more salacious, tales of dalliances with beautiful women in boathouses, of pleasure-seeking at parties among the wealthy. As usual, no genuine evidence was brought to light. But when Parker's wife Eileen decided, based partly on what was being said about the libertinism on the cruise, to divorce her husband, this gave the press the license they needed to turn rumor into news.

A furious Eileen Parker went to the palace and informed the queen's press secretary, Richard Colville, that she was going to divorce her husband, claiming adultery. Colville asked that she wait until the royal yacht had returned to England. But her solicitors did not wait—they informed the press.

Early in January, 1957, Lilibet was faced with a double challenge: the resignation of the prime minister and the strong imputation that her husband, like his companion Parker, had been unfaithful.

Parker's immediate resignation as Philip's equerry only made the charges look worse, as did a hasty statement from the palace that "it is quite untrue that there is any rift between the queen and the Duke of Edinburgh."

If the uproar over Philip's improprieties were not enough, there was a second strong wash of criticism over the way the queen handled her choice of Eden's successor. Instead of following Eden's (informal) recommendation that his able deputy R.A. Butler become prime minister, Lilibet turned to her trusted private secretary Michael Adeane, and to her father's advisers Lord Salisbury and the lord chancellor Lord Kilmuir, to gather Conservative opinion. It appeared, to outsiders, that she was turning to a small palace clique instead of taking the views of a broad spectrum of party members. And when instead of Butler she named the aristocratic, grouse-hunting Harold Macmillan to succeed Eden, she brought on herself the imputation that she had failed to carry out her constitutional duty. That instead of remaining above politics in making her own choice, as she was bound to do, she had allowed the power of the crown to fall captive to a minority faction.

Like Philip aboard his yacht, Lilibet found herself, in the early years of her reign, awash in turbulent seas. Contrary forces tugged at her, her overwhelming sense of duty, at odds with her longing to be out of doors and in old clothes, spending time with her horses and her corgis, her great desire to play her role correctly, always remaining above politics, in conflict with her strong urge to express her views and act in accordance with them. Above all she wanted to reign as her father had, her aim "not to fill the throne but to support it," as she believed his aim had been. She endeavored to reconcile these often conflicting desires, day by day, buffeted by swirling blasts and counterblasts.

Now and then, however, she found herself in the calm eye of the storm. The family's annual holiday at Balmoral often provided that soothing calm, weeks of tramping across the moors and deerstalking, of visiting the nearby village and renewing old acquaintances among the local population.

Seeking that oasis of rest and ease, Lilibet and her family had gone to Balmoral in the fall of 1955, a year before the Suez crisis. They arrived in mid-August, and settled in, doing their best to unwind despite the presence of an unusually large number of tourists encamped in the area and of large numbers of reporters.

Margaret's twenty-fifth birthday was approaching, the threshold of her independence. At twenty-five she no longer needed her sister's permission to marry, and could finally choose as her future husband the man she still loved, Peter Townsend—always provided she obtained Parliament's consent. The huge influx of tourists and of press representatives were waiting to hear her announce her decision. Clamorous headlines implored her to make her decision soon.

Margaret's choice was on Lilibet's mind that fall. She knew, for Margaret had told her, that her sister intended to marry Townsend once consent was given. But no official announcement had yet been made, and Margaret, temperamental, unhappy, certain of Townsend but uncertain where her duty lay, was hard on those around her. What Lilibet herself thought she kept to herself; she did not try to influence Margaret. She knew that her mother and Philip opposed Margaret's choice, making family conferences about the situation awkward, and prompting Margaret to lash out at times.[13]

Festivities in Crathie churchyard offered a chance to escape from the everpresent pressures and spend a little time in the open air. A bazaar was being held, with booths where handcrafts were to be sold. The funds raised were to pay for a new vestry. Under a canvas tent, wooden stalls had been erected where the handmade goods were to be offered for sale. The queen agreed to take part, keeping a stall, along with her mother and Philip and the sensitive, somewhat timid Charles, who was not yet seven years old, and Anne, who had just celebrated her fifth birthday.

The day of the bazaar came, and the fairgoers began lining up behind the temporary barriers provided by the local constables. Far more people appeared than had been anticipated for a small village fair, all of them eager to see the royals, most of them hoping for at least a glimpse of Princess Margaret, at that moment among the most photographed, most celebrated, most closely observed women in the world.

Bravely the royals took their place under the tent, ready to play their roles, the children alongside the adults. But as the crowds swelled and the temporary barriers threatened to give way the family must have become alarmed. This was no small-scale village fête, it looked likely to become a mob scene. They were unprepared for the surge of humanity that swept into the churchyard when the gates were opened and the fair officially began.

Almost at once pandemonium struck.[14] People streamed into the churchyard, a confusion of bodies, there were screams as women found themselves shoved against fences and railings, children fell and began crying.

Cries of "Don't push!" were lost in the melee, as the panic-stricken tried to claw their way back, against the tide of bodies, toward the exit. Clothes were torn, hats pulled off, umbrellas snapped, ankles broken. Police and detectives, overwhelmed and undermanned, did what they could to try to restore order. But the commotion was too great. Some in the multitude went around to the back of the marquee and began pulling it down, still trying to get to the royal booths.

The noise and bedlam, the rush of bodies and the screams of the victims must have terrified Charles, and made even the sturdier Anne cling to her father in fear. Somehow, with the aid of those around her, Lilibet was hustled away before the swarm of people could overturn her stall and reach her. Neither she nor anyone in her family were injured, but all were shaken.

It had been a terrifying, and revealing, moment. The calm, pastoral churchyard with its pleasant bustle had been invaded by a celebrity-hungry mob, clutching and clawing, tearing away at the family's privacy and peace. Robbed of their chance to mingle with the villagers and to share their pastimes, Lilibet and her family had to be spirited away to safety, lest they themselves be knocked down and trampled under, a prey to the ravening throng.

FIFTEEN

Life was getting better. Britons sensed it, felt it, observed it in the increasing material comfort of their daily lives. Rationing of food and clothing had finally ended, wages had risen substantially and, in the late years of the 1950s, nearly everyone who went looking for a job could find one.

It was still difficult, for most lower-and middle-class people, to find a house of their own. But there was more and more public housing available, apartments in high-rise buildings or temporary bungalows or, in an emergency, caravans—mobile homes complete with showers and cooking facilities. Gone were the days of candlelight and

Lilibet at ten years old with a corgi. © GETTY IMAGES/HULTON ARCHIVE

A thoughtful sixteen-year-old Lilibet in the long grass at Windsor. © GETTY IMAGES/HULTON ARCHIVE

Lilibet looks over George VI's shoulder as her father works at his desk.

Lilibet starring in the wartime pantomime "Old Mother Red Riding Boots."

Eighteen-year-old Lilibet at her desk.

Official photo of Lilibet and Philip on their honeymoon in November, 1947

Young mother Lilibet with son Charles at Balmoral. © GETTY IMAGES/HULTON ARCHIVE

Lilibet competing in retriever trials. © GETTY IMAGES/HULTON ARCHIVE

Royal silliness with Prince Charles and Prince
Edward. © GETTY IMAGES/HULTON ARCHIVE

A family marked by distances and silences: the
royals at Windsor, 1969.

A vexed and exasperated Lilibet on a state visit to Morocco in 1980.

© GETTY IMAGES/HULTON ARCHIVE

The queen mother and Lilibet at an outdoor sporting event, c. 1985.

© GETTY IMAGES/HULTON

The aging queen visits the Royal Marines
Commando Training Centre in Devon.

© GETTY IMAGES/DAVID MCHUGH/AFP

Lilibet on her Golden
Jubilee tour of
Canada, October,
2002. © GETTY IMAGES/

KEVIN FRAYER/AFP

Lilibet the horsewoman.

lantern light; most dwellings now had electricity, along with indoor plumbing (outhouses were rapidly becoming a thing of the past), telephones, and television sets. Relatively few people had cars, but that was changing; in the meantime, many had motorcycles, and rode them to work or to the church hall for dancing on Saturday nights or to the cinema where the latest American film, a musical or a biblical epic or a horror story in 3-D, was currently playing.

Many people still had two jobs, but instead of barely providing necessities, the two salaries now paid for sturdier and more fashionable clothes, much better food, and a refrigerator to keep it in. Teenagers bopped to the music of Bill Haley and the Comets on newly bought carpets instead of bare floors. Their parents saved money to go on vacations to the Spanish Riviera, and dreamed of the day, which they hoped would not be too far off, when they would be able to afford a larger apartment or even a house in one of the suburban new towns being built by developers—communities that offered rows of characterless, boxy villas, uniform in style but spacious, solid and above all, modern.

The Britain of 1957 was far removed from the postwar Britain of ten years earlier, the year of Lilibet's wedding. Not only was it more prosperous and rich in material comforts but its population, thanks to television, greater ease of travel and improved communications, was much more interconnected, and better informed. A sense of national participation, of entitlement, had begun to spread, and with it, a rising demand for yet more improvement in the overall quality of life.

For if it was evident that the average Briton was better off, it was equally evident that there was a vast divide separating the wealthy from those of lesser means. The Duke of Westminster, a close friend of the queen's, was said to have a private fortune of twenty million pounds. Sir Bernard Docker, head of the Daimler Motor Company, was so immensely wealthy that he thought nothing of buying his wife a gold-plated car encrusted with eighteen thousand golden stars. ("I hope people won't think it vulgar," said Mrs. Docker.)[1] The landowning classes were said to be declining in numbers, their purchasing power diminishing, but they still commanded vast financial resources compared to the short-hand typist who earned six pounds a week or the laborer who made even less. Stock market investors and real estate tycoons were worth many millions, while middle-class people saved for years to amass the fourteen hundred pounds needed to buy a modest house—if they could find one.

Life might be getting better, but it was not getting safer, rather the reverse. Violence flared in Northern Ireland, and in England, an unprecedented wave of immigration by people of color led to dangerous riots. Racist protesters marched through the streets of immigrant neighborhoods, waving banners and throwing stones, assaulting bystanders and police and wrecking and looting shops. A disturbing undercurrent of anger emerged in plays, novels, even fine art. And the buildup of nuclear weapons on both sides in the intensifying Cold War troubled the dreams of millions, an everpresent menace to the good life with its increasing comforts and prosperity.

Equally unsettling was the mood that settled over the country like one of the thick yellow fogs that from time to time drifted up from the river to smother London, a mood of inchoate frustration and protest.

This was the harshest and most enduring legacy of the Suez invasion, a bitter sense of betrayal. Having thought of themselves as belonging to a great nation, arbiter of global destinies, Britons were suddenly forced to acknowledge that their country had become second-rate. How else could they explain the sudden collapse, under international pressure, of the ill-advised invasion? Victorian Britain, Edwardian Britain, even Churchillian Britain would never have backed down—but then, the Britain of earlier times would not have acted so rashly in the first place, nor would its leaders have resorted, as Eden did, to subterfuge and intrigue.

Eden, who had once seemed an immensely reassuring figure, a figure of international stature who had played a key role in settling the future of Vietnam after the massive defeat of the French at Dien Bien Phu, had so shrunk in popular estimation as to seem a hollow, even a shameful figure, his reactions petty and his tactics ignoble.

To be sure, the diminishing of Britain's might and influence had been going on for years. One by one, former colonies had been granted independence—India, Burma, Sri Lanka, Pakistan—and more would soon opt for self-government. Postwar Britain could not sustain the costs of empire, even if her population had desired to retain vast expanses of foreign territory, which it did not. But even as the roll call of imperial lands grew shorter, the illusion of global imperial reach had remained, sustained in part by the existence of the Commonwealth.* With the Suez disaster, Britons had been forced to confront the inescapable fact that their country, as historian Peter Clarke has written, "was no longer in the great-power league, was no longer capable of playing by its rules, and looked absurd when it tried to cheat."[2]

Distressed, bewildered, resentful, the public was greatly influenced by a strong current of journalistic invective—much of it, in retrospect, healthy—against existing in-

---

*The Commonwealth of Nations, a voluntary association of Great Britain and its dependencies and former dependencies, founded in 1931. Members of the Commonwealth consult together and cooperate, under the informal leadership of Great Britain, but the sovereign members are entirely independent. Commonwealth nations benefit from economic ties, favored trade status and mutual investment and development programs.

stitutions and attitudes. In the course of the ensuing debate, the queen was held up to the light and a damaging caricature of her emerged—a caricature that was to shape the public's view of her for decades to come.

She was pilloried as "dowdy, frumpish and banal," with an offputting upper-class manner and speaking voice in which she delivered "prim little sermons." She was accused of perpetuating "the royal round of gracious boredom, the protocol of ancient fatuity," that her father and grandfather had instituted, and of being neither politically useful nor morally uplifting. In a much-quoted article, Lord Altrincham (as he was then known) gave it as his opinion that the queen was being molded by her advisers into a childish, immature horror, "a priggish schoolgirl, captain of the hockey team, a perfect and recent candidate for confirmation."

According to her critics, Lilibet was at the center of a "royal soap opera," a sop to the adoring lower classes, an artificial substitute for the genuine religion they no longer practiced, since only one in ten Britons went to church. Royalty worship was castigated as a "fatuous industry," a "circus," a "splendid triviality," shallow and gaudy. And the men behind the royal soap opera, the members of the royal household, were accused of being a clique of backward-thinking, unimaginative upper-class time-servers, "a second-rate lot, simply lacking in gumption," who had a vested interest in preserving their own exclusiveness and in preventing the monarchy from moving with the times.[3]

This highly unflattering profile could not have contrasted more sharply with the widespread idealization of the queen at the time of her coronation. "We're all expecting her to work miracles, I think," one corona-tion-watcher had said, summing up a prevalent attitude. Four years later a very large segment of the public—at least a very large segment of those polled—agreed with the queen's critics—though ardent monar-chists threatened the journalists with a vari-ety of ghoulish tortures for their disloyal words.[4]

Even the most ardent monarchist, how-ever, had to agree that Buckingham Palace was a bastion of archaism, an unreal world-within-a-world where tall, sleek, fussily fastidious men in pinstriped suits wearing expensive handmade shoes walked briskly up and down the long ice-cold corridors, carrying out the queen's business.

Servants occasionally fell ill at the palace, aged footmen died, once in a while a despairing housemaid killed herself—but nothing was allowed to interrupt the smooth running of the time-honored daily routine.

At a magnificent state dinner in 1958, the writer Elizabeth Longford (later the queen's biographer) and her husband were present. Turtle soup was served in solid gold soup plates. A dead bluebottle fell into Lady Longford's soup. She pointed to it, and immediately a footman in scarlet livery, without changing his expression, reached for the plate with his white-gloved hand and took it away.[5]

Ambassador Joseph Kennedy was once present at a royal tea where the elderly Lady Elphinstone, Lilibet's aunt, had a heart attack. "It was quite terrible," Kennedy wrote in his diary. But there was no panic, only an orderly response. When Kennedy suggested that he and his wife leave, the lady-in-waiting assured them that they ought to stay and that "Lady Elphinstone was better." The meal was resumed.[6]

Order and decorum mattered above all; any crisis could be handled, as long as proper procedures were followed, proper order maintained. "Disorder would upset the queen terribly," said one of Lilibet's friends. "But if you told her the Japanese had invaded Cornwall, she'd just say: 'I must let the Lord Lieutenant know.' "[7]

Many of the same procedures had been in place since Queen Victoria's time. All messages within the palace walls were delivered by messengers who carried them on silver trays, just as had been done in the time of the great queen. All dishes were washed by hand, laboriously and painstakingly. Footmen's wigs were powdered with the same mixture of starch, flour and soap used in the 1800s. Because Queen Victoria had once requested that a bottle of whiskey be placed by her bedside before she retired, a new bottle was carried to the queen's bedroom every night—simply because no official request to the contrary had ever been made. Elderly staff, remembering how shoes had been polished in the reign of Edward VII and George V, continued to polish the royal family's shoes each night—even the soles.

In the palace's five staff dining rooms, each servant had his or her assigned place at the long dining tables—maintaining an order of precedence in use for decades, if not for centuries. Rigid rules governed who could be addressed by a surname, and who by a first name, who could pass through a certain door and who could not, which member of the staff was entitled to be called "sir" by his inferiors.

There was no end to the minutiae. Officials and visitors were instructed, before they ever crossed the threshold of the palace itself, on what they were expected to wear, how many changes of clothes they were expected to bring, which knee they were to bend when in the presence of the sovereign. Fine points of courtesy had to be observed. When seated at a royal banquet, a guest was expected to keep an eye on the queen, as she conversed with those on her right and left; if she turned her head, everyone else was expected to turn his or her head at the same time, stopping their own conversations in mid-sentence.

If the protocols in use at the palace were

antiquated, so too was the sprawling old building itself. Curtains were falling to pieces, upholstery was frayed and torn, salons that had not been redecorated in a hundred years had patched ceilings and water-stained walls. Hallways were cluttered with old-fashioned statues, walls covered with oil paintings darkened by years of neglect.[8] It was no wonder, amid the clutter of decades, that those in royal service became, over time, removed from reality, embalmed in the past. The passing years, the changes in the outside world, did not penetrate the palace's thick walls; to those who lived out their lives within those walls, time and change ceased to matter.[9]

Too often it seemed, to her increasingly critical public, that Lilibet had succumbed to the same numbing ossification as her staff and household. That she had become fossilized at a young age, her normal development arrested. Instead of the carefree, natural and unspoiled princess the media had once made her out to be, or the dignified, appealing, very attractive young queen she had been at the time of her coronation, she seemed, by 1957, to have taken on a new and contrived persona. She appeared detached, regal, remote, correct. Indurated and incurious, her personality flat and dull. Instead of inspiring a "new Elizabethan age," she seemed uninspired and uninspiring. Her outward appearance mirrored this inner change; her wardrobe, which until the mid-fifties had kept pace, up to a point, with changes in fashion, became much more conservative, an invitation to ridicule. Her hairstyle remained that of the late forties and early fifties. She allowed the taste-challenged Bobo to choose her sensible handbags and unbecoming hats—a particularly unfortunate gaffe none of her advisers could manage to correct. If she had deliberately set out to remake herself along unflattering lines, she could hardly have made worse choices.

Critics focused on the queen's expression—or rather, her lack of expression. She had always been observed to have "severe moments," particularly when listening intently or when deeply moved, and attempting to control her emotions. "Trained like a trooper to resist displays of emotion," wrote BBC reporter Godfrey Talbot, "she brings down an inscrutable curtain of stiffness. . . . Under the limelight of public occasions, her sense of responsibility overlays her innate sense of fun."[10] One observer thought that the queen looked like "an angry thunder-cloud" when attempting to keep her composure; instead of allowing herself to show her feelings, even when they were positive, and would have endeared her to her public, she felt compelled to adopt a carapace of impassivity.[11] Her squarish face tended to take on a preoccupied, solemn look; seen in profile, she looked older, her bright eyes clouded over, her customary animation suppressed.

"The queen's smiles are there, and they're gone, and they come back, and they're gone," Elizabeth Longford thought. "When she's facing you, she smiles and she looks very young—she has wonderful teeth and a lovely expression. . . . She's much younger and more beautiful in front-face than in side-face."[12]

In actuality Lilibet worked hard to keep her face from breaking into any of a dozen emotions, from annoyance to humor to mockery to displays of sentimental feeling or sheer Hanoverian spleen. Expressionless she might strive to be; emotionless she certainly was not. It was an overabundance of feeling that led her to try to adopt an imperturbable mien.

Sometimes she smiled—but she could not always smile. "It's awful," she confessed during her postcoronation tour, "I've got the kind of face that if I'm not smiling, I look cross. But I'm not cross." It was impossible to smile continually; the face muscles hardened and the smiler developed a nervous tic, as the queen had good reason to know. Yet she was well aware that, unsmiling, she was open to the accusation of dourness.

"The trouble is," she told a woman friend, "that women are expected to be smiling all the time; it is terribly unfair. If a man looks solemn, it is automatically assumed he is a serious person, concentrating, with grave things on his mind."[13]

Those close to the queen knew well that when she worked most strenuously to look inscrutable, it was because she was trying hard not to laugh.[14] Her sense of the ridiculous was so keen that laughter was never far away, particularly on solemn occasions. It would never do for her to burst into loud guffaws at a moment of high seriousness, so she did her best to suppress the impulse.

"She has a lovely laugh," one of the queen's harshest critics remarked. "She laughs with her whole face and she just can't assume a mere smile because she's really a very spontaneous person." Others have commented on how, when the occasion permitted, Lilibet "hooted with laughter . . . a lovely, musical laugh, quite uninhibited."[15] As a girl Lilibet had been known to combine "grave responsibility and merry ease." As she entered her thirties that same combination was evident in her, but the ease and merriment were concealed from her subjects. She made no effort to project her entire self, but censored that part of herself that she considered beneath the dignity of the crown.

By 1957, the queen had come to a crossroads: she could either reach out to her people in their restless and increasingly critical mood, and strive to remake herself to suit their taste, or she could take refuge in formality and the reassuring intricacies of outworn protocol, and retreat into what she perceived as an immemorial image of monarchy. She chose to ignore the critical voices, to transcend the chaos of public disapprobation. To take no notice, and walk serenely on.

It was a fateful choice, and one that marked a turning point for the monarchy as well as for the queen herself. As Britain lurched forward into a season of plenty, her populace splenetic and spoiling for further collisions with tradition, Lilibet went into retreat. She retreated behind an inscrutable persona, behind a remote, faintly risible image, behind a phalanx of elite courtiers, behind the solid, square bulk of Buckingham Palace, its iron gates kept tightly shut against the unruly clamor of the modern world.

SIXTEEN

In the cold gray light of a raw January day, Lilibet could be found, in headscarf, old tweed jacket and sturdy brogues or boots, standing with her yellow labradors and cocker spaniels, waiting for the shooting to begin.

When the fat, ungainly pheasants, woodcocks and partridge began to fly up, and the guns to explode, she watched, taking careful note of where the birds fell, and then sent the dogs after them, controlling them in their search by blasts of the whistle she wore around her neck.

The dogs ran out through the underbrush, sniffing eagerly, coming closer in or going farther out in response to the whistled signals. Across streams, through coverts, bounding over tree stumps, the dogs eventually found the dead and wounded birds and brought them back, one by one, and the queen inspected them. With her baton-like stick she dispatched the wounded ones, beating them on the head. Hour after hour she stayed alert, one of the best "pickers-up" on the field, until the last bird was retrieved and put out of its misery and the dogs, loping and yelping, followed her back to the house.

By the late 1950s the queen had become an expert dog handler, and looked forward to the days of shooting at Sandringham in January, eager to run her dogs and compete against other handlers.[1] Training her labradors and spaniels, like supervising the training and breeding of her horses, was a keen pleasure, one she made time for, no matter what other demands she had to fill.

In January of 1960, however, she had to forgo the shooting. She was pregnant with her third child.

Prince Andrew was born on February 19, a sturdy baby, named for Philip's father. His sister Anne was already nearing ten years old when baby Andrew was born, his brother Charles was twelve. Journalists who had published stories only a few years earlier about a growing coolness and estrangement in the royal marriage called Prince Andrew the "reconciliation baby," and focused, not on the long time gap between Anne's birth and Andrew's, but on the significance for the marriage of another royal child being conceived.

Lilibet, who recovered very quickly from giving birth, was soon out with her dogs again, striving to train them to be the best retrievers in the country, and to make herself one of the most capable handlers. She met with master trainers as often as she could, taking instruction, and oversaw the dogs' care with the same avid concern that she showed for her horses. When it came to her special pets, the corgis, she fed them herself, mixing food for each dog in its own silver bowl with a silver knife and fork. She supervised their breeding, inspected the puppies and decided which to keep, made recommendations about their veterinary treatment and, when they grew old, made the heartrending judgment to have them put to sleep, laying the little bodies to rest afterward in the corgi graveyard at Windsor. She made up Christmas stockings for each dog, and hung them by the chimney. She blotted up their messes and tolerated their vomiting, barking, bad behavior, and aggression. When they bit servants or visitors to the palace, she blamed the victims, not the dogs; corgis were, after all, cattle-dogs, as the queen frequently explained to visitors, and they were bred to bite the legs of the heifers and steers they tended.

Occasionally, an obstreperous corgi bit Lilibet herself. She put a bandage on the wound and carried on.

By the early sixties the queen's dogs had become far more than sporting animals and daily companions. They were, like her horses, an absorbing preoccupation, a canine world unto themselves, always underfoot, given free rein and indulged and doted on by their royal mistress.

The corgis became Lilibet's guard and entourage, a cordon sanitaire between herself and the world.

A phalanx of dogs surrounded the queen wherever she went. They went with her from room to room, the scraping and pattering of their feet and their noisy barking a sure indication that she was approaching. No fanfares for Lilibet, rather a scuffling of paws and a chorus of excited yips.

When she sat, the corgis draped themselves over and around her chair. When ministers and foreign dignitaries came to the palace, or distinguished subjects came to receive their honors, they often fell over the dogs, which got in the way. The corgis provided a topic of conversation, a diversion, a focus of interest. Demanding, noisy, aggressive, or watchfully protective of the queen, their moods and behavior were dominant. Like clamorous small children, they could not be ignored.

Some saw in the queen indications of an overconcern, an overinvolvement with her dogs. Servants and officials found it disconcerting that she talked to the dogs, rather than the humans, when both were in a room with her. Her boundless affection for the corgis seemed excessive, part of a dog-centered myopia. Tragedies involving dogs (and horses) aroused in her a far more prolonged and heartfelt grieving and commiseration than tragedies involving people. Dogs she could train, control, understand, while people, especially those in her immediate family, she found to be incorrigible and baffling.

But if Lilibet was overinvolved with her dogs, no one has ever accused her of over-involvement with her children, rather the contrary.

In the case of the athletic, extrovert Princess Anne, whose natural pugnacity carried her blithely through most situations, her mother's limited attention was not crucial. But to Charles, the highly sensitive, shy heir to the throne, Lilibet's neglect was very damaging. Gentle, soft, gauche Charles, kind and well-meaning, needed affection and approval—and got little of either from Lilibet. She designed the upbringing of her eldest son along the lines of her own up-bringing, with rather strict nannies and gov-ernesses to superintend him under her own somewhat distant supervision. As a result, he suffered. He was constantly in want of care, solicitude, nurturing and warmth. All these his grandmother, the queen dowager, provided—but Charles did not live with his grandmother, and had to be content with the brief morning and tea-time visits he and Anne had with their busy, preoccupied mother, and with the notes his mother sent when away on state tours.[2] The rest of the time he was watched over by his brisk, mildly abrasive nanny Helen Lightbody ("No-Nonsense Lightbody," as she was known) and her junior staff.

In Charles's early childhood, Lilibet saw to it that he was provided with some of her old toys—the gesture, one suspects, was more frugal than sentimental. In his nursery was a china cupboard full of the toy soldiers, miniature coaches, worn teddy bears and stuffed mice she had had as a little girl.[3] And according to one sympathetic reporter, writing early in her reign, the queen joined in Charles's and Anne's games.

"She has been an engine driver, a porter or a policeman, an extra hand at snap, a companion on a morning ride," wrote Dorothy Laird, who added that Lilibet talked to her children "easily and naturally as people, never considering that they require a special kind of face or manner, as do some people who are basically ill at ease with the young."[4]

But there was a coolness, even a formality, in her relations with her children. They bowed when they came into her presence, they were not welcomed with open arms, hugs and kisses. When the queen returned from a state visit abroad, not having seen her children for weeks or even months, their reunion would be restrained, even frosty. "A nanny would bring little Prince Charles up and she'd shake hands, or maybe, kiss him on the forehead, and then put him aside," a Canadian government official noted.[5]

What eluded Lilibet as a mother was the ability to create and sustain the cozy, deeply affectionate atmosphere her own mother had brought about so effortlessly in Lilibet's childhood. There were no hilarious morning romps, no jokey outings, no genuine bonding. No cocoon of love; love was subsumed in healthy but often caustic discipline.

"She's a stiffener of backs," the queen's friend and private secretary Martin Charteris once memorably said about Lilibet, and it was true. Charles and Anne were brought up never to cry, never to complain, never to reveal any negative emotions. To do all that was expected of them promptly, cheerfully, and with complete outward composure. To imitate their rigorously self-disciplined mother, in fact. And to suppress the urge to confront or talk about their own emotions, or the grave tensions within the family.

For Charles, there were two thorny sources of tension—and intense suffering. First, he was yoked to and compared with his bold, coarse-fibered younger sister to such an extent that his introverted nature and less evident talents were overshadowed and his self-confidence undermined. Charles and Anne were dressed alike, as Lilibet and Margaret had been as young children. But there the resemblance ended, for Charles, physically soft and yielding, overemotional, clumsy and easily bullied, was cast into the shade by the forceful, fearless, physically vital and volatile Anne, who from babyhood more than held her own with him.

They fought, and Philip spanked Charles for hitting Anne. Charles sulked, Anne gloated—and went on provoking her oversensitive brother. It was a damaging cycle, which grew more damaging as Anne grew older and more boisterous and belligerent—and more adventuresome and courageous—and Charles grew more introspective, thoughtful and spiritually scrupulous.

The siblings were ill-matched, greatly to Charles's disadvantage; in an era when girls were expected to be retiring and sweet and boys to be aggressive and high-spirited, Charles was looked on as a sissy and a wimp.

But Charles suffered from an even greater psychological burden: the extreme disapproval of his insensitive, bullying father.

For the sibling rivalry between Charles and Anne was more than just the inevitable conflict between a gentle boy and his more aggressive sister; Anne resembled her father, and incarnated those gifts of boldness, self-assertiveness and constant dynamic action that Philip admired. Charles was all that Philip disdained, and he made no effort to disguise his scorn. Had Lilibet counteracted Philip's harsh rejection of Charles by giving him her affection and approval, the damage might have been offset, or at least lessened. But by withholding her love and support, failing to intervene between father and son and ignoring the problem, she allowed it to worsen, forcing Charles to turn to his grandmother—the only one in the immediate family to offer him loving acceptance, comfort and solace—to assuage his pain.

Understanding and coping with family dynamics was terrain Lilibet chose to avoid—perhaps because she knew it could prove to be an emotional quagmire that could only drag her down. Untangling psychological knots had never been a theme in the family life of the Windsors; when conflicts or estrangements arose they tended to look the other way. Lilibet saw what was happening to Charles, regretted it—though she was somewhat puzzled as to why it should be happening—and did little or nothing to remedy it.

Indeed the queen gave the impression, as the sixties began, that she was unable to influence or control her family very much. When shortly after Andrew's birth Princess Margaret married the charming, refined, driven Antony Armstrong-Jones, an accomplished photographer with bohemian tastes, and they began to quarrel, Lilibet did not attempt to make peace. She stood by while her beloved sister, ever the beautiful focus of gossip columnists and tabloid reporters, was idolized for her stylish, jet-set glamour but was torn and vexed by what soon became a spectacularly unhappy marriage. The relationship between the sisters, always close, had become corroded by Margaret's increasing bitterness. But Lilibet was steadfast, and tolerated Margaret's quirks and occasional jabs. The two could be seen water-skiing together, or laughing at Balmoral, and Margaret's two children, David and Sarah, were to grow up sharing an intimate bond with their royal aunt.

If the queen remained aloof from Margaret's marital disaster—a disaster that others in the family had foreseen—she also chose not to confront her mother about either her extravagance or her attempt to exert a continuing influence over the sovereign and the policies of the throne. The queen dowager spent lavishly, never counting the cost, and sending the bills to her daughter. She had a generous allowance from the Civil List, and private funds as well. But she overspent, buying costly bloodstock, repairing and redecorating her many residences (the Castle of Mey, Birkhall, Clarence House, Royal Lodge), maintaining a very large staff that included five chefs, three chauffeurs and dozens of footmen, secretaries, equerries, and maids, giving lavish parties that often went on for days at a time. She denied herself nothing, it seemed, not clothes or jewels, not expensive cars, not furnishings or gourmet foods or first-class entertainment. When her bank account became overdrawn, she called on Lilibet to supply the deficit, and Lilibet unfailingly paid.

Frugal herself, the queen nonetheless indulged her mother endlessly—because it avoided a confrontation. When mother and daughter spoke each day, either in person or on the phone, the dowager queen was vocal and demanding whenever changes in palace routine (such as the abandonment of the longstanding rule that palace footmen ought to wear powdered wigs, or the installation of an intercom at Buckingham Palace so that messages between offices did not have to be hand-carried) were proposed. She wanted everything to stay as it had been when her husband was king, and Lilibet, who strove to preserve her father's style of rulership, was sympathetic. But she was not only sympathetic: she was cowed.

"I'd better ask mummy about that," Lilibet was often overheard to murmur. She was made uneasy by the prospect of telling her mother anything that would upset her, and delegated the task of bearing unpleasant news to others. Her filial feelings were strong, and her desire not to upset her mother genuine. But Lilibet was also being self-protective, and choosing to spare herself the stress and vexation of argument. When it came to thorny family issues, she often took the path of avoidance; not that she was unaware, but that, being aware, she chose to look past the problem and ignore it.

And there were many thorny family issues to overlook. Margaret disliked Philip, Philip despised his brother-in-law Tony, Anne was rebellious, Charles lonely and wretched at his school, Cheam, and worst of all, the antagonism between Philip and Charles was curdling into hatred.

The bullying Charles was suffering from his father was far worse than anything he had to put up with from his schoolmates at Cheam, where he enrolled in September of 1957 at the age of eight. Having built his own life and persona around boldness and energetic action, Philip saw nothing but disaster ahead for timid, hesitant Charles, whose inherent sweetness lent itself to ridicule. So when the physically maladroit, flat-footed, plump and awkward Charles attempted rugby football and cricket, his father laughed. Philip himself had excelled at sports as a boy; that his son should do so badly seemed ludicrous. When Charles, who frequently caught colds, was reluctant to swim in the palace pool, and clung to Nurse Lightbody in fear, Philip's vexation rose. The prince went into the pool, runny nose and all, and was forced to learn to swim, like it or not. And when the boy's graceless thrashing through the water was compared with his athletic father's smooth, efficient strokes, observers felt sympathy for Charles—and were embarrassed, for Philip disdained to wear swimming trunks and his muscular, coordinated body was on full display.

The more Philip attempted, through mockery and force, to make a tough, resilient boy of Charles, the more the latter's resentment grew. Having once regarded his handsome, active father as a divinity to be emulated, Charles grew to look on him as a brute whose mockery humiliated him and reduced him to tears. The older Charles got, the more heavy-handed his father's de-

mands and punishing verbal lashings became. If Charles chose to befriend the
headmaster's daughter at Cheam rather
than the boys of his age, Philip was contemptuous; if Charles did poorly in math
(though excelling in reading and writing)
Philip criticized him severely; if Charles
failed to stand at attention during his lessons, or dressed too slowly, or was un-
punctual, Philip would shout at him and be-
little him.[6] Oversensitive he might be, but
Charles was also quite intelligent, and he
knew bullying when he saw it. In time his
deep resentment of his father's harsh treatment became coupled with a degree of
contempt, and a profound dislike. The
prince sought out his mother by preference,
sided with her, and identified with her. And
because his mother was so often unavailable, he sought out his grandmother—and
his favorite male relative, Lord Louis Mountbatten.

Coping with her husband's treatment of
their eldest son was only one aspect of Lilibet's ongoing emotional tug-of-war with her
excitable, restless, virile husband. When at
her strongest, she enjoyed the tussle, the
challenge of his jokey, matey teasing and

goading. She teased back, they understood each other, their physical bond was deep and of long standing—and she never forgot that ultimately, being who she was, she had the upper hand.

But when she was not at her strongest, Philip's vexation and volcanic temper grated on her almost past endurance, while his verbal assaults and ongoing cross-grained behavior tried her considerable patience to its limits and beyond.

They fought, they traded insults, he fulminated, she removed herself from the blistering line of fire. ("I'm simply not going to appear," she would tell her staff, "until Philip is in a better temper.")[7] She maintained her equilibrium amid it all, but at a cost. Among the things that weighed on her was the knowledge that her loyal servants overheard the fierce and prolonged royal quarrels ("truly phenomenal rows," as one of them characterized these battles), and were embarrassed by them.[8]

But as she well knew, there was simply no containing Philip. He was a force of nature, driven to strive, undertake, achieve on a superhuman scale. Patron of a long list of charities, avid polo player, constant traveler, speechmaker, haranguer of palace staff, yachtsman, driver of expensive sports cars (Lagondas, Scimitars), pilot, man of the modern age: that was Philip. Ever in search of a new and dangerous challenge, he flew over the Andes, making stops in Chile, Uruguay, Argentina and Brazil.

The approach of middle age did not slow him down or mellow him, indeed it seemed to urge him on to even greater efforts to excel, and to push others to excel. It was as if, by forcing himself to cram more and more into each day, he warded off a stalking negativity. When he accompanied his wife to an exhibition of paintings by Edvard Munch, and the museum director remarked that Munch "was always preoccupied by death," Philip's reply was, "But everyone is."

Driving near Windsor, Philip had another of his accidents. Lilibet was in the car with him when they struck another car and were pinned down. The owner of a nearby pub heard the crash, came out, and realized that the queen was in need of help. Everyone was extricated from the car, fortunately unhurt. And the driver of the other car was fined.

Driving too fast, risking his life in his

planes or on the polo field, living life on the edge—that was the exciting, exasperating man she had married, and Lilibet knew it. She had made him a prince of the United Kingdom in 1957, and three years later she declared, "after further consideration," that the family name would be Mountbatten-Windsor. It was a meaningful concession, though she meant it to apply only to her great-grandchildren, and only to those of them who would not be Royal Highnesses.[9]

The urgencies of family politics, it seemed, had triumphed over palace protocol.

But the royal marriage, like many an aristocratic marriage, continued to be blighted by the canker of Philip's infidelities. Proof there is none—to date—yet the suggestive evidence is persuasive, indeed all but overwhelming. Gossip and scandalmongering aside, and Philip's vehement denials notwithstanding, most responsible researchers have concluded that the queen's husband continued to enjoy a private love life outside his marriage, and his wife knew it, and in public, looked the other way.[10]

What marital rifts and tensions this caused can only be guessed at, but the heated quarrels overheard by the palace staff and servants give a strong indication. Lilibet lived in tension with Philip, theirs was a stormy marriage. Yet his frequent long absences, and her time-consuming preoccupation with her horses and dogs, not to mention her deliberately chosen rigorous working schedule, meant that husband and wife could, to an extent, live separate lives. It made for a workable compromise, or so it would seem. Philip performed his public duties as the queen's husband with charm and efficiency. Both knew divorce to be impossible—if not unthinkable. No private diary, no letters have come to light to witness to the humiliation, heartache, and loneliness Lilibet must have suffered. It is entirely possible, however, that given the queen's robust common sense and somewhat coarse-fibered nature, by the 1960s she had long since ceased to lament or to be wounded by her husband's waywardness. Perhaps she had found a way, psychologically, to dismiss what would otherwise have given her pain, to take refuge, as she did in other family troubles, in passivity and regal unconcern.

Even so, somewhere deep within her, the

ongoing affront of Philip's flirtations must have eaten away at her peace, a nagging undercurrent within her unsettled family life. The tasks of queenship she performed with admirable aplomb; the more delicate, less straightforward tasks of wife and materfamilias she shirked, lacking the skill to perform them well, and the commitment and tenacity to find a way to work all the problems through.

The shooters at Sandringham in the chilly January of 1964 stood in the harsh cold, rain drizzling down, waiting for the beaters to flush the birds. Alert, ears pricked up, the dogs waited to hear their trainers' whistles, the signal to go after the wounded and dead birds and bring the warm, still fluttering bodies back to lay them at their masters' feet.

Lilibet's labradors and cocker spaniels were as excited as the rest, keen to run and fetch their quarry, eager to be off bounding through the underbrush and across the streams. But their mistress was not there to send them. She was once again pregnant, in her eighth month, and she had to stay off her feet and keep warm.

The inactivity was frustrating, but she accepted it as necessary. Her sturdy common sense told her to do as her doctors said she must, to remain inside, in the warmth, and not take her usual place as picker-up and dispatcher of wounded birds. Besides her advanced pregnancy, and the preparations for the new baby, she had much on her mind as the new year 1964 opened. Political separatists in Quebec, bent on seceding from Canada, had threatened her life—and the security forces assigned to protect her were taking the threat seriously, for the American president John Kennedy had been assassinated only a few months earlier and that tragedy had profoundly shocked the British.

The government was tottering, with high unemployment and a declining economy creating increasing dissatisfaction with the Conservative leadership of Sir Alec Douglas-Home, who had succeeded the discredited Harold Macmillan. Spy and sex scandals led to a corroding disillusionment among the electorate, and made Britain the butt of jokes worldwide. The opposition of de Gaulle had so far kept Britain out of the European Economic Community, which she vitally needed to join. Privately, Lilibet had been informed that her tall, blond third cousin Anthony Blunt, an art connoisseur who held the official post of Surveyor of the Queen's Pictures, was an agent of the Russian KGB; instead of quietly dismissing him from her staff, she kept him on, on the advice of her ministers.

"I find that I can often put things out of my mind which are disagreeable," she told a friend. Putting disagreeable thoughts aside as best she could, while continuing to confront, in her hours of daily paperwork, the mounting discord and violence in the world and the demands for change at home, Lilibet entered the final weeks of her pregnancy. On March 10, 1964, she gave birth to another son, Edward Antony Richard Louis.

The hours of labor, and the overwhelming effort of childbirth, left her drained and exhausted. Only a few years earlier, after Andrew's birth, she had recovered quickly. But this time her body was overstrained, and weakened. She was ordered to rest, and her private secretarial staff went to work clearing her schedule.

Suddenly, unexpectedly, the tireless, dependable queen had to take a long break from her daily routines. Resting at Buckingham Palace, reading, doing crossword puzzles, watching her favorite sport ("all-in wrestling") on television, her corgis spread out at her feet, she gradually recovered her vitality. Tiny Edward, healthy, pink and appealing, gazed up at her when she held him in her arms. And gradually, as the weather grew warmer, she was able to spend long weekends at Windsor and take walks on the palace grounds, her dogs at her heels.

SEVENTEEN

It was breaking out all over Britain, the new mood of irreverence, unbridled license, freedom. Moral norms were loosening, hemlines rising, the sweetish smell of burning marijuana spreading. Suddenly all that had gone before, the world of stiff, formal manners and aristocratic privilege and conventional class hierarchies, seemed archaic, indefensible, ridiculous. And the monarchy most of all.

The Beatles sang of love and harmony in a peaceful, utopian world. The Rolling Stones sang of sex, primal and glorious. Communes sprang up, university students rebelled vocally, husbands and wives went their separate ways in a rising tide of divorce. And with the advent of the pill, attitudes toward abortion began to change and, at the same time, the number of single mothers began to grow.

Britain was changing, inside and out. The empire was all but gone, transmuted into a Commonwealth of new nations and a congeries of fledgling republics. British Africa was a thing of the past, and a white supremacist government came into being in Rhodesia. The United States and the USSR were locked in a Cold War for global domination—and for the domination of space as well. Dwarfed by the two superpowers, Britain was still a world financial center, but her military muscle was gone, and her international prestige had fallen enormously, thanks in large part to revelations of rampant security risks in the intelligence community.

As if to mark the passing of the nation's former greatness, Londoners in the last days of January, 1965, gathered to attend Winston Churchill's funeral. His coffin lay in state in Westminster Hall, while tens of thousands passed by, waiting many hours in freezing weather in long lines that stretched across the Thames and down along the south bank. Among the mourners were the members of the royal family, the queen's face frozen into a mask of somberness, all signs of her deep affection for Churchill subsumed under a rictus of solemnity. Disguising her feelings in public had become second nature, yet like so many others who mourned the great leader's passing she must have felt not only grief but dismay, musing on the vast contrast between the prevailing culture, with its pop and flash and contempt for conventional values, and the stalwart, self-sacrificing values of Churchill's wartime heyday. Her own passage through adolescence, her formation as a young woman, had come during that wartime era, and despite the intervening years, she had not changed much.

Indeed Lilibet appeared to set her face firmly against the encroaching tide of modernity, to ignore it, as she would a troublesome child or an errant spouse.

The queen, A. N. Wilson has written, was "so unmodern that she does not even know what it is to be modern."[1] But the comment takes no account of Lilibet's keen, shrewd acuity; she knew very well, in the mid-sixties, what it was to be modern, and she wanted no part of it.

To be sure, some concessions were made. Her skirts were shortened to above the knee. The royal family's first divorce, that of the queen's cousin Lord Harewood, son of her late Aunt Mary, was quietly permitted. And in a significant thawing of the decades-old frostiness of the royal family toward the Duke of Windsor, Lilibet actually went to visit her uncle when he was admitted to a London hospital. He was seventy-one, frail and in failing health. She spent half an hour with him, and with the duchess— once the most widely hated woman in Britain—in a gesture of family peace-making.

Through the exciting, turbulent mid-sixties, with Britain in the creative vanguard of the remarkable youth culture that spread its reinvigorating, naively hopeful values (and its appetite for drugs and for communitarian yet anarchic social arrangements) world-wide, the queen went on working at her old-fashioned desk. She sat in the mahogany

Chippendale chair her father had given her, with the seat he had embroidered himself, methodically going through the papers sent to her. She went on tours, she opened Parliament, she held garden parties and receptions and teas. To her subjects, she came to seem, at best, a remote, marginal figure, middle-aged and dull, swept aside by the rock stars and political agitators of the era, just as Britain itself was shunted aside in public consciousness by the moral quagmire of the Vietnam War and the shrill American antiwar protests.

Sucked under amid the maelstrom of change, the monarchy came under assault from critics on the left, who condemned it as reactionary and obstructionist, an outworn obstacle to the inevitable full democratization of British society. When Labour won the October, 1964 election by a narrow majority, many of the ministers, especially the Minister of Labour, the urbane, cosmopolitan Richard Crossman, were archly contemptuous of the court and dismissive of the sovereign.

But when they met Lilibet, their opposition began to thaw.

Coming to Buckingham Palace for the official swearing-in ceremony for the new government, the Labour ministers expected to be confronted by a stiff, ossified figure, remote and haughty, full of chilly regality; instead they were greeted by a bright-eyed, quick-moving, energetic little woman with a warm attractive smile and a ready wit. She was disarming, chatting to the ministers about her corgis, about how often people stumbled over them (two fat brown corgis were lying at her feet as she spoke), going into some detail—as she invariably did with visitors—about how corgis were Welsh dogs bred for cattle-herding.

On another occasion Lilibet chatted to the ministers about her livestock. "The queen got on to talking about cows," Richard Crossman wrote in his memoirs, "and said how terribly pleased she was when she had entered for the Dairy Show for the first time and won the championship for Jersey cows."[2] She went on to talk about Charles, and his school and exams, and generally kept the conversation to rather mundane, homely topics. "It was a fairly forced performance," Crossman recalled, but he could not help but be pleasantly surprised at the sovereign's naturalness and unaffected charm. Palace etiquette was followed, to be sure, but there was none of the rigid archaism or stuffiness the Labourites had been expecting. On the contrary, there were times when the queen became so relaxed and unbuttoned that the contrast between her grand, stately environs and her lively spontaneity was startling.

At a privy council meeting she was in "tremendous form," Crossman recalled. She was describing a wrestling match she had watched on television the previous day. "An all-in wrestler had been thrown out over the ropes, landed on his feet, and after writhing in agony had suddenly shot back into the ring, seized his opponent and forced him to resign." The unexpected turnaround had delighted Lilibet, who recounted the match to the ministers, telling them what "tremendous fun" such matches were. "It was interesting to hear what a vivid description she gave of the whole scene," Crossman wrote, "writhing herself, twisting and turning, completely relaxed. It was quite an eye-opener to see how she enjoyed it."[3]

The queen was even more at her ease with the prime minister. Harold Wilson, forward-thinking, forceful and professional, impressed Lilibet even as he made her laugh. He became a favorite dinner companion, and his weekly audiences with the queen, audiences during which he was struck by her wide knowledge of Commonwealth affairs and her command of current governmental issues, were a pleasure for both Lilibet and her prime minister. As Wilson's tenure went on, the weekly meetings became longer and longer, an hour at first, and then an hour and a half, and then two hours or more.

"She's the only person in this country who I can talk to about anything, because she's not after my job," the prime minister said. She had been a discerning observer of global affairs for so long, her acquaintance with world leaders was so wide, that Wilson could learn much from her, and she from him. He enjoyed their exchanges more and more as time went on. "He became more excited by them," biographer Philip Ziegler noticed, "and he'd come back with a kind of glow of satisfaction."[4] They conducted business, and then they chatted, gossiped—and shared a few whiskeys.[5]

A favorite topic of gossip was the French premier Giscard d'Estaing, who was rumored to be ignoring politics for dalliance. The newspapers were full of stories of how, having spent the night carousing, the premier would supposedly "ride back home in the early hours on a milk cart, having been womanizing somewhere." Tales of Giscard's driving around the countryside in the company of demimondaines led Lilibet to rock with laughter and call out "Ho-ho, Mr. Wilson!"

When the prime minister went to France, and returned to give the queen his account of his official meetings, she leaned forward expectantly at the conclusion of their business and asked, "Ho-ho, Mr. Wilson?"

"Ma'am," he replied, "there was no ho-ho; everyone went to bed early."[6]

In May of 1967 Lilibet found time to make a private visit to Normandy to see the French bloodstock standing at stud. She had looked forward to the trip for several years, ever since de Gaulle invited her to come while talking with her at Churchill's funeral. Her career as an owner had fallen on hard times; although Aureole's colts and fillies had become big winners in the early 1960s, making Aureole leading sire in England for several years in a row, in the latter half of the decade Lilibet's horses had made lackluster showings, and even Aureole, aging and cantankerous, had become dangerous and attacked his groom and nearly knocked him out. A mysterious cough had spread among the queen's horses in her stables at Freemason Lodge, making them unfit to race. Her racing manager and trainer were at the end of their careers, and her old friend Lord Porchester was moving into the role of adviser, in hopes that new leadership would reinvigorate the royal stables.

Porchey was with her now, as the queen flew to Tours and was met by the British ambassador, who accompanied her as she made her rounds. Madame Elisabeth Couturié's stud at Le Mesnil came first, then the French National Stud, where the French horse Baldric II, winner of the Two Thousand Guineas, was on display. Baron Guy de Rothschild took the queen around his stables at Meautry, near Deauville, and

Comte François de Brignac showed her his stud farm Haras de Verrerie.

For several days a happy, relaxed Lilibet did what she loved, watched horses and talked about them, observed at first hand and made the acquaintance of stallions she had never seen but to which she had sent her mares over the years, and discussed, in her excellent French, the fine points of bloodlines, feeding practices, and veterinary care with other knowledgeable owners and breeders. She may even have had a chance to ride—she still rode whenever she could at Windsor, Sandringham and Balmoral—and to examine the feet of her mounts afterward, as she invariably did at home, to make sure no stones had lodged themselves in the shoes.

At forty-one, she was still active, energetic, "strong as a horse," as she frequently liked to say. Her stamina and vigor impressed her French hosts, as they impressed all who encountered her. She had no gray hair, no harsh lines in her face, and was still fairly slim, though she relied on a skilled Hungarian corset maker to provide her with girdles and specially designed bathing suits to camouflage the thickening of her waist and hips. She walked rapidly and, when pressed for time, ran with agility, though not as fast as she once had. When in the countryside she chopped wood vigorously, stopping only when she pulled a tendon. Sinusitis continued to bother her, and her feet ached constantly, as Philip once confided to her shoemaker; after a long day of reception lines and public appearances, during which she shook hundreds of hands, her own hands hurt a lot, and she wrung them over and over in an effort to restore the circulation.[7]

If Lilibet was "hugely strong," as one of her ladies-in-waiting has said, and radiated energy and robust good health, it was in part because of an intolerant attitude toward illness. Illness was not allowed in her world, either in herself or others. Insofar as possible, it was ignored (though the queen mother, who shared her daughter's general intolerance of anything but good health, had to acknowledge that she needed a colostomy in 1966). Lilibet was a great believer in homeopathy, the practice of treating disease with small doses of drugs that produced the symptoms of that disease. A homeopathist, Sir John Weir, had been among the royal family's physicians for decades, and in the sixties the queen added new homeopathic doctors to her staff. When she traveled, Lilibet took with her a black leather case with small doses of white arsenic, snake's venom, deadly nightshade and other such compounds in case of need. If she injured herself slightly when out riding, she had arnica cream on hand to apply to the wound.[8]

Her attitude toward illness and preference for nontraditional medicine did not prevent the queen from recognizing the need for surgery in emergencies. When Arthur Simmons, the traveling head lad of her stables at Freemason Lodge, was diagnosed with a brain tumor, she arranged for her own surgeon to remove it at once—saving the man's life.[9]

Those who met the queen in the late sixties, in an informal setting, discovered in her an unexpected, behind-the-scenes self, a self characterized by her deep, rich laugh, lusty and carefree—the sort of laugh that bubbled up from earthy depths. Her great-great-grandmother Queen Victoria, outwardly a stickler for etiquette and propriety, had the same sort of laugh, uproarious and with a bawdy edge. But unlike the intellectually pedestrian Victoria, Lilibet had a dry wit and a droll manner of speech, her remarks full of subtleties and understatement. Those dignitaries, making small talk with the queen at official gatherings, who claimed to find her conversation bland and shallow (Crossman's "fairly forced performance") were not encountering the real woman, only the royal façade. In private, among friends and family, Lilibet could shine and sparkle with fun.

She made fun of people, imitating their speech, criticizing their clothes, grimacing and talking in false voices. She did a hilarious impression of the Concorde landing. She sang off-color songs. She made jokes about herself, describing how hats "made her look like a sheep." "Why should I want to look like a sheep?" she asked, deadpan. Reputedly, she enjoys being teased—but who, outside the immediate family, dares to tease the queen?

She loves silliness, and has trouble keeping herself from giggling at formal occasions. When Prince Charles was invested as Prince of Wales in 1969, both mother and son had to struggle not to burst out laughing. The princely crown was too large, it sank down too far over Charles's head, and that struck Lilibet and Charles as very funny. Among the stories Lilibet likes to tell is about the time she broadcast her Christmas message from the Royal Mews, standing in front of a horse.[10] As she was speaking, the horse bared its teeth, right into the camera. The entire broadcast had to be redone.

If the queen's deep vein of humor and strong sense of the absurd, a sense she shares with Philip who can be very funny, was evident to those who met her informally, it was evident to her staff that that sense of humor helped to carry her through her very long work days.

She did not slack off, or lessen the number of her engagements, after turning forty, but continued to fulfill the same taxing schedule as before. It was a routine she chose, not one thrust upon her, for apart from the precedent set by her parents, there was no tradition of constant royal engagements and frequent state trips abroad. Lilibet had simply decided to make herself in her father's mold, as sovereign, and what he had done, she continued to do.

But the effort it required was far more draining than any outsider could imagine, or so the queen's private secretary, Sir Michael Adeane, told a parliamentary committee in 1971.

"Nobody who does not carry such a burden of responsibility is in a position to appreciate the strain it imposes," Adeane said. "The queen is never absolutely free to do as she likes in the way that ordinary men and women are, or to take a complete holiday."

He described how the red boxes of papers arrived from the government ministries twice every day, and how it took his royal mistress two or three hours to read the state papers they contained, in order to remain current with whatever problems the government was addressing just then. "And always at the end of the day," Adeane added, "there are papers to sign and read and the queen is never too tired to deal with them."

When asked whether anyone could possibly be that consistent, whether there were not some times when the queen simply could not do what was required and had "to leave work aside," the private secretary's response was that Lilibet was remarkably conscientious.

"If she does not do [her papers] on Monday she has to do them on Tuesday. . . . If there is anything outstanding at the end of the day it goes into a red box and it goes upstairs and in nine cases out of ten when I come in the following morning the box has been done and is sitting on my table. If it is not sitting on my table I know that the queen will do it after breakfast."[11]

And there was not just the strain of the focused, careful reading of the papers, and thoughtfully integrating their contents with what had been read the day before, the week before, even years before, the whole forming a great body of information to be stored in memory and called up in moments of crisis. There was not merely the anxiety caused by the queen's intimate knowledge of the day-to-day dangers of the Cold War, with Russia gaining ascendancy over the Western democracies in the rivalry over nuclear supremacy and the conquest of space. There was not just the repeated shock of encountering, routinely, the details of every border conflict and minor civil war, every horrific act of terror, every thorny international dispute and potential diplomatic rift in the world. There was the added physical effort of many hours devoted to granting audiences.

Besides receiving ambassadors, ministers and Commonwealth representatives by the dozen, the queen gave audiences to distinguished citizens by the score. A random list, from the early years of her reign, included the retiring bishop of London, whom she invested with the OBE, her principal naval ADC, the governor of Virginia and his wife and a group of other prominent Virginians, the Supreme Allied Commander of NATO in Europe, justices of the high court, whom she knighted, and her retiring stud groom, to whom she presented, in recognition of his fifty-six years of service, a gold Royal Victorian Medal.[12]

Throughout her long day, when not on her way to make an official appearance, Lilibet had to be available to confer with staff. The lord chamberlain came to see her to talk over questions of precedence, or the details of styles and titles, or to obtain her approval for the flying of flags or for ceremonial arrangements for weddings and funerals. All new appointments to the household of three hundred–plus were approved by the queen. She also approved or amended the daily menus sent to her by the head palace chef, and discussed catering with the master of the household. The keeper of the privy purse came to talk over finance and issues regarding the royal estate.

So many decisions had to be made, with no time to really ponder any of them, there was so much minutiae to absorb and retain, so much variety in the matters she had to deal with. There must have been times when, feeling tired and overburdened, Lilibet wanted to throw up her hands and walk away from it all. But according to her loyal staff, she never did. Even when the mass of papers, facts, particulars merged, in her tired mind, into a swirl of chaos, she hung on and handled it all, methodically, doggedly, competently.

Part of the strain of her daily tasks came from the climate of unceasing scrutiny in which she labored. Someone was always watching Lilibet at her various tasks, she was continually being photographed, filmed, televised. Painters captured her likeness, and a film crew, authorized to make the first television documentary about the royal family, hovered in the background of her life for the better part of a year. The press had become much more intrusive during the past few years, eroding the queen's small margin of privacy. She was always on display, always having to be conscious of what effect she was producing.

Nor was this only true when she was in the capital, or on visits abroad. "The strain of a long day in a provincial town, Adeane told the parliamentary committee, "taking a lively interest in everything, saying a kind word here and asking a question there, always smiling and acknowledging cheers when driving in her car, sometimes for hours, has to be experienced to be properly appreciated."[13]

A journalist who watched Lilibet closely wrote that she was like an opera singer or an actor, always performing, always emoting—and at the same time, reining in her emotions. In the brief intervals between performances, the journalist thought, the queen was like a performer waiting in the wings after a taxing solo or soliloquy, "drained and exhausted."[14]

Stage fright hindered her. "I always have

butterflies when I open Parliament," she admitted. Before appearing to make even the briefest of television speeches, she became very tense, "so worried," she confessed, "that I could not bear to think about it." "It is so absolutely irrevocable," she confided to a member of her household.[15] Even when coached thoroughly, and reassured that she invariably performed adequately, the fear recurred.

When the tensions, and the negative emotions they generated, became too great, the queen liked to seek refuge in weeding the garden, pulling up great handfuls of ragwort, or in chopping wood, or simply in getting away by herself for even a short while. When at Buckingham Palace, she liked to order some bread from the page of the backstairs, then go out to the duck pond and feed the ducks and swans, the geese and pink flamingos. In quiet communion with the animals, she found peace. And at the end of a strenuous day that was hard on the nerves she liked to bathe by candlelight, or retire to bed to write in her diary and read, especially detective stories.

Few of her subjects could have imagined, before 1969, that their queen was funny, full of energy, enormously hardwork-ing and overburdened with the tasks of reigning: in short, that she was human. They saw her as an icon—or as a target. They made fun of her, mercilessly, they dis-missed her as an irrelevance. They took her picture off their walls and rarely sang "God Save the Queen." When on vacation abroad, they read about her in the continen-tal press, reports that she was about to ab-dicate, that she was about to divorce Philip, or even (much to her annoyance) that she was pregnant again.[16]

The chorus of loyal, reverent voices of those who still looked on the monarchy as an institution to be revered, and on the monarch as an anointed being to be vener-ated, was all but drowned out by the much more vociferous chorus of disdain. The pre-dominant view was that the queen was aloof, unconcerned, a parasite on society. A fossil, petrified and disposable.

In the course of a single night, June 21, 1969, that view was altered.

The documentary Royal Family aired, and something like seven out of ten Britons watched it. There was the queen, a little woman, cheerfully alert and bustling, making salad at a family picnic, standing with her daughter, watching her horses run in an early morning workout, driving Andrew and Edward to the kennels to see hound puppies. There was the royal family, watching an American sitcom, laughing and relaxed. There was the queen's office, her desk a jumble of papers, family photographs and flowers; there were toys on the floor, and overall an aura of work in progress, amid a domestic atmosphere.

Viewers watched Lilibet chatting with Richard Nixon, Lilibet touring Brazil, discussing arrangements for future tours. Lilibet showing Andrew and Edward pictures in a family photo album, and talking to them quietly, giving them encouragement. Lilibet feeding carrots to her horse. Lilibet ignoring Charles at a party and giving her attention to a group of women athletes instead. In scene after revealing scene, the queen appeared, stripped of her monarchical trappings, her public mask abandoned. She was appealing, capable, likable—if not regal.

In immediate response to the film, public perception of the monarchy became more sympathetic—though what remained of the awe accorded to majesty was permanently tarnished. And the more sophisticated segment of the viewing audience, realizing that *Royal Family* was not the true-to-life, authentic record of royal life it appeared to be but a carefully edited, polished, artful work of persuasion, if not quite outright propaganda, were made cynical. Insiders knew that the making of the film had been suggested by an expert in public relations, Nigel Neilson, one of several hired to improve the monarchy's public image.[17]

Lilibet was reportedly pleased with the positive public reaction to the documentary. The television cameras, which intimidated her so much when she had to make a speech, had proven to be a useful ally.

A month after the airing of *Royal Family*, the queen sat down in front of the television to watch the American moon landing. Neil Armstrong was about to step down onto the moon's surface, the first human to make contact with another world.

Armstrong began his descent, the queen sat forward on her sofa—and suddenly the screen went blank. Something was wrong with the set. Television, that ally of the monarchy, that global unifier, so powerful it could even penetrate into the depths of space, might be a remarkable tool of progress, but as Lilibet was to find, it could also let her down and go terribly wrong.

EIGHTEEN

"One day when I was driving out of the palace," Lilibet told the painter Norman Hepple, "the car stopped just outside the gate and an old lady came up and peered in at me and said"—here the queen put on a cockney accent—"'she ain't very like her pictures is she.'"

It amused her, the queen told the painter, that the old lady had complained about her not being like her portraits instead of the portraits being unlike her.

Monarchy invariably carries with it a whiff of the unreal, and Lilibet was well aware of it. She joked to her friends that she is seen, not as herself, a unique person with problems, triumphs, yearnings, weaknesses, hopes and dreams, but as a "Jungian archetype," an embodiment of the idea of a queen that all people carry deep in the unconscious. Archetype or not to others, by the time Lilibet reached her mid-forties, and probably long before, she knew herself well.[1]

She was the sovereign, to whom everyone bowed and curtsied. She was the royal employer whom her household servants addressed as "Ma'am." She was the figurehead, the icon, always ready "to see and to be seen," as she often said. She was the countrywoman, happiest when in old comfortable clothes, walking across open fields, or deerstalking at Balmoral with a broken rifle across her arm or wildfowling at Sandringham. ("I heard from Balmoral that there is snow on the ground there and berries on the holly trees," she remarked to some reporters early one fall while on one of her royal tours. "A sign of a cold winter—that is, if you believe the old wives' tales."[2])

She was her father's faithful successor. She was a successful breeder of horses. And as sovereign, she was, in her own words, "a personal and living bond" between the crown and the Commonwealth.

As such, she traveled, tens of thousands of miles a year, to all parts of the globe. By 1970 she had visited, among many other places, India, Ceylon, Pakistan, Nepal, Iran, Canada, Ethiopia, the Sudan, the United States, the Caribbean, the South Pacific, as well as Europe and North Africa. In Australia, on her tour in the early 1950s, nearly three-quarters of the country's population saw the queen in person. In Canada, the royal train stopped at many small provincial towns, allowing thousands of rural Canadians to encounter the monarch at close range.[3]

The shocks, adjustments, discomforts and cultural vagaries of her many journeys were an ongoing challenge. On her tour of Nigeria, there was the long daylight flight from London to Tripoli, then another long night flight—Lilibet hates to fly—over the Sahara, then the sudden and severe impact, on landing, of the hot, wet tropical air, a humidity so staggering it made many newcomers faint. The excessive cold of her air-conditioned bedroom at Government House in Lagos was enough to wither all the flowers given her in token of welcome, and her vulnerable sinuses were soon under severe assault.

While the maids in her entourage went to work unpacking the clothes, family photos, special feather pillow and hot water bottle, boxes of white gloves, solid gold brushes, combs and mirrors from her blue trunks with their gold-lettered label "The Queen," and Bobo began ironing the wrinkles from her mistress's suits and gowns, Lilibet began four strenuous days of special events. Crowds of chiefs, emirs, leopardskin-clad warriors passed in parade before her, horsemen in plumed helmets, officials in high feather crowns, African kings in ermine and velvet. Red dust rose in thick clouds over the noisy rejoicing, staining Lilibet's pale dress, matching hat and immaculate white gloves, settling on Philip's white uniform and making spectators and performers sneeze.

At the immense Lagos Durbar, or ceremonial court, the fifty thousand spectators, stirred by the incessant drumbeats and by the sight of so many colorfully gowned dignitaries, began to jump and dance, raising more dust; before long the heat, dust and noise were stupefying. Into the earthshaking chaos came more din. Great hosts of armored warriors charged at full gallop, shouting at the top of their lungs. As the hours of celebration continued, the drums grew louder and the cacophony of instruments more spirited. Under the relentless afternoon sun, long speeches were made and gifts exchanged.

Lilibet, wilting, besieged by mosquitoes, persevered until at last, her feet aching and her hand hurting from shaking so many foreign hands, she retired to her icy rooms to rest, comforted, no doubt, by the knowledge that her blue traveling trunks always contained China and India tea, Malvern water, barley sugar (for energy, and to feed the local horses), sausages from Harrods and fruitcake and shortcake biscuits.[4]

Leaving Lagos, the royal tour went on through the sweltering low-lying Niger Delta, a landscape of sluggish canals and marsh, toward Ibadan, where more displays, parades, and noisy celebrating went on. Reporters from the *Daily Telegraph*, the BBC, Tass, Agence France-Presse, and *Asharq Al-Aswat* noted how Lilibet, unlike other European visitors on formal tours, did not seek out the white residents exclusively but "broke away. . . to talk to Nigerians and constantly broke through the difficulties of race and custom."[5] Tour arrangers always did their best to keep the queen away from areas where disease was epidemic, but Lilibet, knowing that Hansen's disease (leprosy) was not contagious and that most Nigerians believed that it was, went to a settlement of Hansen's disease sufferers on the Oji River and visited every housing compound and many classrooms at the settlement school. By her presence she demonstrated to Africans that it was safe to show compassion for those afflicted and to offer them companionship. She quietly made arrangements to "adopt" several of the children at the settlement and underwrite their medical costs and education.[6]

If the queen was sure of her identity as the personal link between the throne and the Commonwealth, she was equally secure in her role as the natural center of royal ceremonial. She took it for granted that she would preside at ceremonies at the Cenotaph in Whitehall, that she would open the Highland Games at Braemar, that she would take the salute at the Trooping the

Colour ceremony on Horse Guards Parade. That each year during Holy Week she would distribute purses of coins to the poor. And that, each fall, she would drive to the Palace of Westminster in the Irish State Coach, be met by the lord chancellor, the lord great chamberlain and the earl marshal, and then, having put on her crimson robe of state with its ermine, and wearing the heavy imperial state crown with its freight of costly gems, she would make her way to the House of Lords in procession, the pages of honor bearing her long train.

It was a mini-coronation, this robing, processing, delivering of the short speech to the combined houses of Parliament amid much solemnity and awareness of tradition. It recalled the past—and for Lilibet in particular, it recalled her stammering father, for whom any speechmaking was torture and who practiced long hours in his study before his annual appearances before Parliament. She remembered him, sitting at his desk, the heavy crown on his head (he practiced wearing it, reaccustoming himself to its weight), going over the words he would say in an effort to ensure a smooth performance. Remembering her father, the queen declined when offered the option to wear the lighter St. Edward's crown; he had worn the heavy one, and so would she.

The queen knew herself, defined herself realistically and defined and carried out her role sure-handedly. But for others, as the new decade of the seventies opened, there were questions about who she ought to be, and in particular, about how much she, her family, and her large establishment ought to cost.

It was a delicate subject, this matter of the queen's upkeep. The cost of the entire royal establishment—the salaries of the household and servants, the sums paid to the sovereign and her relatives annually, the supplements paid to the court by various government departments—was very high, and growing sharply higher each year. Questions were raised by both the Labour government and, after June, 1970, the Conservative government under Prime Minister Edward Heath, about why the crown should not be more self-sufficient. After all, it was pointed out in the course of debate, the queen was among the wealthiest women in the world. The palace vaults were full of priceless jewelry in untold abundance, on the palace walls hung priceless works of art. Every time the queen went abroad she received valuable gifts. Her estates, including the immense landholdings of the Duchy of Lancaster, yielded a very high annual income. And her private fortune, on which she had never paid any income tax, was imagined to be almost incalculably high.

Speculation about the queen's personal wealth became, in the early 1970s, rampant, and the debate over the cost of the royal establishment rancorous. Royal officials refused to disclose the queen's actual worth, claiming that to make such an estimate would invade her privacy. Yet such secrecy only led to more speculation—and more resentment.

Was she worth fifty million pounds, a hundred million? Or was the true sum far higher, in the billions perhaps, making her nearly rich enough to buy and sell her own realms several times over?

The wealthier Lilibet was imagined to be, the more vociferous the debate became. Why, it was asked, were public moneys being voted by Parliament to subsidize, among other things, the royal yacht *Britannia* at upward of five million pounds a year when Philip, according to *The Times*, owned at least four yachts of his own, plus countless expensive cars and racing boats and other rich men's toys?[7] Why was the queen paid a salary (for such her annual Civil List allotment seemed to the average Briton) at all when she spent so much on her racehorses and her many mansions?

It was useless to point out, as advocates of the monarchy tried to do, that the queen's privy purse, paid to her under the Civil List Act, was given in exchange for valuable crown lands which she had turned over voluntarily at the start of her reign. Thus the monarch was in fact subsidizing the government (since the crown lands yielded far more than what was given back to her), and not the other way round. It was also useless, when tempers ran high and voices grew shrill, for the prime minister to urge patience and to disclose that the entire question of the royal finances had been under quiet discussion between Treasury officials and members of the queen's household for months, and was on its way to resolution.

In the public mind, the line between what was subsidized by the government and what the monarch paid for out of her private fortune was blurred; the only thing that mattered was a widespread suspicion that the very rich royal family was costing the taxpayers far too much, and carrying far too little of the cost themselves.

The discussion could hardly have been more topical, for Britain was in a steep economic decline as the 1970s opened, a decline much sharper than that experienced by any other nation in the developed world. Great increases in the price of oil led to alarmingly high inflation. Food and housing prices rose so fast that the public became unsettled, then frightened, as more and more workers lost their jobs and the hoped-for industrial recovery, which had seemed a possibility in the late sixties, gave way to depression. During the prolonged strikes by coal miners, power and fuel supplies ran very low. Homes and public buildings were chilly, some department stores actually sold goods by gaslight. When the garbage collectors went on strike in sympathy with the miners, mountains of uncollected trash accumulated in the streets. Protest marches, clashes between workers and employers, mass picketing, ultimately a state of emergency declared by the prime minister: these were only the outward and visible signs of a deeply troubling inner decay in Britain's economic life, a decay pessimists predicted would not be arrested in their lifetimes.

Optimists pointed to Britain's admission to the European Economic Community in 1973 as offering hope for a reversal of the negative trend, and when the first North Sea oil flowed in 1975, it was expected that the realm's dependence on foreign oil would be greatly reduced, if not eliminated. But the initial impact of Britain's EEC membership was to cause more inflation, not less, and by the mid-seventies it was becoming clear that no single remedy, not even the much anticipated availability of domestic oil, could stop the economic rot. Income taxes had been raised, the pound devalued, yet poverty was spreading, and the introduction of decimal currency seemed yet one more symptom of an irreversible change, for the worse, in the state of the economy.

Amid the widespread hardship the queen and her court received substantial increases in funding, over much parliamentary opposition. In 1975 the Civil List raised the combined royal allowances to nearly two million pounds a year, with a provision in the act that annual increases would become automatic. Subsidies for the royal yacht, the Queen's Flight, the royal train, maintenance of the castles and palaces and a long list of minor costs (for flowers, garden parties, official gifts, horses for ceremonial occasions) were provided—with the monarch supplying any deficit out of her own accounts at Coutts Bank.

To those who made the Atlantic crossing with her in 1976, aboard the *Britannia*, Lilibet seemed positively buoyant despite all the country's difficulties.

"Wheeeeeee!" she cried, excited and smiling, extrovert and unrestrained, holding on to a sliding door and sliding with it as the royal yacht pitched and rolled wildly in turbulent seas just east of Bermuda. Many of the guests aboard were seasick, but the queen, one of them thought, looked "philosophical, almost merry," and enjoyed the wild ride. She particularly enjoyed the discomfiture of her spouse, whose face was "less fresh than usual, ashen and drawn."

The tossing of the ship grew less extreme on the following day, the gales having abated, and Lilibet was again merry at lunch. "I have NEVER seen so many gray and grim faces around a dinner table," she said, referring to the night before. She added, grinning, "Philip was not at all well. I'm glad to say." She giggled.[8]

Sometimes, as those around her thought, a look of "immense delight" came over the queen's face, a pure and childlike happiness. Informal photographs capture that carefree, laughing look of pleasure, the "great gaiety" she showed to her intimates and favored guests. She had not lost the capacity to jump for sheer joy when one of her horses ran well in a race, or to dance energetically late into the night, her effusive good humor infectious.

But at other times she looked, the journalist Ann Morrow thought, "strained and unhappy," as though she had been through many an ordeal. Her face then revealed her age, and she appeared weary, worn down by her burdens and by the "fretwork" that her father had observed at work in her.

In the early seventies she was fretting about Margaret, who was not aging well. Instead of making a graceful transition into her forties Margaret was regressing, growing more and more temperamental, alternately moody and fractious. Like a refractory child she sulked—or shouted in a violent temper.

"Don't take any notice of Margaret," the queen mother advised those present when her younger daughter threw her purse across the room or shouted at the top of her lungs in rage. But how could anyone fail to take notice of the once beautiful Margaret, now visibly going to seed, blowsy with too much makeup, drinking too much, noisily carrying on or snarling and snapping petulantly? Uncomfortable family friends and guests turned away tactfully from the sight of Margaret embarrassing herself; on one memorable occasion, at a luncheon, the princess chose not to eat or socialize but sat stonily facing a wall, refusing food.[9]

Her marriage to Tony Armstrong-Jones had become a toxic battleground. Explosive arguments and tantrums corroded whatever love there had once been, and both partners were unfaithful. Tony, reportedly, had lovers of both genders and Margaret had a series of boyfriends, one of whom, the artistic bipolar nephew of the prime minister Alex Douglas-Home, com-

mitted suicide, giving rise to very unflattering gossip.

Alternately loose and giggling and explosively angry, Margaret lurched into middle
age, still married but restlessly and un-
happily searching for her lost youth. She
thought she had found it when she met
Roderick Llewellyn, a devastatingly bad
choice of partner. Not only was the twenty-
five-year-old Roddy unstable, the survivor
of two suicide attempts; not only did he occasionally dress in the leather-and-chains
trappings of the sadomasochist; not only
was he a sometime male model but he was
hard up for money, and Margaret was rich.

Whatever the truth of their liaison (which
may have been mostly platonic), it was certainly indiscreet, and inappropriate for a
married member of the royal family, fifth in
line for the throne. Public sympathy for the
princess evaporated when pictures of her
with Roddy on her private estate on the
Caribbean island of Mustique were published. She was seen as nothing more than
a pathetic, self-involved, pampered woman
who happened to be the queen's sister, a
costly superfluity, her behavior a stain on
the Windsors' generally wholesome image.

But it was not just that Margaret had floundered into scandal; the scandal had a sordid edge. And Margaret, jittery and overly uninhibited, was clearly ill.

Lilibet stood by, worried but able to do little, as her unstable sister went along her self-destructive path. She took Margaret's children, especially her niece Sarah, under her wing. Meanwhile the chain-smoking Margaret succumbed to pneumonia and had part of a cancerous lung removed. At one low point she reportedly swallowed sleeping pills, but not enough to be fatal. Her physical and mental fragility were so evident—yet Lilibet, sturdy and robust herself, had difficulty empathizing.

"The queen found it hard to cope with Princess Margaret," one of her friends has said. "She wondered, what am I going to do with her?"[10] Lilibet's closest advisers became accustomed to listening to her talk about Margaret and her illnesses, her disintegrating marriage, her ongoing ties to Roddy and the pain the liaison caused.

"How can we get her out of the gutter?" the queen asked bluntly. There seemed to be no obvious answer.[11] Meanwhile the scandal was inviting more and more prurient press coverage. The story of the princess and her degrading love affair was given more space than the change of prime ministers. The public wanted to read every detail: how Roddy was broke ("Margaret's Darling Angel on the Dole"), how she visited him at his shabby commune and spent the night, how the two frolicked together in the tropics. Unethical journalists published altered photos of the two from which other people had been removed, giving a false impression of privacy and intimacy.[12] Servants were paid large sums to come forward and tell what they had witnessed, intrusive photographers kept up a wearying, relentless surveillance.

The family was under scrutiny as never before. But Lilibet, outwardly unfazed, retained her calm—if not always her inner serenity—and continued to anchor the family with her down-to-earth manner and common sense.

And with the familiar, comforting ritual of afternoon tea.

The late afternoon procedure of tea-making, like the late afternoon feeding of the corgis and the morning serenading of the queen by her pipers, was an exercise in grounding, a calming and reassuring rite with its own rules and protocols. Whatever else was going on, at whatever stressful pace, all came to a halt during the interval set aside for tea. The queen presided, the flavorful brown liquid was poured, and for the better part of an hour time stopped and the world and its demands were held at bay.

NINETEEN

Lilibet carefully spooned her preferred Darjeeling blend from the jade tea caddy, exactly one spoonful per person, and boiled the water in a Victorian silver kettle that Philip had electrified. The spoon was an heirloom, as was the silver cream jug in the shape of a cow which had been passed down through the generations from Queen Victoria's uncle William IV.

Brewing the tea Lilibet regarded as an exact procedure, akin to brain surgery or diamond cutting, and she did not allow anyone else to take charge of it. Not Philip, who had already forced her to compromise with tradition by wiring the kettle, and not her mother, who with charming insouciance would have used tea bags, as she did when making tea by her bedside at Clarence House. ("Don't tell my daughter," the queen mother admonished an interviewer when confiding that she drank tea made from tea bags. "She is very Puritan about these things.")[1] The making of tea would never be delegated to Charles—he was not yet ready for the responsibility. Anne lacked the exacting care and precision to do a good job, and Andrew and Edward were too young as yet.

No, the queen had to preside, in order for the ritual to be carried out to perfection.

Lilibet had observed that a small-leaf Darjeeling was best when brewed for three minutes, while a larger-leaf blend required six minutes; after scrutinizing the leaves she decided how much time to allow the tea to steep. When the time was up she poured, the soft growling of the feasting corgis in the corridor outside providing a counterpoint to the gurgling of the poured tea going into each cup.

Not a leaf was allowed to escape; the queen herself refused to drink tea with even a single leaf floating in it. Moreover, she refused to drink hot tea, it had to sit until it was tepid, then she drank it. While it was cooling she managed to ignore the plates of egg and watercress sandwiches, cookies, muffins and gingerbread brought in by the page of the presence. With iron self-discipline she watched her family eat, intent rather on hearing what they all might have to say.

But they said little—or rather, they said little that was either informative or self-revealing. They were not a close-knit family; in fact the opposite. They were physically separated. Each had his or her own suite in the immensity of Buckingham Palace, the suites separated by long corridors. Each had his or her own agenda of activities, Philip and Lilibet traveling, usually apart, the queen mother in Scotland or at Clarence House, Anne, from 1973, with her own establishment and husband, Charles in the navy and often at sea, Andrew at Gordonstoun and Edward at Heatherdown. Beyond the physical separation, they were emotionally distant, the relationships between them full of strain and unspoken grievances and festering disappointments—as well as costive affection.

There were mechanisms at work among them to lighten the atmosphere and camouflage the resentments—family jokes, banter, the ongoing preoccupation with horses and dogs, shooting and fishing and similar country matters, gossip about others. But they shied away from saying what was really on their minds, and did not ask the probing questions or raise the thorny issues. They did not allude to troubling thoughts or feelings. Family teas were uncomfortable, especially for Lilibet, who complained that "her children never talked to her," oblivious of the dampening effect of her controlling perfectionism, her everpresent example of close-mouthed, tightly held self-discipline and her inescapable aura of regality.

As tea was served the task of keeping up a semblance of communication fell to the queen mother, who was emollient and pleasant, and to the opinionated Philip, against whose dominant remarks the others braced themselves. Anne, bluff and imperious, was least fazed by her father and had no hesitation in contradicting him or showing her exasperation with him.

In her mid-twenties Anne was unshakably self-confident, full of physical vigor and with an intimidatingly authoritarian nature. She was the family champion, notably successful as a horsewoman, having won the European Three-Day Event championship in 1971 and devoting herself to the eventing circuit. Anne dreamed of competing in the Olympics. The inbred, closed, snobbish world of competitive riding had become her milieu, and had done nothing to mellow her driven and aggressive temperament or soften her irritability and brusque manner. Nor had it brought her closer to her brothers, toward whom she was disdainful and dismissive, seeing Charles as wimpy and Andrew and Edward as spoiled and coddled.

When Anne chose as a husband another competitive rider, Captain Mark Phillips, her parents were far from elated but saw the advantage of the couple's sharing an avocation. Anne's lavish wedding was televised and the British public, drawn in by the rich ceremonial and the social cachet, were well content, knowing nothing of Mark's dull wits, social limitations or his liking for puerile practical jokes. (He became known in the family, as he had been at school, as "Fogg.")

Charity work undertaken on behalf of Save the Children improved Anne's public image by making her appear more altruistic, and less narrowly equine in her preoccupations. And in March, 1974, an incident occurred that turned Anne into a heroine.

As Anne and Mark were being driven along a busy London street, a gunman stopped their car, shot the princess's bodyguard and chauffeur along with several others, and tried to grab her and pull her out of the car. Anne fought back, demanding angrily of her would-be captor, "What good is this going to do?" She held her ground, and was eventually released unhurt. The kidnap attempt was thwarted. Witnesses applauded Anne's calm and fortitude.

Lilibet was proud of her daughter, but not close to her. During Anne's teen years her stubbornness and opposition had exasperated her mother, who had called in her sympathetic lady-in-waiting Susan Hussey as mediator and surrogate.

Susan Hussey was also at hand when Charles needed a confidante, or when his usual supporters the queen mother and

Louis Mountbatten were unavailable. She was sitting beside him one night at the opera when he turned to her and said, his tone almost plaintive, "Will I ever be able to choose the girl I want to marry?"

"We'll see," Susan said, patting his hand reassuringly.[2]

By the mid-seventies the question of whom Charles would choose to marry, and how soon, was crowding out every other concern in his life. He had brief, ultimately unsatisfying affairs with many women, fell in and out of love with equal ease. Sex was all too readily available. Young girls, actresses, wellborn ladies, some of them married, were eager to arrange assignations with the Prince of Wales, and Charles's friends offered their estates as safe places for rendezvous.[3] But sex did not bring either love or reassurance, and Charles was in desperate need of both.

Charles was wrestling with a seemingly impossible dilemma. In 1970, at the age of twenty-two, he had met a woman who satisfied his every need, the slightly older, far more experienced Camilla Shand. But he could not marry her; though she came from a landed country family, she did not fit the

royal ideal of a bride for the next king—an innocent, virginal girl, sheltered and protected
from the corroding effects of sophistication.
And besides, Camilla was in love with Andrew Parker-Bowles, one of Princess Anne's
former boyfriends. Camilla married Parker-
Bowles in 1973, and Charles went on with
his free-wheeling love life.

Lilibet saw clearly how adrift her eldest
son was, how lacking in confidence, how
socially gauche and prone to self-pity. If she
had any pity for him, for his extreme discomfort in the role into which he was born,
with all its restrictions (for that, at bottom,
was what ailed him), she seems not to have
shown it. To sympathize would be to
weaken him, what Charles needed was to
become tougher, more thick-skinned. Sympathy would only make him needy and
emotional and self-absorbed.[4]

Impatient with the complexities of
Charles's nature, and repelled by what she
saw as his weakness and self-indulgence,
Lilibet chose to look past the warning signs
that Charles was suffering and in trouble.
She loved her son, but could not understand him; what she saw most clearly was
that he appeared to be shirking his primary

duty, which was to marry and continue the Windsor line.

The clash between the queen's outlook and that of her heir could hardly have been more sharply etched. It had never occurred to Lilibet, from childhood on, not to do what was expected of her. Charles, on the other hand, seemed to be rebelling against doing what was expected of him. To be sure, he had studied at Cambridge, served in the navy, taken his place at public engagements. But in essential ways he remained an outsider to the critical tasks of monarchy, and had not adopted the prevailing values of his social class.

Nor did he seem to be at home with the times he lived in. He felt a nostalgic longing for the age of Victoria, for the era of "men of action," as he put it, and wished that he could have been born a century earlier so that he could lead a cavalry charge. At the same time, he looked forward with the fervor of a spiritual seeker to the future, when a purer ethic might prevail, one influenced by non-Western philosophies and devoted to peace and the sparing of all animal life.

To the practical, present-minded Lilibet, who with the rest of her family regularly shot, stalked and ate the animal life of Balmoral and Sandringham, not to mention roasted rodent in Belize and smoked reindeer in Finland, Charles's wistful utopianism seemed eccentric, especially when he grew a beard—the queen hated beards—and began talking of traveling to Asia to study Hindu philosophy at close range.

Charles's intellectual and spiritual preoccupations seemed to be driving him further from settling down and choosing a wife. His mother knew that he continued to see Camilla, despite her marriage, and that, frustrated in his yearning for her, Charles was showing signs of rebellion, shouting at the servants, throwing angry fits and stamping his feet, becoming furious on the slightest pretext. His vitriol was symptomatic of his gnawing sense of futility, of the purposelessness of his life. He was becoming capricious, neglecting his desk work as Prince of Wales, playing polo instead of attending scheduled events, spending more and more time at long weekend house parties where his indiscreet liaisons invited tabloid exploitation. Lilibet's staff, who kept her well informed, warned her that the prince's free-and-easy love life could lead to damaging publicity for the family. That he was jeopardizing his own and the family's good name, and risking the sort of notoriety that Princess Margaret had acquired, must have made the queen angry, though she did not intervene.

Compared with Anne and Charles, her two younger boys presented her with few challenges as a parent. Boisterous, energetic, talkative Andrew was enjoying his teen years, unhampered by angst or self-doubt, physically robust and aggressive like his sister. He was shaping up to be a man's man, capable of handling himself in a fight but not quarrelsome; on the contrary, Andrew was genial, got along well with others and, except for his arrogance, was likable and had many acquaintances if few close friends. At Gordonstoun he was no scholar, but performed adequately, while proving himself to be sturdy and independent. Observers thought he was the queen's favorite.

Edward, still a child in the mid-seventies, was a quiet and sweet boy, a sensitive, studious introvert but without Charles's over-sensitivity. Against the backdrop of his much more colorful siblings little Edward receded, distinctive only for his youth. He was Lilibet's lastborn, her "ewe-lamb," as she liked to say, referring to his gentleness and obedience. Some said Edward was his father's favorite.

The tea was drunk, the sandwiches and cookies and muffins consumed. What conversation there was turned on superficial topics—Lilibet's favorite mares Highclere and Escorial and Albany, with their newest foals, shooting prospects at Sandringham, the yearlings at Polhampton stud farm, of which Lilibet had become one-third owner in 1972. Politics was avoided, as were other subjects, closer to home, that were on the minds of all but the youngest in the family, chiefly Margaret's disintegrating marriage and her fragile health and the queen mother's extravagance and betting losses.

The queen drank her lukewarm Darjeeling, from a large cup (she disdained dainty teacups), and resigned herself to another uncommunicative family tea. Rather than resent or regret the absence of close connection, which she was after all habituated to avoiding, she may well have recalled with a smile another family tea, one with a great deal of jollity.

On this former unforgettable occasion, the queen was pouring out and a footman had just brought in a trolley with cakes and sandwiches. He pushed a button on the trolley, intending to raise a wooden extension on the side. But he pushed too hard— and suddenly the wooden flap rose too high, too fast, sending all the food flying through the air. A gooey cream cake landed on Lilibet's chest, leading to an explosion of loud laughter from everyone.[5] That story, and the renewed laughter it evoked, enlivened many a family tea for years afterward.

TWENTY

They had been waiting in the rain since the day before, standing, sitting and lying in the street on piles of soggy blankets, watching for the queen to come out of St. Paul's Cathedral to greet them. It was Jubilee Day, June 5, 1977, the official day designated to celebrate Queen Elizabeth II's twenty-five years on the throne.

Hundreds of thousands of people had turned out to see the queen, crowded into the narrow streets, lining the roadway ten deep, singing "God Save the Queen," "Rule Britannia" and "It's a Long Way to Tipperary" to pass the time. They drank tea poured from thermoses into Jubilee Mugs, waved special Union Jacks sold for the occasion, wore Jubilee hats and teeshirts. While they waited they joked and laughed, shook themselves like dogs in a futile effort to dry off, cheered whenever a trio of police came riding by or walking along on patrol.

Among those gathered near St. Paul's the mood was jubilant despite the rain, and the crowd kept getting larger and larger. They were waiting for the ceremony of thanksgiving to be over, and they could hear, from within the immense cathedral, the sounds of singing and of trumpets playing fanfares and descants. At last they heard a final singing of "God Save the Queen," and before long Lilibet herself was approaching, with Philip walking behind her and a phalanx of police and bodyguards as her escort.

She was on foot, a small, smiling woman in a dress of bright apricot, long white gloves and pearls, with a matching hat trimmed in little apricot bells. In her arms she carried a bouquet of white orchids. She was graying at the temples, and her once vivid deep blue eyes had taken on a softer hue. But her stride, as she approached her subjects, was vigorous, her stamina evident.

A roar went up from the crowd as she came closer, hundreds of hands were stretched out toward her, hundreds of miniature Union Jacks raised aloft and waved enthusiastically.

"Liz! Liz!" voices cried out. "Over here, Liz!"

Excitement surged through the crowd in the queen's presence, a primal response to the chill, numinous glory of majesty. For this was not just a smiling middle-aged lady in a bright dress, this was royalty, and royalty evoked awe; Elizabeth was an anointed queen, who carried within her the power of the transcendent.

She touched a hand here, an arm there, singling out individuals in the sea of radiant faces. A wave of sentiment followed her, there were no strident voices from among the densely packed spectators.

"We have come here because we love you!" came a shout from a young woman.

"I can feel it," was the royal response, though she kept her feelings well in check, a slight tremor in the muscles of her neck the only hint of emotional tension. "And it means so much to me," she was overheard to add.

On she walked, toward the Guildhall, along the cordon holding back the delighted onlookers. She continued to speak to a favored few, and beamed on all, her pleasure in their outpouring of affection unmistakable. Her feet hurt, the muscles in her cheeks burned from so much smiling, but she was content, and her reticent manner did not camouflage her satisfaction.

She was content—but very tired. During the first five months of the Jubilee Year, 1977, she had already undertaken more than three hundred engagements within Britain in addition to touring large areas of the Commonwealth. And hundreds more engagements, along with tens of thousands of miles of international travel, lay ahead.[1]

On her visit to Fiji in February, where a fierce tropical rainstorm soaked the entire royal party, she had had to contend with thousands of tiny frogs, spawned during the heavy rain, which leapt onto her dress and lodged themselves in her shoes, her handbag, even the scarlet poppies of her soggy hat. In Tonga she had dined in a hut made of banana and coconut leaves with the king, the enormously fat Taufa 'hau Tupou IV, served her own curly-tailed piglet cooked whole in an earthen pit. In Australia she listened to military bands and heard speeches and attended teas and civic events by the dozen—and was rewarded by being promised a thoroughbred foal.

Provincial events within the United Kingdom had tested her patience and fortitude. She had sat through amateur musicales, walked through acres of muddy grass to attend local sporting events, toured castles, presided at banquets, opened exhibits, listened to operas (she hated opera), watched bicycle races and met with groups of orphans, veterans and the disabled.

Everywhere she was met with hundreds of expectant faces, enthusiastic applause, appreciative comments. And no matter how tired she was, she managed to look gratified and interested, benevolently engrossed—without appearing patronizing. She had not laughed at gaffes or absurdities, though there were quite a few of these, nor had she allowed her boredom to show.

Jubilee Year was a revelation to Lilibet. Time and again she remarked to those around her how surprised she was to find herself the object of so much love, so much sincere appreciation. A hundred thousand letters had reached the palace, letters of congratulations and thanks to the queen personally. Twenty-five years of dedication, of self-denying, self-deprecating professionalism had won her far greater rewards than she had ever envisioned. She had been met by large crowds for years, of course, and they had been welcoming and enthusiastic. But in the past, she had assumed that the welcome and the enthusiasm were not for herself, but for what she represented: the monarchy, the realm. She had always seen herself, in her public role, as a symbol. Now, however, the adulation was unmistakably personal. An expression of affectionate gratitude for her years as queen. She had won her people's favor, she had been found worthy of their heartfelt acclaim. It was remarkable—and all the more remarkable coming as it did at a time when Britain's fortunes were at their nadir.

For Lilibet's twenty-five years had been, on the whole, years of economic downturn, and during the seventies, neither Conservative nor Labour governments had been able to arrest the sharp decline. The massive unemployment, violent labor disputes and severe inflation of the early and mid-seventies were worse than ever in Jubilee Year, their disastrous effect made more troubling by a series of IRA bombings in which many civilians died.

Terrorism was becoming part of everyday life, as was increasing poverty and a sense of economic doom. Upwards of two million Britons were out of work in the year of the queen's Jubilee, prolonged strikes were becoming dangerously politicized, prices were continuing to rise very rapidly and only a large infusion of cash from the International Monetary Fund kept the nation solvent. To add to the general air of crisis, for the previous two years the rain had stopped falling. Green England had quickly turned brown, formerly lush meadows and vernal fields were replaced by a dry desertscape, full of dead plants and dusty earth. Supplies of drinking water ran very low, the Thames fell and grew shallow in its upper reaches.

Change was needed, a respite from the vociferous demands of the powerful labor unions and the menace of the violent strikers. James Callaghan's Labour cabinet struggled to control the widespread industrial unrest and bring stability to the fragile economy, but in the winter of 1978–79 it seemed, to many Britons, as though no force, political or otherwise, could contain the rancorous disunity unleashed by the severe recession.

Workers stopped working, plants closed, state and city services came to a halt. With no one to collect the garbage, bags, boxes and bins of it piled up, forming stinking hillocks in the middle of dirty streets. Traffic came to a stop, schools and municipal buildings shut down. Not only was there a threat to public health, but hospitals all but ceased to run, as hospital staffs, medical workers, even ambulance drivers were all on strike.

The bleak early months of 1978 came to be known as "the winter of our discontent," a wry borrowing from Shakespeare's *Richard III*. The poet had envisioned a transformation to "glorious summer" following the winter of unrest, and Britain was soon to witness such a transformation. In May of 1979, the Callaghan government was defeated by the Conservatives led by the most forceful political personality since Churchill: Margaret Thatcher.

Forthright, intrepid, self-assured, Margaret Thatcher "radiated authority," in Peter

Clarke's just phrase, and as head of the Conservative Party she galvanized a new coalition of traditional Tories and the lower bourgeoisie. Thatcher set herself firmly in opposition to all things large—large labor unions whose demands paralyzed the country, large corporations that were losing money without gaining productivity, large government that was paying out billions in welfare but achieving no lasting improvement in people's lives. Her bold if ill-advised free-market policies—radically cutting government spending, intervening to control industry and reduce inflation by manipulating the money supply, lowering taxes on the richest individuals—offered hope and did, for a time, reverse the decline in Britain's economic output, albeit at great social cost. She harangued Parliament, labor bosses, industrialists, indeed anyone who opposed her, with a powerful populist rhetoric drawn from the age of Queen Victoria, a rhetoric that stressed the virtues of self-reliance and the evils of the welfare state, much of which, over time, she and her political allies dismantled.

In a television age, it was the image of Prime Minister Thatcher, professional, stalwart, resolute, strident, that worked itself deep into the consciousness of Britons. It contrasted sharply with the other principal image of female authority, that of the queen. Thatcher was sleek, modern, aggressive; Lilibet was unstylish, conservative, reserved. Thatcher was scrappy, Lilibet coolly above the fray. Thatcher was, or appeared to be, all that was current and contemporary, while Lilibet stood for the immemorial.

It was perhaps inevitable that two such significant women should be expected to lock horns, and that their ongoing relationship would be given exceptional media attention. In the early seventies, after all, the queen had been the most admired woman in Britain, according to formal polls, while by 1975 Thatcher had taken her place. Even during the queen's Jubilee celebrations onlookers had expected Thatcher, who was not yet in office, to upstage her. ("Where's Mrs. Thatcher?" voices in the crowd were overheard to call out. "She'll arrive in the Golden Coach instead of the queen, you'll see!"[2]) Thatcher, the fresher and more colorful personality, was stealing some of the queen's aura, and the latter, largely unperturbed, was too secure in her own position to perceive the challenge, much less try to meet it.

Or so it appeared to the public. Privately Lilibet found Thatcher to be baffling, and not a little disturbing.

At their weekly meetings, the long-winded prime minister, according to the queen, held forth without letup, and "never listened to a word she said." Listening to Margaret Thatcher lecture was an unwelcome contrast to Lilibet's enjoyable and congenial meetings with the previous prime minister, James Callaghan. On warm summer evenings Callaghan would make his weekly report to the queen while walking around the palace gardens with her, their mutual give and take a pleasure for both.[3] The humorless Thatcher lent herself to mimicry; it was said she brought out Lilibet's talent to imitate.[4] But Mrs. Thatcher's style, and political philosophy, were at the same time deeply puzzling to the queen. She was used to bluster, thirty years with Philip had made certain of that. Yet the brisk, dismissive manner Thatcher adopted ("Why does she always sit on the edge of her seat?" Lilibet wanted to know), at once deferential and patronizing, left the queen confused. At one level, she simply couldn't figure out who Margaret Thatcher was, and what her attitudes were meant to convey. When the prime minister sent her rubber gloves as a Christmas present, was that merely a gesture of practicality, or was there a hidden meaning in the gift, a subtle reprimand ("ordinary people, who are not royal, use these when they do the dishes, you should too")? Was the exaggerated respect Thatcher demonstrated ("nobody would curtsey lower," a friend said) merely a deeply ingrained byproduct of her pro-monarchist lower-middle-class origins, or could there have been a hint of mockery in it?

It was well known that, to Thatcher and her avid political followers, the monarchy was nothing more than the decadent, useless tip of a rotting iceberg of aristocratic privilege. An institution to be kept as marginal as possible, its influence to be ignored. As a self-made woman (who had married a multimillionaire; Denis Thatcher's money made his wife's political career possible), Thatcher tended to be contemptuous of the highborn queen, who had had every advantage of wealth and royal birth. But beyond this, she had a fundamental inbred prejudice against all privilege, and against the attitude of the privileged toward the disadvantaged.

To the prime minister, the monarchy was the ultimate font of paternalism, perpetuating the inequalities of the class system by making charitable gifts to the poor. In a more just society, one in which resources were more equitably shared, there would be no need for such lofty generosity; therefore it was harmful. To Lilibet, who had devoted her whole life to fulfilling the ideal of noblesse oblige, Thatcher's view was profoundly incomprehensible. Of course there were wealthy people, and of course they would try to help others. Lilibet was, and always had been, kindhearted and generous, particularly toward the needs of individuals. If she did not fully perceive the enormous and widening gap between the wealth of the monarchy and the deprivation of her subjects, it was not a willed blindness, a hardening of the heart.

The prime minister, on the other hand, seemed positively opposed to any sort of charitableness. "I'm against compassion! It's so patronizing!" Thatcher was overheard to say, and her words reached the queen, who found such sentiments not only profoundly uncongenial but hard to forgive.[5]

As the prime minister's term went on, the gap between the two women widened. Lilibet went on trying to fathom Thatcher ("Is she religious?" she asked those who knew her. "Do you think she will ever change?") Weekly meetings were correct, but perfunctory, with the sovereign, reportedly, slightly rigid and icy and the prime minister increasingly wordy and imperious. Lilibet, though politically neutral, could not sympathize with the Thatcherite agenda, which seemed to her heartless and overly extreme, while those around her were convinced that she found the prime minister herself very hard to take.[6]

As the troubled decade of the seventies came to a close, Lilibet drew satisfaction from the afterglow of her successful Jubilee, rejoiced in some racing successes—in the Jubilee Year, her filly Dunfermline won the Oaks and St. Leger—and took pride in having become a grandmother.

"We might well expect it to have four feet," said Lilibet of her first grandchild, when Anne shared the news that she was expecting. Peter Phillips came into the world November 15, 1977, and the queen went that evening to St. Mary's Hospital in Paddington to greet her grandson. A sizable crowd was waiting outside the hospital to cheer her, and the princess and the new baby. Earlier in the day there had been a forty-one-gun salute fired from the Tower of London.

It was a turning point, the arrival of a grandchild, a subtle shift in the balance of the generations. Another crop of Mountbatten-Windsors had begun to arise. And their grandmother, strong and energetic as she was, had to acknowledge her seniority. Not that she was very conscious of her age in years. Commenting on her mother's excellent eyesight and her own advancing presbyopia, Lilibet remarked "It's extraordinary, my mother doesn't need glasses at all, and here I am fifty-two, fifty-six, well whatever age I am, and can't see a thing."

In 1979 she was in fact fifty-three, one year younger than Mrs. Thatcher. Middle age had caught up with her, but hardly slowed her down, much less made her cautious, as a dramatic event in the spring of the previous year had shown.

A large group of spectators had come to watch the Royal Windsor Horse Show in May of 1978, enjoying the intervals of sun between showers, the parade of fine mounts, the displays of skilled riding and driving of horse-drawn vehicles. Lilibet was there, as she had been every spring since her girlhood, ready to award the prizes, dressed in a suit, hat and high heels. She was enjoying her afternoon, absorbed in watching and judging the skills of the riders and drivers, when suddenly something went terribly wrong.

One of the coaches, drawn by a team of overexcited strong young horses, over-turned. The horses, wild and out of control, began to gallop, dragging the disabled coach along behind them, with the passengers still inside.

The crowd hardly had time to react when, to the amazement of all, Lilibet walked out into the path of the onrushing horses, shouting at them to stop. Never flinching, planting her feet in their awkward high heels into the turf, she reached out and managed to seize the slack reins as the team reached her, coming close to riding her down. Meanwhile there were shrieks of terror from the onlookers, who were certain that the queen was about to be trampled. And in fact she came close to being injured, if not killed. The horses slowed, but did not stop, and had Philip not come running down onto the course and grabbed the reins along with his wife, helping her to restrain and calm the frenzied animals, the incident would have ended differently.

There were shouts of relief from the crowd, applause, turmoil as the reporters present hastened to record the queen's bravery and the rescue of the bedraggled passengers from the overturned coach. Lilibet took all in stride, retaining her customary aplomb, slightly out of breath but otherwise unperturbed. Having smoothed her skirt and cast a rueful eye over her muddy shoes, she prepared to take her place at the judging stand to award the afternoon's prizes.

TWENTY-ONE

The fishing boat *Shadow V* slipped out of the harbor of Mullaghmore on the west coast of Ireland late on the morning of August 27, 1979, past the wharf and out into the sparkling blue waters of Donegal Bay. There was little wind, the ocean was calm and the fishermen were out checking their lobster pots. The skipper of the *Shadow V*, Lord Louis Mountbatten, stood at the helm with his teenage grandsons Nicholas and Timothy near at hand. On board were his daughter Patricia and her husband, John Brabourne, and John's mother Lady Brabourne, who like Lord Louis was in her seventies.

The *Shadow V* cleared the jetty and turned north, hugging the coast. Mullaghmore was only twelve miles from the border with Northern Ireland, where the extremist Provisional wing of the Irish Republican Army was known to be active, but Mountbatten had never been concerned about his or his family's safety. He was well known to all the local families around Mullaghmore, having vacationed at nearby Classiebawn castle for decades. He felt admired and accepted. And there were security guards on watch at the castle twenty-four hours a day.

The quiet lapping of the water against the shingle, the crying of curlews, the slap of the small waves against the side of the fishing boat and the hum of the engine were the only sounds in the peaceful bay. Then, all of a sudden, came a powerful explosion. The *Shadow V* blew up, the seven people aboard were all thrown violently into the water, where they floated, bleeding and dying, amid shards and splinters of wood.

So startling was the terrifyingly loud blast that the villagers of Mullaghmore did not at first understand what had happened, or react. Fishermen who had seen the boat burst into pieces hurried to lift the broken bodies out of the water, and once they got them ashore, two doctors did what they could in a hastily assembled emergency room by the quayside. Lord Louis, his legs all but blown off by the explosive, could not be saved, and his grandson Nicholas and the hired Irish boat boy Paul Maxwell from County Fermanagh also died. The dowager Lady Brabourne survived only a few hours. The others, Patricia, John and son Timothy, were badly and permanently injured.

Having threatened the royal family for years, the IRA had finally made good its threat. "The IRA claim responsibility for the execution of Lord Louis Mountbatten," said an official announcement from the Provisional IRA in Belfast. "This operation is one of the discriminate ways we can bring to the attention of the English people the continuing occupation of our country."[1]

To Lilibet, losing the avuncular "Dickie," who had been an ebullient, dominant, life-enhancing member of the extended royal family for as long as she could remember, was a profoundly upsetting threat.[2] She needed no reminding of the peril in which she herself and the family stood; IRA bombs had killed two thousand people over the previous decade, the majority of them civilians, and injured tens of thousands more.

The dilemma of the English in Ireland was an old and unhappy one. The Irish Republic had become a sovereign state but Northern Ireland remained a part of the United Kingdom, its Protestant majority wanting to remain under the rule and protection of Westminster while its Catholic minority, severely underemployed, poor, and determined to attain union with the Irish Republic, engaged in a determined campaign of deadly violence. No one was completely safe, and when Lilibet flew over Northern Ireland in a helicopter in 1977, it was not only airsickness that made her pale.

Now that violence had come closer than ever before, carrying off Lord Louis and maiming Lilibet's childhood friend Patricia Mountbatten, once her companion in the Girl Guides, and leaving Patricia grief stricken over the loss of her father, her son and her mother-in-law. The queen attended the Mountbatten funeral, and consoled Patricia who was present in her wheelchair. As sovereign she extended her mourning to include the dozens of others who had died within hours of her relatives, also victims of IRA bombs: eighteen British soldiers killed in a blast beside Carlingford Lough in Ulster, and four more injured in Brussels.

The stalwart Margaret Thatcher flew to Belfast, risking attack herself, in a display of courage, a gauntlet thrown down to the rebels. But Lilibet withdrew, returning to the remote tranquillity of Balmoral, and to autumnal pursuits of hunting and stalking, seeking solace in the familiar rhythms of the season.

"If someone really wants to get me," she remarked to friends and staff in the aftermath of the Mountbatten assassination, "it is too easy."[3] And she was indeed an easy target, going on "walkabouts" and chatting with people in the crowd, driving out in her private car to visit friends in London suburbs, riding unescorted in Windsor Great Park, sitting in the stands at the racetrack. On foreign tours IRA supporters got close enough to squirt her with ketchup, but might just as easily have fired pistols or thrown bombs.

On her tour of Morocco in the summer of 1980, the usually tight royal schedule had to be abandoned more than once because of security concerns; King Hassan was worried, having presided at a banquet at which a hundred guests had died in a bomb attack. He wanted to avoid risk at all costs, and allowed extra time for taking precautions. Even so, security in Morocco was disturbingly lax. And even in peaceable, efficient Switzerland, where formalities were held to a minimum ("They don't even wear dinner jackets there," was the queen's disconcerted aside to a friend), Lilibet had to ride in a train through the manicured countryside, discouraged from taking long walks in the open air by gatherings of shouting demonstrators sympathetic to the IRA. Police used tear gas to disperse them.

Everywhere she went, it seemed, the queen was reminded of the increasing polarization of society, and the hostility it produced. It became harder for her to stay aloof from controversy, to transcend political and social quarrels. Her very image, the ladylike conservative clothes, old-fashioned (as they now seemed) hats, gloves and pearls, the eternal short curly hairstyle that never varied: this image seemed an affront to feminists seeking a radically deglamorized unisex look and adopting an acidulous, aggressive tone in demanding their rights.

In the midst of all the violence and stridor, with the economy growing ever more crisis-ridden and the government's policies creating a backlash of bitterness, one issue at least was on its way to being resolved: the Prince of Wales had made up his mind, at long last, to marry.

The decision had been long in arriving. In 1980 Charles turned thirty-two, but seemed even older, in some respects curmudgeonly and middle-aged. He was absorbed in a major task, the restoration and redecoration of Highgrove House, his 350-acre estate in Gloucestershire, and this undertaking seemed to provide an anchor for his previously unsettled life. His emotional anchor was Camilla Parker-Bowles, his married mistress, and when he lost his surrogate father and mentor Mountbatten he wanted Camilla to divorce her husband and come to live at Highgrove with him.

Such an arrangement would have satisfied Charles, but it would have meant that the throne would pass, in time, to Andrew and his heirs, for the church would not permit or recognize any marriage Charles might make to a divorced woman. Lilibet found her son's continuing evasion of his clear duty intolerable; she did not mind his relationship with Camilla, but she did mind his failure to marry and start a family.[4] His continuing liaisons with other women, especially the difficult but alluring Anna Wallace, displeased Lilibet, who may have feared, as Mountbatten did, that Charles would settle for becoming a polo-playing playboy, a melancholy wastrel like Edward VIII.

In January of 1981 Lilibet let her son know that "the idea of this going on for another year is intolerable." He must marry, and soon. Finally giving in to the pressure, Charles made up his mind.[5] He proposed to the young woman his grandmother favored, the nineteen-year-old Diana Spencer, and she eagerly accepted him. The engagement was announced in February.

Whether or not the queen knew, or came to suspect, that the coy, coltish Diana was a less than ideal mate for her son, she was nonetheless relieved and pleased that he had made his choice. She cannot have entirely overlooked his lack of enthusiasm about the engagement, and the odd, enigmatic response he gave when asked by reporters if he and Diana were in love ("whatever 'in love' means"). It cannot have escaped her vigilant notice that Diana, relatively unworldly though strong-willed, was emotionally brittle, with quicksilver moods, adolescent quirks and a habit of jumping into Charles's lap at inappropriate moments.

How much Lilibet actually knew about the young woman who was about to become her daughter-in-law can only be guessed. But she was well informed about most things, relying on Bobo, and on her staff, to pass on vital information. Sifting gossip and rumor, and even after dismissing what seemed implausible, the queen must have heard enough about Diana to bring on misgivings. That before becoming involved with Charles she had had at least one lover, and probably others, that she had a tendency to exaggerate the truth, and invent things, that she was bossy and demanding (this the family witnessed during the engagement period), and that she seemed compelled to draw attention to herself. That she was of only average intelligence and had been inadequately educated was of less concern than that she seemed to be wilting under the relentless hounding and scrutiny of the press, who delighted in her attractive shyness and with whom she developed a strong ongoing rapport.

"She's going to have to learn to get used to this sort of thing," was the queen's comment about Diana's sensitivity to being besieged by reporters. Diana must toughen herself up, learn to be brave and rise above all the harassing press attention: such was Lilibet's tonic advice. But she failed to perceive the complexities of Diana's nature, just as she had failed to acknowledge the complexities of Charles's nature. Both Diana and Charles lacked self-confidence, both had a tendency to sink into low spirits. And in Diana, there was a deeper pathology at work, one that led her into bulimia, severe anxiety and self-destructive behavior.

In the months following the official announcement of Charles's engagement to Diana, as the elaborate planning went forward for the gala wedding, both the future bride and groom became more and more unhappy and uncertain that they were doing the right thing. Charles, observing Diana's moodiness and erratic demands, her dislike of his friends and the lack of any developing rapport with his family, became disenchanted, and unnerved by Diana's tantrums. Diana, having become aware of the strength of Charles's emotional entanglement with Camilla, became more insecure than ever. She tried to persuade Charles to sell Highgrove, which was less than twenty miles from the country estate of Camilla and Andrew Parker-Bowles. When thwarted in this attempt, she sulked, threatened, ranted.[6] Bravely, Charles talked to Philip about his doubts and was told simply that he had to decide, one way or the other.

The entire situation was artificial, the emotions of all involved distorted by the overheated public and press excitement over the forthcoming wedding. The ceremony, which was scheduled for late July, had taken on a life of its own as the great social event of the summer. Television contracts had been signed, guest lists drawn up, parties planned, caterers and dressmakers engaged. Thousands of people were affected, directly and indirectly, by the royal wedding, hundreds of thousands of pounds invested in it. Publicists, journalists, royalty-watchers around the globe were jubilantly focused on what they chose to see as a "fairytale wedding," the outcome of a storybook romance.

Diana's imminent entry into the royal family was the most thrilling, rejuvenating event in the monarchy's recent history, causing an immense boost in popularity—and creating an important, if shallow, distraction from the social disintegration that was making headlines nearly every day in the spring of 1981.

With all that the wedding seemed to offer the kingdom and the monarchy itself, and given the continual family pressure to take a bride, even a flawed one, Charles decided he could not back out of his promise to Diana. If he did not marry her, he would be caught in the same dilemma as before, facing an urgent need to find someone else to marry, and there was no other candidate in view to take Diana's place. Diana, for her part, confided her doubts to those close to her but lacked the certainty to give up her dream of marrying the prince, return his costly diamond and sapphire engagement ring and spring free from the tightening bonds and restrictions of membership in the royal circle—restraints she felt keenly, and instinctually sought to escape.

Lilibet chose this tense time to hold a reunion for the women she had gotten to know in the final weeks of World War II, when she had trained as a driver and mechanic. Of the eleven others who had taken the course with her, all were still living, now in their sixties. One or two of them she had seen, by chance, or had had news of over the intervening years. It was a nostalgic meeting, an opportunity to forget the fraught present and compare memories of the happier past.[7] The women laughed over pictures of themselves, remembered the nineteen-year-old Lilibet, "delightful and so pretty," recalled "Parents' Day" at the instruction center when the king and queen had come to inspect their daughter's progress.

Did Lilibet, in the company of her old acquaintances, think of the contrast between her life at nineteen and Diana's? Of how she had been in love with Philip, and wanted to marry him, of the terrible sorrows, fears and sacrifices she and her family had borne because of the war, of her own relative naïveté and her overriding concern with duty and responsibility? Diana, at nineteen, raised amid far greater comfort if lower rank, appeared to be ambivalent about her engage-

ment, unsure about Charles, not at all acquainted with sacrifice (though she did
know sorrow, having been all but abandoned by her mother at the age of six and
having known the dread of coming close to
losing her father to grave illness), fairly
worldly, and unproven as to her capacity for
entering into the duties required of a Princess of Wales. If Lilibet thought about the
contrast between her life and Diana's, her
reflections are undiscoverable. But she did
not warm to her daughter-in-law-to-be, and
even the queen mother, who had encouraged Charles to take Diana seriously as a
possible wife, began to wonder whether
she might have made a mistake.[8]

If the spring of 1981 was a season of expectation, with the upcoming royal wedding
the central focus of attention, it was also a
time of escalating violence. The Provisional
IRA issued new threats against the royal
family—who were still mourning the loss of
Mountbatten and his grandson and the injuries to other family members—and assassination attempts were in the news, with the
shootings of President Reagan and Pope
John Paul II. A letter bomb was sent to
Charles, but experts managed to defuse it

before any harm was done. The queen, visiting the British Petroleum oil terminal at Sullom Voe in the remote Shetland Islands, felt a shock and a jolt under her feet. The ground shook as a tremendous explosion struck the facility, damaging buildings and equipment and disrupting the flow of oil. It was an IRA bomb.[9]

Barely a month later the queen was riding her black mare Burmese along the Mall in the Trooping the Colour parade. It was an act of courage, she had not wanted to yield to intimidation by riding in a protected vehicle, nor did she want her family to change their routines to avoid danger. Just ahead of her, Andrew rode in an open carriage with Diana, while Philip and Charles, mounted, rode just behind. The queen was riding side-saddle, as she always did, in the birthday parade, which gave her somewhat less control over Burmese and a less secure seat. She had just turned Burmese into the narrow lane leading to Horse Guards Parade when she saw, in the midst of the crowd, a handgun being raised and pointed straight at her.

She was in the direct line of fire, none of the guardsmen escorting her were near enough to shield her. The gunman was very near, perhaps ten feet away. He held the black revolver in both hands, taking careful aim.

The brief second during which she grasped what was happening must have seemed an hour. There was the assassin, ready to fire, and no one to stop him. Then she heard the shots. There were two distinct shots, then four more in a rapid cluster. Burmese began to toss her head and rear as people in the crowd screamed, their shouting drowning out the music of the military band.

The queen did not duck or flinch. While trying to calm her horse, and avoid falling off, she worried about Charles and Philip; she had not been hit, but had they? And were there more shots to come?

Two cavalrymen were riding toward her.

She shouted at them, abruptly and profanely, still struggling with the shying prancing Burmese.

"Are you all right, ma'am?"

"I was until you came—you're upsetting my horse!"[10]

The only sign of the queen's distress was her extreme pallor, stark against the red guardsman's jacket she wore. No more shots were fired. The man with the gun was seized and led away, to shouts of "Hang the bastard! Kill him!" Charles and Philip came up on either side, helping to calm Lilibet's horse. The commotion began to subside. People who had ducked or run away returned to their places behind the wooden barriers.

Lilibet smiled and nodded to the guard in the column ahead, indicating that she wanted the parade to go on, aware that there might be other shooters in the crowd. There were no further disruptions, the parade came to an orderly end.[11]

Once again, as when she stopped the runaway horses at the Windsor Horse Show, Lilibet had shown much bravery. But it would take more than physical courage to deflect a determined assassin. (As it proved, the seventeen-year-old opponent of monarchy who fired at the queen in June of 1981 was not a terrorist, and he fired blanks.) It could only be hoped that security at Charles and Diana's wedding would be adequate to protect the entire family, their guests and entourages.

Seven hundred and fifty million people all

over the world watched Charles marry Diana on July 29, 1981, and another quarter of a billion listened to the ceremony on the radio. No royal event had ever been carried out on such a lavish scale, with such far-reaching impact—or with such heavy security.

The queen rode in an open carriage to St. Paul's Cathedral, looking relaxed and unconcerned about her safety. Inwardly, as she confided later, she felt tense, thinking "Please don't let anything go wrong today."[12] Nerves were still on edge from the alarming incident at the Trooping the Colour parade; the queen mother, now eighty-one, had been so upset by the attack that her health was affected and Lilibet was concerned about her. Not until evening, at a post-wedding party at Claridge's Hotel, was the queen able to put aside her worries and enjoy herself. She laughed when she saw a video of the day's events ("Oh, Philip, do look, I've got my Miss Piggy face on") and danced happily, to the music of a New York band, until one-thirty in the morning. "I'd like to stay and dance all night," she said as she left.[13]

It was a long, grim summer with ugly riots

in Brixton and Liverpool and Manchester and looting and arson in a dozen other cities—everywhere the depressed economy led to desperation and the policies of the Thatcher government provoked hostility. In the fall, Lilibet embarked on an extensive tour of Australia and New Zealand, only to find that conflict followed her. The IRA threatened to attack the royal party in Melbourne, and there were loud and angry demonstrators waiting to harass the queen every time she disembarked from the yacht *Britannia* or was driven to a school or town hall or park to meet the public. The strain of the past few months was evident in her face. "She is tired, not well," the *Australian Woman's Weekly* announced. An abdication was a possibility, so Australian journalists thought.

"Are they trying to put me in my grave now?" was Lilibet's sarcastic response to the speculation in the press. Her staff knew how strong she was—she led them, nimbly, on seven-mile hikes for recreation—and were in awe of her stamina through the arduous days of official appearances.[14] But she came down with a cold, and her strong gait slowed slightly, and by the time she left for New Zealand she was ready to put lively, brash, raucous Australia behind her and rest in the relative peace of Christchurch.

Even here, however, the mood of unrest stalked her, the crowds sparse, the receptions lackluster, and the everpresent demonstrators inescapable.

In Dunedin, outside a museum, she was verbally assaulted by a host of placard-wielding, shouting picketers and had to walk along a narrow path between two walls of angry faces and noisy epithets. Feverish and muzzy-headed, dosed with homeopathic cold remedies, Lilibet was not her usual steady self and the angry Maoris, Black Panthers and homeless demonstrators unnerved her. Popular resentment was at such a pitch that it unnerved her security guards as well, and the local police.

The royal party was scheduled to fly on to Wellington that night and embark on a further round of official appearances. But something—an alert, some suspicious activity, a tip given to the Wellington constabulary—led to a change in the schedule. The queen and her entourage flew to Wellington, but did not keep to the original itinerary once there. Lilibet got into the black Rolls-

Royce that was waiting to drive her from the airport into the city—and waited for the chauffeur to start the engine.

It was nearly an hour before the limousine left, a precious hour as it turned out. Had there been no delay, the black Rolls would have crossed the Petone bridge at about a quarter after ten—just at the time a bomb went off under the bridge amid showers of stone shards and hunks of twisted metal.

TWENTY-TWO

It was a season of contention. Everywhere the queen looked, it seemed, there was strife. In the inner cities, young people by the thousands, out of work and angry at the government, looted shops and torched buildings; decay and squalor spread as rapidly as the unemployment numbers, which reached an all-time high of three million.[1] Crimes, especially violent crimes, were increasing faster than the statisticians could count them. The unraveling of conventional moral norms was more difficult to chart, but everyone was aware that it was happening, a breakdown in the ordering of life, along with an upsurge in racial hostility.

Mass demonstrations against the severe cuts in social spending by the Thatcher government brought more tens of thousands of the discontented out into the dirty, littered streets, with their aging shopfronts and cracked pavements. The crowds were protesting the lowering of public assistance and the cutbacks in government jobs, the empty rhetoric (as they saw it) of the prime minister who sermonized about a return to values of thrift and self-help while pushing the country deeper into poverty, increasing the numbers of homeless beggars and the high rates of mortality from malnutrition, disease, even suicide. The "Thatcherite" became a hated icon of the early 1980s, an expensively suited bureaucrat, young and pitiless, out to make his own fortune at the expense of the poor and working classes. The prime minister's brisk, no-nonsense manner and thrusting, self-aggrandizing style seemed to infect all her subordinates, while her policy of reducing the tax bills of the rich increased class resentments and further widened the yawning abyss dividing haves from have-nots.

Closer to home, Lilibet could not but be aware of the abyss that was opening between Charles and Diana. They had fought violently, with smashed furniture, cracked mirrors, slashed bedcoverings, within a month of the wedding, and there were said to be many issues dividing them, from Charles's disapproval of his wife's extravagant spending to Diana's objections to Charles's beloved but incontinent old dog Harvey to Charles's liking for Diana's hated stepmother Raine.[2] Quarrels blossomed constantly between them; they did not entertain, so bitter was the atmosphere and so strong the rancorous feelings. The Waleses' household staff began leaving, there was gossip, the couple's friends talked and rumors of a rift spread. Nor were the rumors squelched when, in November of 1981, four months after the wedding, Diana's pregnancy was announced.

Diana was carrying Charles's child, the child who would one day rule the realm. She was the mother-to-be of a future king or queen, and would one day be queen herself. Yet she was desperately unhappy.

She knew, for Charles had told her right before the wedding, that he did not love her. And she had ample evidence that he was still in love with his longtime companion and

mistress Camilla Parker-Bowles. Shortly after the honeymoon, Charles and Diana were
at Highgrove, about to have lunch, when the
local hunt came trotting through the Highgrove garden. Charles, knowing that Camilla
was in the hunting party, got up from the
table and went in search of her. While Diana
waited, hurt and angry, he talked on and on
to Camilla, providing yet more evidence of
his attachment to her—and of his utter lack
of consideration for his wife.[3] It was one of
many reminders of their sad mismatch, and
of the hopelessness of their situation, yoked
in a loveless union. As Charles was to put it,
they knew that their marriage was a "bloody
awful mistake."

The queen was only too aware that it had
been a mistake, but given her view of how
people ought to behave, she was slow to
recognize just how severe the consequences of the mistake were likely to become.

Early in 1982 the increasingly unstable,
pregnant Diana, in a fit of despair, threw
herself down a staircase at Sandringham.[4]
Instead of responding to this act of desperation with empathy and a firm insistence
that Diana receive expert psychiatric help,

Lilibet seems to have thrown up her hands and done nothing. Another family might have embarked on family therapy when one of its members showed such overt evidence of acute anguish. But facing and confronting family problems had never been the Windsors' style; such issues were too murky, too complex, too fraught with dense and unpleasant emotions.

"That girl is quite mad!" Lilibet is said to have exclaimed about Diana. "She simply did not want anything to do with that impossible girl," was the view of the queen's longtime friend and sometime private secretary Martin Charteris.[5] And possibly her attitude was sensible; Diana's problems were very serious, and the environment in which she found herself, an environment in which spontaneity and personal expression were expected to be subordinated to form and protocol, was making them more so. It is possible that no amount of therapy would have helped, and that opening doors into the darkness of unspoken family conflict might have led to damaging estrangements, though ultimately it might also have led to healing.

"She's mad, she's mad," Lilibet muttered

when again and again Diana ignored the long established customs of the royals and simply did what she liked. She did not fit in comfortably at the ritual of afternoon tea, with Lilibet presiding and measuring out the spoonfuls of Darjeeling; the careful silences and surface chat made her uncomfortable. She often did not come to meals at all, or if she did, she wore earphones and listened to pop music while the others dined and made efforts to converse. She did not join the ladies after dinner, she made no effort to talk to anyone (disliking their usual subjects, horses and sport, and lacking the ability to make small talk), she cared nothing for such minor but vital acknowledgments of her mother-in-law's status as never retiring to bed before the queen did or never arriving anywhere later than the queen did.

While actually saying little, Lilibet conveyed that she had doubts about Diana, and "seemed very cool" about her son's marriage.[6] According to "one of those who saw a great deal of Lilibet at Balmoral and Sandringham," the queen "very early on, had misgivings about the marriage. She did not express it directly, she just seemed very cool about it."

Month by month her misgivings increased, as Diana showed further symptoms, not only of not fitting in with the royal
family, but of breaking out of the royal mold
in unpredictable and potentially damaging
ways. Instead of staying above stairs in
Buckingham Palace, she descended into
the kitchens, and sat, in jeans and sweat-
shirt, chatting with the servants—whom she
called by nicknames.[7] On board the yacht
Britannia she declined to keep to the upper
deck as the queen did but fraternized with
the sailors, going to crew parties where she
played the piano until steered back to the
royal quarters by shocked officers. To Diana, Balmoral seemed stiflingly ceremoni-
ous, embalmed in antique etiquette, a ludicrous monument to bad taste with its stags'
heads and ugly tartans and clutter of bric-a-
brac. Having to stay there during the endless weeks of the annual family vacation
bored her past endurance until she felt she
had to break away to London for an orgy of
shopping.

Self-discipline, the Windsor trait par ex-
cellence, was lacking in the princess, who
could not contain her physical restlessness
or her often inappropriate reactions. At for-

mal public occasions, when she was on display and expected to maintain reasonable decorum, she occasionally burst into hysterical laughter and was unable to stop. At sporting events she could not hide her sense of tedium behind a placid facade. And in her many unguarded moments, she looked wary, hunted, and very unhappy. A secret fear haunted her, the fear that, at any moment, she or Charles might cross paths with Camilla—who was part of the small, tightly knit aristocratic circle of hunters and riders, all of whom knew one another and were part of one another's social lives—triggering another episode of jealousy and ill feeling.

Overshadowing Diana's behavior and Lilibet's disappointment in her was the inescapable fact that the Princess of Wales had become an international press phenomenon. How Diana looked, what she wore, where she went and how she spent her time became the object of intense international interest. She was on the cover of countless magazines, the subject of daily press stories. Legions of fans copied her style and were eager to learn her secrets. They adopted her preferences in everything from fashion to fitness to food to maternity clothes. Her hairstyle was to be seen on thousands of heads, and her engaging, smiling, polished public image became synonymous with all that was vital, youthful and current.

Having been upstaged once by her prime minister, Lilibet was now upstaged a second time, and with far greater impact, by her daughter-in-law, whom she knew to be troubled and likely, sooner or later, to cause havoc within the family. With her customary superb poise, the queen bestrode the disturbing situation, month by distressing month, trying in vain to convince the hungry media to give Diana some peace during her pregnancy. When this effort failed, she simply turned a cool but watchful eye on events.

While Diana waited out her pregnancy, actively roaming the palace corridors with her headphones on, the international situation overtook domestic concerns and by April, 1982, the United Kingdom was at war.

The tiny outpost of British sovereignty known as the Falkland Islands—called the Malvinas by the Argentinians—had long been administered as a crown colony, but the Argentine government had traditionally disputed the British claim. On April 2 Argentinian forces captured the islands, and the Thatcher government, after considerable internal debate, responded energetically.

A large naval task force left Portsmouth, bound for South America, with Britain's two aircraft carriers, the *Hermes* and the *Invincible*, and dozens of vessels carrying some ten thousand troops. In a display of naval power reminiscent of the great days of the British empire, the armada made its way south, while the prime minister gave voice to the nation's pride and confidence. ("Failure? The possibility does not exist," Thatcher said, echoing Queen Victoria in an earlier conflict.) The prime minister's splendid rhetoric was matched by an upsurge in national patriotism; Britain might be crippled by a dismal economy, and in the throes of social conflict, but at least she could still flex the muscles of a great power, in a small war for a few small islands.

Small war it might be, but the danger, for those involved, was great. And one of those involved was Prince Andrew.

Good-looking, jovial, warm, talkative Andrew, handsome in his officer's uniform, was a twenty-two-year-old sub-lieutenant in 829 Naval Air Squadron aboard the *Invincible*, flying Sea King helicopters, when the war began. There was no question that he would serve; it was his duty.[8] But his mother worried about him.

"Do you think he'll be warm enough?" she asked two days after Andrew's deployment. "Do you think we should send him some extra clothing?" She was in her private study at Windsor Castle, talking to the ousted British governor of the Falklands, Rex Hunt, and his wife. There was no one else in the room, no secretary or staff. "She was just like any other mother," Hunt recalled later, "worried about the role that her son was going to play."

The queen had never been to the Falkland Islands herself ("It's the only territory of mine that I haven't visited"), the Foreign Office advised strongly against it, knowing the Argentinians would see a royal visit as a provocative gesture.[9] But she imagined that it would be freezing cold in the South Atlantic in April, autumn in that southern latitude. Andrew would be sailing through the Roaring Forties, some of the roughest, coldest, stormiest seas on the globe. And the fleet was very vulnerable; not only was there only limited air protection for the vessels—only as many planes as the two aircraft carriers could accommodate—but the Argentinians had a devastatingly effective weapon, the sea-skimming Exocet missile, which could be launched from either planes or boats and which could easily sink a large ship.

Andrew's role was to fly his Sea King out from the carrier as a decoy, to attract Exocets. He was to serve as human chaff, to confuse the missiles and prevent them from destroying the ships. While he and his fellow pilots flew out into danger, battle was joined and, over a period of some six weeks in May and June, several dozen British ships were damaged, the *Sheffield*, *Ardent*, *Antelope*, *Coventry*, *Galahad* and *Fearless*, and the *Atlantic Conqueror*, a container vessel, all sunk by missiles or aerial bombs. Were it not for the fact that so many of the Argentinian bombs failed to explode, many more British vessels would have been sunk. The Argentinian cruiser *Belgrano* (formerly the USS *Ranger*, a veteran of World War II) was sunk by the British, with the loss of three hundred Argentinian sailors.

Daily, sometimes hourly, reports reached the palace and Lilibet read them all, grieving over the casualties and scanning the news for word of the *Invincible* and Andrew. She had sent a message to her Falklands subjects early in May, assuring them that they did indeed belong to the British crown and would be defended. However, as everyone knew, the success of the British venture rested on the preservation of the two aircraft carriers—and on the covert U.S. support President Reagan had agreed to lend his friend and fellow conservative, Margaret Thatcher. Had one or both of the British carriers been crippled or sunk, the Americans would have had to rescue British interests by overt action against Argentina—an unwanted diplomatic complication.

Then, on June 14, after more engagements and with several more British vessels lost, the capital of the Falklands, Port Stanley, was secured by British troops and the war was swiftly brought to an end.

That evening, Andrew called home.

"My mother was in," he told reporters. "She was surprised to hear from me. She asked [me] to pass on how proud she was of everyone and to say how marvelously all the troops had done."[10]

Britain was jubilant. The British public, weary of economic depression and social unrest, had had a cleansing catharsis: in a few short weeks they had gone from indignation to anxiety to pride and a sense of victory. They loved it all: the old-fashioned John Bull belligerence, the prime minister's granite confidence, Prince Andrew's heroics. And the queen's visiting the wounded, which she did as soon as they were shipped home from the South Atlantic. The spirit of the Old Britain lived on, it seemed, beneath the veneer of confused modernity, a bedrock of tradition. And at the core of that tradition was the monarchy.

To set the seal on the nation's mood of triumph, word came from St. Mary's National Health Hospital in Paddington that the Princess of Wales had given birth to a son, Prince William Arthur Philip Louis, on June 21, 1982. The seven-pound, one-and-one-half-ounce baby boy, with his thin quiff of fair hair and blue eyes, became the second in line for the throne, the guarantor of the continuity of the royal line of Queen Victoria and Edward VII, of George V and

George VI and Elizabeth II. The line that would, barring accidents of fortune, stretch forward into the future, through the reigns of Charles III and William V and to untold monarchs to come.

The queen went to the hospital to greet her grandson and congratulate his parents. But she did not linger. More wounded were being brought back from the Falklands, and she went to see them, asking each one how he was feeling, where in Britain he came from, how soon he expected to return home. She was solicitous, kind, well meaning. For a few brief weeks, she seemed to stand on equal footing, in the press, with the mother of the new prince and the Iron Lady who had led the realm in time of war.

TWENTY-THREE

The intruder climbed over the iron fence onto the grounds of Buckingham Palace a little before seven in the morning, dressed in jeans and an old teeshirt that read LONSDALE. He was disheveled, unshaven, slightly drunk from the bottle of whiskey he had shared with a neighbor four hours earlier, and he had been up all night. He looked terrible.

He wasn't the first to scale the garden wall of the palace; in the previous year three German tourists had been discovered on the palace grounds and escorted out, and there had been several other such incidents. But this intruder, Michael Fagan, was to become infamous.

He was on a mission. He wanted to talk to the queen. He wanted to tell her just how miserable his life was, out of work, low on money, facing a pile of debts. He felt certain his wife was sleeping with other men. His four children and stepchildren were going without and feeling the family tensions, even his parents were suffering.

The queen would be his salvation. He knew she would sympathize with his troubles, and help him end them. He had only recently been released from Brixton Prison, from the psychiatric ward. The judge had sent him there after he slashed his wrists with a broken bottle during his court hearing on charges that he had stabbed his teenage stepson in the neck with a screwdriver.

He knew there were bound to be guards at the palace, and that they might try to stop him from seeing the queen. But his voices were leading him on, the voices that told him not to be afraid, but to dare. The same voices that had told him to do brave things in the past, to climb the girders and towers of the bridges spanning the Thames and to challenge himself by stripping off his clothes and diving into the Grand Union Canal.[1]

His voices led him on, and his visions. He was weary, not having slept, and he felt disoriented, out of balance, clouded in mind. Yet his purpose was unwavering. He walked through the dark streets, staggering slightly from drink and fatigue, until he approached the looming square stone edifice of the palace, with its gabled classical pediments and its black wrought-iron railings separating the imposing royal precincts from the encircling street. Without hesitation he climbed the fence and dropped down into the grounds, almost entirely unnoticed and without arousing any of the guards.

Had the intruder carefully researched palace security, and planned the timing of his entry, he could hardly have chosen a better hour to break in. The cleaning staff was just arriving, and to accommodate them the inner doors had just been unlocked. The police officer who sat on watch in the corridor outside the queen's bedroom all night had just gone home. And the corgis, those hypervigilant, everpresent guardians of the royal person, had been taken out for a walk in the gardens by a footman.

Fagan located an open window and let himself in.

He found himself in an unoccupied room, filled with display cases and cabinets. The priceless stamp collection that had once belonged to George V was kept there, but that was of no interest to the intruder, who was eager to get to the queen's suite. He went back into the courtyard, noticed a drainpipe leading upward and gazed at it in a reverie. Seeing the drainpipe reminded him of the previous time he had broken into the palace, about a month earlier. Then he had climbed a drainpipe in fear, shinnying up it very rapidly and feeling an immense exhilaration.

"The drainpipe was at least fifty-five feet," he was to tell interviewers later, "and I climbed it in seconds. I felt I could do anything, touch the sky, anything. I was a Prince of the Earth."

On that earlier occasion, on the evening of June 7, 1982, Fagan had alarmed a chambermaid by entering her room and then making his escape. The maid had screamed and run out of the room to get help, but even though she told the officer on duty what she had seen, the security staff had not managed to find Fagan, who lost himself in the maze of long chilly corridors and remained at large for quite a long time. ("I idled my time walking up and down the passageway," Fagan later said. "I was at my leisure, looking at the paintings and wandering about the corridors."[2])

On that earlier visit, Fagan had made the palace his own, going where he liked, staying as long as he liked, finding a bottle of California Riesling and making off with it before letting himself out through a window and going home to Highbury.

Emboldened by his earlier success, and having been obsessed with the thought of returning to the palace for the past month, the intruder now found himself once again at the bottom of a wall, staring up at a long drainpipe. He climbed it, and found himself this time in the office of the master of the queen's household. He had taken off his sandals and socks, and his hands were black with tar from the drainpipe. He looked even more like the unstable derelict he was. Had the master been at his desk, he would have lost no time in seizing Fagan and having him ejected immediately.

But the master was not yet at his labors. His office was empty. Fagan was free to roam through it at will.

Electronic detection devices had meanwhile begun to register signals in the palace security headquarters. The signals were noticed, but discounted; the police sergeant whose job it was to monitor the alarm system had often seen such signals before, and knew them to be the result of some malfunction. He ignored them.

Fagan left the office and resumed his quest for the queen. "I'd been through every kind of fear you could imagine," he recalled later, "and I just wanted to see the queen by this time. It was a burning ambition."

Still barefoot, he roved the long carpeted hallways, surprised to come upon one of the maids vacuuming.

"I just gave her a wave," he remembered, "said 'Good morning,' and walked on."

Fagan now stumbled into the Throne Room.

The vast, high-ceilinged room with its three large imposing chairs was illuminated by weak early morning sunlight. Fagan walked toward the thrones, but before sitting down he wiped his tar-covered hands on the curtains. They were very old; no one had touched them for years. According to Fagan, they crumbled to pieces in his hands.

He sat in each of the grand throne chairs in turn, trying each on for size. Overall, he was not impressed. "In fact the palace didn't live up to my dreams of what a palace should be," he remarked afterward. Having reached the Throne Room without being apprehended, he now had the remarkable luck—from his viewpoint—to accidentally press a hidden spot in the wall paneling that opened a special door into Lilibet's private apartments.

He was close now, the queen had to be nearby. He wanted more than ever to talk to her, and not only to talk to her, but to do something to draw her attention to the extremity of his difficulties. He decided to do what he had done a few weeks earlier, in court; he would slash his wrists. On that occasion he had used a broken bottle. What could he use now? Entering an anteroom, he found a glass ashtray, and smashed it. Taking one of the glass fragments he cut his thumb. Blood began dripping down onto his trousers, his bare feet, the carpeting.[3]

Back in the corridor again, the intruder saw bowls of dog food, and knew that he had to be very close to the queen's own bedroom, for the queen and her corgis were never far apart for long. What he needed to find was a bathroom, but, seeing none, he relieved himself in the dogs' bowls. Then, a short way along the corridor, he came to a door, opened it, and found himself in a dimly lit room decorated in blue.

It was a simply furnished room, the blue carpet and wallpaper matching the blue silk draperies above the bed's headboard. In the bed, under the white blankets, was the small figure of a sleeping woman, her rest as yet undisturbed by the sound of a vacuum cleaner being operated in the next room.

He walked to the window and pulled open the curtains, to let in more light. The woman in the bed woke up, saw him and, according to Fagan, "looked really disturbed." She was uncomprehending at first, then shocked.

"What are you doing here? Get out! Get out!" she said firmly, her voice imperious.

She was commanding, and in possession of herself, but the person who confronted her frightened her very much. Not only was he holding a fragment of glass, and bleeding, but he looked deranged. According to Fagan, he said "I am not here to harm you. I think you are a really nice woman," adding "I love you, I love you."

None of this was reassuring. Disturbing thoughts must have tumbled over one another in Lilibet's quick mind. Would he attack her with the glass? He was a slight man, thin and wiry, but bigger and stronger than she was. What on earth did she have at hand with which to defend herself? And how had this crazy man gotten in?

Could he be a terrorist assassin, disguised as a derelict? The IRA had threatened her many times. They had managed to evade security and to plant a bomb that killed Dickie Mountbatten only three years earlier. Had they now sent this madman to kill her?

Fagan walked up to the bed and sat down on the white blanket, staining it with his blood, still holding the fragment of the ashtray. According to Lilibet she got out of bed, put on her dressing gown and slippers, "drew herself up to her full regal height, pointed to the door, and said again, 'Get out.' "

What followed, it seems, was a tense conversation between the two—Fagan said it was very brief, Lilibet that it lasted perhaps ten to fifteen minutes—during which the intruder poured out his troubles, and the queen listened attentively, watchful, no doubt, for any sudden moves on his part and twice interrupting the conversation to call the palace switchboard from her bedside phone. "I want a police officer," she said distinctly. But no police appeared.[4]

Whatever had been his plan beforehand, Fagan now decided not to slash his wrists. But he was very disillusioned. The queen wasn't anything like what he had expected, and he felt "badly let down." He was tearful. The encounter with his sovereign had not brought him comfort or reassurance, but depression.

What happened next is unclear. The maid may have come in with the breakfast tray, though Fagan did not remember her afterward. Eventually the young footman came back with the corgis, all eleven of them, barking and whining, agitated from their walk. They upset the intruder, and Lilibet tried to keep them away from him, no doubt fearing that he might hurt them. During the confusion the queen asked her footman, Can you give this man a drink? Fagan was escorted, uncomplaining, out of the queen's bedroom and into the Page's Vestibule where he was kept occupied with whiskey and cigarettes.

Lilibet made her way to her study and, according to the footman, screamed her complaints to the switchboard operator from there. "I have never heard the queen so angry," he said.

Before long a cordon of officers ran up the staircase, apprehended the intruder, and took him away. It was all over very quickly, but Lilibet's deep and abiding anger was slow to cool. She complained, and some in the security staff were fired. The Home Secretary, William Whitelaw, was denounced in the press and in Parliament. The number of police at the palace was tripled, and there were no more intruders.

Seething, and in increasing pain from an impacted wisdom tooth, the queen went to the hospital for the first time in her reign and had the aching tooth pulled. Her swollen cheek hurt afterward, and she went to Windsor to nurse her pain, giving strict orders that no uninvited guests were to be tolerated on the castle grounds.

TWENTY-FOUR

There were those who asked, in the aftermath of the break-in at the palace, where
Prince Philip had been when his wife was
confronted by the unstable Michael Fagan.
The answers given were varied and contradictory. Some said he was asleep in his own
room, two rooms away from the queen's
bedroom, and that he slept through the entire incident. Another story was that he had
left the palace very early in the morning for
an official engagement. Still another account was that he had slept in a different
bedroom from his wife "as he had to be up
early to take part in horse-driving trials in
Scotland." Insiders claimed that Philip had

not spent the night at the palace at all, but at his club.[1]

Anyone familiar with the prince's crowded schedule of trips, speeches and appearances would not have been surprised to find him unavailable on any particular morning. During the first six months of 1982 he had visited fourteen countries, attended countless formal lunches, dinners and committee meetings and raised a great deal of money for his many charities. Though he made himself available to his wife when needed—for example, to accompany her when she opened Parliament, or to travel with her on state visits, or to be present at family occasions—he kept his own hours, and lived his own life. She had even built his own house for him on the Balmoral grounds. She had long since come to terms with this element in their marriage; at sixty-two he was unlikely to change, nor was she likely to demand that he change. It was an embarrassment to her that when the newspapers reported on her encounter with Michael Fagan, they noted that Philip was not with her, and wondered why.

Her marriage was her own business, a private, delicate matter that involved no one but her husband and herself. Palace staff guarded the details of Philip's personal life carefully, and he, as a onetime friend put it, "was a genius at keeping his own secrets."2

A more pertinent question than why Philip was not in bed with Lilibet when the intruder broke in was why Bobo was not nearby.

The seventy-eight-year-old Bobo, gray-haired and shrunken in size, but still doing her best to watch over Lilibet and control her environs, was a much more ubiquitous presence in the queen's bedroom than Philip. Her brittle bones were frail, she could no longer work every day and was turning over more and more of her duties to her assistant Peggy Heath. But she still seemed ubiquitous at the palace, despite taking long vacations in Venice and spending more and more time with her sister and brother-in-law in her grace and favor house in Marlborough House mews. With her hunched shoulders and beetle brows, her frowns of disapproval (frowns that could still intimidate others among the household staff), Bobo Macdonald ruled the queen's apartments, and some said she ruled the queen.

Certainly there was a surprising similarity in their crisped, frizzled hairstyles—they shared the same hairdresser, Charles Martin—in their square unstylish handbags, in their preference for sensible flat laced shoes and practical plain raincoats. Lilibet still listened when Bobo criticized her for behaving frivolously or for forgetting to put on a coat or sweater when she went walking outside. It was to Bobo that the queen turned, as she dressed in haste for an evening out, and called, "Get out my thing, would you?" The "thing," which Bobo retrieved, was a jeweled clip with an immense diamond. Lilibet fastened it on, wrapped herself in a black mink coat, and was ready to go.[3] Bobo too had a valuable fur coat, made for her by the queen's own furrier, with "Margaret Macdonald" embroidered on the lining. She also had a sparkling brooch with twenty-five diamonds, a gift from the queen on the fiftieth anniversary of Bobo's royal service.[4]

It was Bobo who sat on the white plastic toilet seat in Lilibet's bathroom and talked to her while she bathed, Bobo who, it was said, was still capable of chastening her, even of making her cry. Journalists whispered that the queen was "mesmerized by Bobo," that their rapport was so extraordinary as to be "almost telepathic."[5] Telepathy failed, of course, on the morning of Michael Fagan's intrusion into the royal bedroom. Possibly Bobo was away, staying in her mews house, or she may have been ill. Her anger at the failure of the security system must have been formidable; her tongue-lashings were probably more severe than her mistress's.

Reporters and television journalists were quick to seize upon the story of a man breaking into the queen's bedroom and exploit it from every angle. Had the queen been frightened, or was she courageous and calm? How dangerous was the trespasser? What did Philip's absence mean about the state of the royal marriage? Where were her bodyguards, the palace detectives? (The spotlight was turned with special brightness on the detectives, one of whom, as it turned out, was put to shame, and resigned, reflecting badly on the palace; as a direct result of the negative publicity surrounding the breach of security it came out that he had had a relationship with a male prostitute.)

The massive, sensationalized coverage was indicative of a shift in media focus, a newly emerging set of attitudes toward the monarchy and the royal family on the part of the press generally. And with it came a shift in public perception, one that was to have long-range consequences.

Partly because of the immense popularity of the Princess of Wales, partly because of the bracing but divisive tone set by the prime minister and her colleagues, and their domination of the news, partly the result of a pervasive ferment in cultural values that afflicted Britain in the eighties, a change occurred in how the queen and her family were regarded. Royalty and celebrity became interchangeable; the symbolic, semi-sacred role of queen counted for far less than her fame, her notoriety, her topicality as the object of popular esteem or derision. Her value was perceived to lie far less in her exalted character as an anointed monarch than in her enormous wealth and peerless social standing, the allure of her title and its fairytale mystique.

With this new, far more hollow and fragile image of monarchy went a venal appetite to find and expose lurid melodrama around the throne: personal tragedy, conflict, intrigue, romance, self-destructiveness, saintliness and martyrdom, wickedness and vice. It was no longer enough to report ordinary doings of the royals; now a new breed of media owners demanded a constantly evolving, larger-than-life story, punctuated by thrilling or shocking theatrical events.

The queen, and her family, lost stature. And it has never been regained.

But for a time, it appeared that the royals had been elevated in significance, because their visibility rose. When Lilibet and Philip went to the Caribbean, Mexico and California in 1983–84, there were thousands in the press corps, instead of the dozens or at most hundreds in previous decades. Fleets of television trucks followed the royals throughout their day, and press conferences had to be held in amphitheaters to accommodate the huge numbers of reporters and cameramen. When the queen, in her tiara, her gown flashing with shiny beads, got out of her limousine to attend the state dinner in her honor in San Francisco, it was a display of glamour worthy of Hollywood. In Hollywood itself, a dinner was held on the 20th Century–Fox lot for the queen and her entourage, with entertainment by Frank Sinatra and George Burns.

Lilibet, caught up in the excitement, allowed herself to be carried away, not yet perceiving the potential harm caused by media excess. She made excited phone calls to Margaret, telling her all about California: the movie studio, the swank of Beverly Hills, the drive from San Francisco to Yosemite with its immense mountains and towering cascading waterfalls, the friendly crowds and warm semitropical climate.

When Reagan's press secretary Michael Deaver suggested that the queen and Philip go to a San Francisco restaurant, Trader Vic's, Lilibet's response was immediate and electric.

"Oh, a restaurant! That's wonderful!" She turned to her husband, Deaver recalled, and said "Philip, Mr. Deaver has this wonderful idea about going to a restaurant!"

"A restaurant?" Philip replied. "Surely you are kidding. A restaurant?"

"We'll talk about it tonight and I'll tell

you," the queen said to Deaver. Eventually they went to Trader Vic's, with its imitation Polynesian atmosphere, stage-set tropical banana trees and coconut palms, rattan furniture and pineapple- and coconut-flavored cocktails. They had fun.

"Thank you, Mr. Deaver," Lilibet told the press secretary after he delivered the party back to the shabby-genteel old St. Francis Hotel on Union Square. "That was a wonderful evening. It was the first time we have been in a restaurant in seventeen years."[6]

Thirty-three hundred reporters, photographers, and commentators followed the queen during her days in California. But at the same time, more thousands were following the daily activities of the Princess of Wales, whose second child, Prince Harry, was born in September of 1984.

Diana had become a staple of media coverage. One couldn't pass a magazine rack without seeing her picture, every newspaper carried a story about her, or so it seemed. When Bishop Hugh Montefiore said of Diana that "she was a phenomenon; she was the most famous woman in the world," he was only stating what everyone had come to believe.[7] Her blond good looks, deep blue eyes and sanpaku gaze, sweet, faintly wistful smile and svelte, athletically toned body clad in becoming designer fashions were an icon of female beauty. Women throughout the world wanted to look like Diana, wanted to watch Diana as she moved through her charmed life.

And she was not only famous; she was revered. The same empathy and warmth that had initially drawn Charles to her drew millions of others, who admired her for her striking personal qualities, as well as for her sincere compassion. "I understand people's suffering, people's pain," she declared, and she set out to minister to the suffering and the afflicted. Like a modern Florence Nightingale she seemed to set a new pattern of charitable empathy among the highborn and well-connected; like Mother Teresa she sought out the most shunned of the suffering and dying, especially victims of AIDS, and gave them her hands-on love. And the cameras were nearly always present to record her works of mercy.

Diana was maturing, motherhood and sorrow and frustration (and her ongoing struggle with bulimia) as well as her widening charitable outreach were maturing her. She was turning inward, seeking spiritual or occult guidance, becoming convinced that she had lived before. When asked how she knew this, she replied, "Because I'm a wise old thing."[8] Consultations with her astrologer Becky had convinced her that Charles, whom she had grown to detest, would never succeed his mother as king. Her son William would be the one to reign after her mother-in-law. These welcome insights, however flimsily derived, deepened Diana's sense of mission and lent an air of gravity to her public demeanor.

Charles, meanwhile, was barely civil to his wife in public and seething in private. Screaming, furniture-destroying tantrums were a symptom of his loathing of Diana and—so it was widely believed—of his jealousy of her. She had stolen the spotlight completely, though there was some measure of sympathy for Charles on the part of royal-watchers who saw in Diana, behind the revered icon, a spoiled diva bent on self-advancement.

Some said it was in order to deflect potential criticism from herself that Diana introduced Sarah Ferguson to the unmarried

Prince Andrew, who in 1985 was twenty-five and becoming known as a playboy, having already established himself during the Falklands War as a hero. Handsome, arrogant, self-confident Andrew, far less complex than his older brother Charles and secure in his mother's strong approval, was said to be harmless and well-meaning but callow and boorish, accustomed to being the center of attention and unaware of how tedious his demanding, rather shallow personality could be. (Andrew, it was said, would capture center stage at a dinner party by tapping his knife on his glass and shouting "I want to tell a story, I want to tell a story!"[9])

Outgoing and good-natured, flamboyant and funny, Sarah was wellborn but not wealthy, very much a woman of the world. Far more than the aristocratic Diana, whose father was an earl and whose family lineage was lofty, Sarah at twenty-six had had wide experience of life, with a middle-aged boyfriend and a history of party-going and hedonistic enjoyment. She was hearty and amusing, down-to-earth and likable, with no obvious neuroses and without Diana's moodiness and exercise mania. Sarah smoked and drank, spoke her mind, made her own rules—as many young women of her generation did—without reference to traditional mores. She was intelligent and curious, daringly self-confident. When Andrew proposed to her and she accepted, Sarah seemed largely unconcerned about meeting any obligations she would be taking on as Duchess of York, or any standards of behavior the palace might try to apply. She loved Andrew—she fell in love easily—and looked forward to being Diana's sister-in-law. "I'll just be myself," was her airy response when asked about any changes she would need to make.[10]

Lilibet warmed to Sarah as she never had to Diana. She liked Sarah's straightforward, earthy manner and her wit and humor. They were on common ground when it came to the queen's favorite preoccupation: horses. Sarah liked to ride, enjoyed the outdoor life and was happy at Balmoral and Sandringham. Her father, former Guards officer Major Ronald Ferguson (called "The Galloping Major" for his fondness for horses and women), was a public relations executive as well as Prince Charles's personal polo manager; horses were a big part of his life, and

Sarah had grown up around them and on them. All in all, Lilibet was pleased with her son's choice and was content to see Andrew and Sarah married, amid much fanfare and splendor, in Westminster Abbey in July of 1986.

Sarah fitted in, as Diana never had. She and Andrew got on well, had boisterous fun together and laughed a lot. Sarah enlivened things, she stirred up the stodginess in the family and lightened the atmosphere. To be sure, the traditionalists among the palace staff dismissed her as déclassé—Martin Charteris called her a "vulgarian"—but they couldn't help liking her. Sarah's good cheer offset Diana's mercurial swings of temperament. She diverted press attention, the paparazzi began chasing her, reporters following her.

"My mother's a star; my daughter-in-law is a star. Where does that leave me?" the queen is said to have asked out loud in the mid-eighties.[11] Now there was yet another media star in the family. But Sarah, buoyant and undemanding, jokey and energetic, was a welcome twinkle in the royal firmament. Her arrival was a hopeful sign, pointing toward greater consensus and understanding within the fragmented royal family. Or so Lilibet may have hoped as she watched her favorite son and his wife exchange vows before the high altar of the abbey, and silently wished them well.

TWENTY-FIVE

The red deer had been growing in numbers, overrunning the Balmoral hills. Each day when Lilibet rode over the estate she saw them, many of them, does with half-grown fawns and antlered bucks, clusters of animals grazing, twigs snapping as they ambled through the thick underbrush. The deer greatly outnumbered the thin, shaggy-haired Highland cattle, and the small, dainty fell ponies that picked their way along the narrow tracks on the hillsides. Foresters planting patches of new pine seedlings had to build high fences to keep the deer out, and even then they managed occasionally to jump over the fences and break them down, so eager were they to get to the tender young greens.

Musing over the deer problem was a diversion for Lilibet, who had much on her mind this fall season of 1987. It was at Balmoral each August and September that she rested, mentally, from the daily demands of her vocation. On her long rides and walks and deerstalking jaunts she turned things over in her mind; the wide landscape invited reflection, and offered, if not serenity, at least an illusion of calm.

The slow changing of the season, the yellowing of the birch leaves, the purple heather against the blue and dark green conifers was comforting and familiar, if faintly tinged with melancholy. It was harvest season, ripe and rich, but the brisk chill air was a reminder that winter was coming. The animals were gorging, fattening while they could, and starting to put on their winter coats and plumage; food would be hard to find once the hills were buried under a carpet of snow, and they would need thicker fur and deeper coats of feathers.

Lilibet too was marking a change of season in her life. In 1987 she was sixty-one, the gentle frosting of gray in her hair covered by a discreet brown dye, the lines in her still attractive face deepening, her erect carriage slumping ever so slightly though she still moved quickly and with vigor. With her crimped hair and increasingly dowdy clothes she had taken on the prim, no-nonsense look of a retired schoolmistress or governess; she still wore long white gloves and pearls in the afternoon, as she had in her youth. When watching her horses exercise, in tweed skirt, twinset and raincoat (and the everpresent pearls) she peered through bifocals carrying a camera and wearing an unflattering scarf tied around her head, fastened inelegantly in place with bobbypins. Clothes interested her less and less, especially at Balmoral. Walking out with her many corgis, watching them chase rabbits, she was free of the need to look polished or even presentable. No one cared, except perhaps her mother and Bobo, and they too relaxed their standards when the family was in the country.

The years were closing in on Lilibet, little by little. She was a grandmother now, her two grandsons William and Harry were aged five and three. She no longer rode Burmese in the annual Trooping the Colour parade, she and Burmese had retired together in 1986. She deputed Charles to give out some of the thousands of honors and decorations royally bestowed each year instead of giving them all out herself. In other ways she eased her burden slightly, adjusting for occasional infirmity—and for the effects of stress.

For by this fall of 1987, she was under stress from many sources: from the ongoing dilemma of Britain's unrelieved economic decline; from her concern over the triad of woes facing working Britons, high inflation, high unemployment, and what analysts were calling "deindustrialization"; from the disturbing currents of Thatcherism with which she disagreed (or so *The Times* said in 1986), especially the government's harsh treatment of workers and its cavalier attitude toward the Commonwealth.

And there were other strains, deeper and seemingly intractable.

The palace staff were out of control. Beneath the surface decorum, the complex set of rules and procedures and the elaborate hierarchy of staff, there was a hornet's nest of intrigue, rampant thievery and a squalid underworld of bullying and sexual exploitation, full of unsavory cliques and frantic efforts, some of them illegal, to keep the whole sordid mess from coming to light.[1]

One former employee was found to have purloined a large number of valuables from the underground vaults at the palace, including Queen Mary's engagement ring and silver knives and forks from the time of George III. There were souvenirs as well as heirlooms, sheets from Windsor Castle and a Royal Standard, for instance, were found in the guilty man's apartment. And the thief, who knew a great deal about the inner workings of Buckingham Palace, told journalist Andrew Morton that he was not prosecuted because of fears in high places that he might reveal embarrassing secrets.[2]

Princess Anne's love letters were stolen, almost certainly by a palace insider whom she trusted. Anne wanted the thief found and prosecuted, but Lilibet, quite possibly in an effort to avoid unsavory publicity and damaging revelations, intervened to prevent this.[3] Even so, some seventy servants were fingerprinted and interviewed by detectives.

Two footmen contrived an elaborate plot to use the palace as a warehouse for explosives, which they stole from mine stock-piles.[4] Sticks of gelignite were brought in in a stolen Land Rover, and stored where the thieves thought no one would ever find them. Eventually the dangerous cache was found, causing much alarm. (Were the footmen IRA terrorists, planning to blow up the royal family?) Both men were jailed.

Illegal, furtive goings-on within Lilibet's household put her under much strain, but there was a wider source of stress, for the erosion of her authority at the palace was paralleled by a more general decline in her ability to command. Symptoms of decay were everywhere: in the failure of the press to heed the queen's request that the Michael Fagan incident be kept from public knowledge; in the dismissive attitude of many in the government who, to judge from their actions at least, found the queen and the monarchy generally to be a cumbersome vestigial organ in the operations of the state; in the near-total collapse of public reverence for the crown; and in the ceaseless prurient hounding by the disrespectful press.

Personal snubs and discourtesies reminded Lilibet that she was becoming an irrelevance. When she arrived in Morocco for a state visit the king went off to play golf rather than greet her and offer her a welcoming meal. (QUEEN IN RAGE OVER SNUB cried one London tabloid.)[5] Three days of repeated rudeness in Morocco left her angry, but unable to improve the situation; she assumed an air of inscrutable reserve and eventually made a dignified exit.

When President Reagan visited the queen and they went riding together in Windsor Great Park, surrounded by the ubiquitous press, the president turned the occasion into an impromptu press conference. Disregarding Lilibet's attitude—which was a blank refusal to respond to shouted questions—and choosing to ignore the fact that he was a guest in her home, in her private riding park, Reagan responded good-humoredly, making the queen so furious that she turned her horse and rode off. Not long afterward, when the president ordered his troops to invade Grenada, he did not bother to signal his intentions to the queen, who was the island's sovereign. It was not lost on her that the charming Reagan was willing to discuss horses with her quite amiably, and to admire what he called her "forward seat" and her mastery of her mount, but over-looked the prerogative of her sovereignty entirely.

Realist that she was, Lilibet was aware that she counted for less and less. Successive prime ministers, Margaret Thatcher most of all, had leached away much of her residual influence, her power of command had been greatly reduced, even her moral influence diminished. The difference was intangible, but unmistakable. Where once others had deferred to her aura of sacred majesty, they now ignored it—or denied its very existence.

Meanwhile her daughter-in-law Diana, and to a lesser extent her daughter-in-law Sarah, had greatly eclipsed Lilibet herself as celebrities. Her mother, the "queen mum," was more loved by the public than she herself was, especially as the dowager queen reached her late eighties. Lilibet's children did not obey her, did not confide in her, and did not model themselves on her. Above all, the traditional cordon of respect that had protected Lilibet and her family for decades had been shattered, perhaps irreparably.

And her exasperating, perplexing, feckless heir Charles was set to inherit her lowered authority, her lessened power and control. Already he was showing himself to be unable to manage his staff. An allegation of rape had been made by a junior member of his household against one of his closest aides, and the accuser had left the palace employ with a large check.[6] Charles disliked the grueling paperwork of monarchy, the hours-long daily task of painstakingly reading and signing stacks of government documents. He neglected this work, he pleased himself. When he should have been tending to business he played polo. ("Without polo," he said, "I'd go stark, staring mad.")[7]

He might have added: without Camilla he would go stark, staring mad. For by this fall of 1987, his marriage to Diana was little more than a legal formality. Charles had returned to his nurturing, understanding mistress, this fact had been public knowledge for some time.[8] Leaving aside propriety and morality, and the pain Charles was causing his emotionally fragile wife, the situation was an exceedingly awkward one for Lilibet. She knew Camilla, and her husband, she could not help encountering them at Anne's equestrian events, or at race meetings—anywhere horse-loving aristocrats met. Officially she had no reaction to the resumption of Charles and Camilla's longtime intimate bond, officially the queen was above noticing or reacting to such things, in a sphere apart. But in actuality the situation troubled her, not least because it upset the always delicate balance within her family.

All family gatherings now had an increased undertone of tension. Holidays were corroded by rifts, slights, petty revenges. Diana was sullen, Charles insensitive and gauche. Certain subjects had to be avoided. No one knew when the smoldering hostility between Charles and Diana might burst into singeing flame, scorching everyone nearby. Camilla was a silent, unseen but constant presence, on everyone's mind.

And the queen mother, who unlike Lilibet blamed Diana, not Charles, for all the anger and dissension, made things worse by constantly taking Charles's side, giving him a refuge and a sympathetic ear. When Charles and Diana's estrangement took on a particularly bitter edge during the long autumn season at Balmoral, Charles fled to the neighboring estate of Birkhall, where his grandmother stayed, and remained with her, sometimes for weeks at a time, while Diana was on her own, stranded in the rustic environment she hated. ("BOR-RING" was her comment about Balmoral to her friend and lover James Gilbey.[9])

Diana's resentment of the queen mother was yet one more unpleasant emotional crosscurrent blemishing the Balmoral holiday. According to Diana's aides, the princess "regarded the queen mother as a very tough operator who frequently got at the queen and told her, 'Diana is fouling up all you stand for.' "[10] The queen mother was poisoning the well, Diana thought, and Margaret and Philip were drinking from it—and joining in the chorus of condemnation. Diana felt that she was being likened to that most hated of all interlopers, Wallis Simpson, the despised American who, in family legend at least, had committed the unforgivable sin of enticing Uncle David to give up his throne for her.

Rightly or wrongly, Diana felt persecuted—and she blamed her mother-in-law for failing to intervene. She had learned over the years that the queen was weak where family problems were concerned. She ducked the issues, or ignored them.

She deferred to her mother. She let discord fester, hoping it would go away.

Now, however, Lilibet was coming to realize that she had to take charge. Too many situations had gone too far out of control. It was time to act, and decisively. The herd of red deer would have to be culled, the palace staff brought more firmly to heel. If there were limits to her ability to regain her overall authority, she would at least take a firm stand with Charles and Diana; their irresponsibility would have to stop.

In the last days of her Balmoral holiday, enjoying the pleasures of stalking and shooting, riding and walking through the coarse, drizzly grass and springy heather, listening to the calling of the curlews break the silence of the hills, Lilibet armored herself internally, as best she could, against the winter to come.

TWENTY-SIX

In the fall of 1987 the queen summoned Charles and Diana to her private sitting room at Buckingham Palace and sat them down together, insisting that they listen to what she had to say. It was not often that they sat together any more, their sharing a room was in itself a not inconsiderable step in the process of what Lilibet hoped would be a rapprochement, albeit one imposed from outside.

The prince and princess were well aware of why they were being brought together into the royal presence for a talk. The gossip and press speculation caused by their behavior toward one another had reached a

damaging extreme. Many in the realm wondered whether they would divorce. An inspiring dream—the dream of a fairytale
wedding, followed by married happiness
and the birth of two fine sons—had been
shattered, and the public's disillusionment
was in need of repair, for the good of the
nation and for the sake of the monarchy.

In the queen's view, the couple's duty to
the country ought to come before anything
else, certainly it ought to outweigh personal inclinations or affinities. Marriage was
sometimes difficult, as she herself had good
reason to know. But the difficulties could be
surmounted. All it took was self-discipline
and an act of will.

It was this self-discipline that seemed to
be lacking in both Charles and Diana. Now
Lilibet insisted that they pull themselves together and put things right, in order to stop
all the speculation. There was enmity between them; well, so be it. But for the sake
of their all-important public responsibilities,
they had to muster the grace to mask that
enmity beneath a carapace of assumed civility. The ability to put on a suitable, dignified and gracious public face was a hall-

mark of royalty. Lilibet herself had modeled this ability for six decades.

Diana was clearly in need of correction. Her erratic behavior—a departure from the maturity she had seemed to achieve earlier—had led to renewed gossip. At a society ball a few months earlier, she had danced with a good-looking young man for hours, ignoring Charles, who left the gathering early and went home alone. Even more recently, Diana had gone by herself to a London party and when she emerged from the fashionable Queensgate Mews house where the party was being held, had made a spectacle of herself, dancing in the street, squealing in mock terror like a schoolgirl when a car driven by a male friend approached her. A photographer took her picture and, when Diana's detective tried to confiscate the film there was a loud confrontation and a scuffle.

Diana, in tears, begged the young cameraman to give her the film, in effect pleading for mercy. If his photos were published, she sobbed, her life would become even more unbearable than it already was. She poured out her heart to this young stranger, telling him how wretched she was, all but bereft of friends and so constrained in her day-to-day existence that she rarely had any fun.

She won the cameraman over, and he relinquished the film to the princess's wrathful detective.[1]

Diana was foolishly indiscreet, but Charles! Charles was exasperating, wrongheaded, and deeply disappointing. Family friends and staff were convinced that Lilibet and Philip both blamed Charles for the breakdown of his marriage, and the contretemps in the fall of 1987 was in many ways a culmination of years of increasingly sour psychological estrangement between the heir to the throne and his parents.[2]

Confident and decisive herself, the queen had never been able to excuse or empathize with her perpetually anxious, highly strung son. Fretful, overstrained Charles, who was inclined to feel besieged by the world, and who was plagued by incessant internal debates, vexed her by his timid petulant nature. He was nearly forty, surely maturity ought to teach him to conquer his inner doubts and to grasp his responsibilities.

But maturity, at least maturity as the queen understood it, seemed to elude

Charles. He took his teddy bear everywhere he went, even on long trips abroad. (When, on one overseas journey, his staff forgot the bear, he was beside himself with petulant vexation; the beloved teddy was rushed to the airport and sent to him on the next jet.[3]) He had tantrums. He felt sorry for himself. He indulged himself—extravagantly, in his mother's view. He groused about having to go to London (he much preferred High-grove, or some other rural retreat), about noisy toilets and leaking air conditioners, about people who smoked and servants who could not set a table properly or pro-vide him with his preferred oversize bath towels.

To Lilibet, whose personal needs were modest (despite living in a palace) and who avoided inconveniencing or exploiting—much less haranguing—her servants, Charles's fussy, demanding ways seemed shamefully spoiled. And she looked on his attitudes and behavior as a husband in the same light. With Diana, she assumed, he was tense, childish, querulous, self-pitying, explosively angry and demanding—as well as unfaithful. It was no wonder the marriage had veered toward estrangement.

But now, she informed Charles and Diana, as they sat before her, all must change. They had to find a way to restore harmony and live together amicably. They must work things out between them, observing discretion, preventing gossip, preserving the appearance of sharing a contented marriage. William and Harry, aged five and three, could not be allowed to grow up in an environment clouded by scandal and corroded by marital conflict. In due course, Charles would come to the throne, Diana would be his faithful helpmate, and together they would prepare William for his own future reign.

It was a comforting image, an image of order restored, good feeling regained, positive, purposive living reestablished. It satisfied Lilibet's enduring need for tidiness, and her sense of herself as family matriarch—a role she hardly ever assumed. As a final indication of her vigilance, Lilibet sent one of her footmen, Paul Burrell, to Highgrove to serve Charles and Diana as butler. Burrell was to be a link between the Waleses' establishment and the palace, and, if need be, a conduit of information; as events turned out, the butler became Diana's trusted confidant and loyal, longsuffering admirer.

If the Prince and Princess of Wales took heed of the queen's words, even fleetingly, they soon forgot them, Diana ignoring her mother-in-law's authority, Charles angry and alienated and rebelling, heedless of his ever-worsening reputation in his future subjects' eyes. Diana, while enjoying an ever widening celebrity and using her fame to further worthwhile causes, continued to be miserable with Charles and to seek emotional comfort and sensual pleasure with other men. Charles held fast to Camilla. And the sniping, wounding battles raged on, with the prince and princess at odds over childrearing, and with Diana manipulatively keeping the children away from Charles and seeking revenge in other ways for his maintaining his ongoing menage with his mistress.[4]

Meanwhile a second royal marriage was reaching its end. Early in 1989 Princess Anne and Mark Phillips, both of whom had turned to others as their bond to each other frayed, were legally separated. Lilibet reluctantly gave her permission for their formal separation, realizing that a reconciliation was unlikely. Lilibet was sympathetic to Anne, liked her boyfriend, palace equerry Timothy Laurence, and was not at all inclined to intervene as divorce between Anne and Mark became inevitable. By the end of the 1980s, nearly half of all marriages in Britain were ending in divorce, though the Church of England still taught that marriage was indissoluble. Prevailing attitudes and behavior were changing so rapidly, and institutions could not keep pace.

Andrew and Sarah too were headed toward separation, though without the enmity and bitterness that divided Charles and Diana. For most of their marriage, Andrew had been away at sea, and Sarah, with two children, Beatrice and Eugenie, found the prolonged separations tedious. Her youth was passing her by, she felt, and meanwhile she was expected to live in stultified seclusion, deprived of her husband's company, in the beautiful but isolated estate bordering Windsor Great Park that her mother-in-law had provided for her and Andrew. Feeling "nervous" in the great house on her own, as Sarah confided to friends, and made uncomfortable by the many security devices installed there, Sarah moved to apartments in Buckingham Palace, with Beatrice and Eugenie occupying the second-floor nursery.[5] But this meant exchanging the nervous isolation of her rural estate for the long gloomy corridors, old-fashioned shabbiness and unwelcome formality of the palace, and there too Sarah was discontent.

By the time Eugenie was born, however, in March of 1990, Sarah had begun diverting herself with infidelity, first with the very wealthy Texas playboy Steve Wyatt and then with another Texan, John Bryan. Both affairs led to damaging talk and eventually to tabloid scandal. The queen talked to Sarah, whom she continued to like for her jokey cheeriness, and attempted to apply moral suasion, but her counsel made no difference. In the last days of 1991 Andrew and Sarah informed Lilibet that they had decided to separate.

She asked them to do nothing for six months, but their announcement saddened her. None of her children had made lasting marriages. Edward, who was twenty-seven in 1991, had not attempted marriage at all—and was rumored to be gay. The next generation was well launched, the succession was assured. But the continuity of enduring, stable family life was broken. Irregular unions, improvised arrangements were becoming the norm. In lieu of the sequence of generations, following one another rank on rank, there was only a state of flux. In lieu of cordial, or at least civil, unions (within which discreet intimacies could be indulged), there was only incompatibility, which led to rancor, then to estrangement. The children were left to find their way as best they could through this emotional wreckage.

And all this was coming into being over the queen's expressed objections, and despite the example she tried to set.

"I can't understand my children," she admitted, and the admission must have caused her as much pain as frustration.[6]

But the following year, 1992, was to bring much more than pain and misunderstanding. It was an anniversary year, the fortieth anniversary of the queen's accession—and the fortieth anniversary of her beloved father's death, that great shock she had received in Africa so long ago. There were more shocks to come.

An angry Prince Andrew, wounded by the discovery of compromising photographs of his wife and her lover Steve Wyatt, told his mother he had made up his mind to divorce Sarah without further delay. The couple's formal separation was announced in mid-March. Then early in June came the first installment of the book that was to change the way the royal family was regarded—not only in Britain, but worldwide.

Andrew Morton's *Diana: Her True Story* horrified readers with its dark tale of the "inside" story of the Princess of Wales's marriage. Diana, the much-admired public icon, was according to Morton a victim of wretched depression, who had been driven to attempt suicide no less than five times by her adulterous husband's mistreatment and by the heartless indifference of the royal family. Diana's bulimia was revealed, along with her visits to therapists, her miserable relations with her royal in-laws, and her desperate struggles to survive in the hostile environment of royalty, an environment presented by Morton as a gilded snake-pit.

Lilibet was on a state visit to France when the sensational Andrew Morton revelations were published. She heard about them, swallowed her deeply startled reaction, and proceeded with her tour, greeting officials, appearing before crowds, looking self-possessed, though she knew that many in Paris were aware of the headline-making details. Her automatic response to embarrassments was to ignore and rise above them, seeming not to notice. But this was a mortification that struck deep: even though Lilibet cannot have been shocked or surprised by Morton's actual disclosures concerning Diana's weaknesses and fragility (she was far too well informed for that), she seems to have been disconcerted by Diana's complicity in bringing them to public knowledge. Diana's personal anguish apart, her allowing Morton to tell her unadorned, sensational story was nothing less than a full-out assault on the family that had honored Diana by making her a royal princess and tried—at least Lilibet had tried—to make a place for her. The degree of Diana's anger and desire for revenge were laid bare.[7]

On her return from France the queen tried once again to bring pressure to bear on Charles and Diana to hold their marriage together. She asked them, as she had asked Andrew and Sarah, to wait six months before making any decision about their future. They should make an official trip together, demonstrate to the international press that they were working things out.

She did her best to command. Insiders said her tone was "imperious." But most likely it was already too late for any amount of scolding or insisting to make a difference.[8] Too much damage had been done, too many hurtful details had been revealed. The royal family would not be the same ever again, no matter what the queen did or didn't do.

For the royals were about to be swept under by adverse publicity on an unprecedented scale, and the widened notoriety would change everything.

The enormous commercial success of Andrew Morton's bestselling book about Diana invited imitation. Journalists searched intensively for more secrets, informants came forward seeking to be paid well for salacious stories. Old tales, once thought too far-fetched or too thinly substantiated to report, were brought out and reexamined by editors avid to cash in on the growing public hunger to know more about the Windsors.

On August 20, 1992, when the family was at Balmoral, the *Daily Mirror* published photographs of Sarah and the man referred to as her "financial adviser," the American John Bryan, embracing at Bryan's rented villa. The duchess was topless, Bryan was sucking her toes, the air of casual, cosy sensuality was clear for all the world to see and interpret in the most lurid light. Only a few days later, on August 24, the *Sun* published transcripts of a taped conversation between Diana and her lover James Gilbey, a conversation that had taken place nearly three years earlier when the two were together in Gilbey's car late on New Year's Eve. Diana told Gilbey that her life was "torture," that Charles and his whole "fucking family" were against her and that even the queen mum upset her by staring at her "with a strange look in her eyes." The tape confirmed what Morton's book had affirmed: that the princess was miserable, hated her husband and her royal in-laws, and had been unfaithful—or so it seemed from the degree of her intimacy with Gilbey, who called her "Squidgy"—with other men.

That these disclosures could easily have called the legitimacy of the succession into question seemed the least of the issues they raised. The family, gathered in tense togetherness in Scotland, fell into a degree of disarray unknown since the abdication crisis of 1936.

Sarah left for London. Charles, reportedly "deeply offended," and "in a state of shock," looked lost and in very low spirits.[9] Lilibet, who had been furious and glum earlier in the summer, showing a degree of bad temper very unusual for her, looked "really shattered" after the late August scandals, according to one of her senior courtiers. "The queen looked ashen and completely flat," he recalled, though the reaction was to be relatively short-lived.[10]

It was not only that the palace seemed to have lost all semblance of control over the media, and that the media, focused on bringing more and more sensational stories to light, had lost all sense of propriety and proportion. It was not only that the public tended to believe what it was told, however unlikely or far-fetched, or that jokes about Sarah and her "financial adviser," or about "Squidgy," were circling the globe. It was the certainty that more embarrassing secrets were in unfriendly hands, waiting to be revealed. The hostile Rupert Murdoch press had disclosed, only the previous month, that its news organization possessed very prejudicial information about the royals, and that it was keeping this information locked away—for the time being.

The queen knew that there was much more that could come to light—the whole shadowy sexual underworld within Buckingham Palace, the alleged crimes that had been covered up, quite possibly other secrets which have yet to be brought before public scrutiny at this writing. There was more, and it was only a matter of time before the truth stood revealed.

The enormity of what had happened was there on the queen's normally unreadable face, in her pallor, in the lines of weariness around her dark-ringed eyes and downturned mouth, the look of defeat in her blue eyes. "She looked so awful, I felt like crying," said one of her household staff.[11]

The load she carried had suddenly become heavier. Not only was she concerned about her kingdoms, with Britons suffering under the worst recession since the 1930s, and with a new and rather tentative Conservative prime minister, John Major, in office (the redoubtable Margaret Thatcher having been forced out of power toward the end of 1990), but she was both angry and heartsick over Sarah's foolish, reckless philandering and Diana's more calculated acts of revenge. She worried about Charles's stability, about her grandsons and granddaughters, caught in the meshes of marital conflict and in danger of being permanently harmed by the resultant scandals. In her darkest moments she must have wondered whether, amid the inescapable ridicule and shame to which her family was being subjected, and the mounting clamor on the part of republicans, her throne might be tottering, and her reign might see the end of Britain's ancient monarchical system.

For the monarchy itself was under renewed scrutiny, harsh and unsparing. For decades dismissed as a genteel archaism, all but powerless and primarily ceremonial in form and function, fading into obsolescence, the monarchy had more recently been seen as having a much more central, and more sinister, role in Britain's difficulties and destiny.

Monarchy, argued the influential republican Tom Nairn in his book *The Enchanted Glass*, was at the heart of an outdated national British identity which was holding the nation back from coming to terms with postmodern realities.

"The monarchic trance," Nairn argued, with all the fossilized ideas that accompany it, keeps Britain in thrall to a nostalgic image of itself—an image that must be discarded if Britain is to thrive once again. Royalty-worship perpetuates damaging myths of Britain's greatness and of an overarching social and moral order that never existed; royalty occupies, Nairn says, the niche in the national psyche once filled by the idea of Providence. Until monarchy goes, the myths will continue to hold Britons back from seeing themselves as they really are and attaining meaningful progress.[12]

Intellectuals and anti-monarchists read Nairn's book and agreed with it. Republican sentiment expanded in influence, fueled by exasperation and shame. Jokes about "Elizabeth the Last" were told and retold. And beneath the surface chatter, the conferences on the nature of monarchy and the inquiries into its appropriate future as Britain approached the threshold of the new millennium, the vast public arrived at its silent verdict.

As for Lilibet, pale and temporarily laid low by the news stories and photos, she demonstrated a remarkable resilience. Throwing off her crestfallen mood (or at least disguising it well), within days she resumed her Balmoral routine, riding and walking, stalking and hunting with ferrets. The same staff member who had felt like crying when confronted with her dejection was astounded to see her "absolutely transformed, smiling and happy."[13] Cares laid aside, the sixty-six-year-old queen tramped off into the woods, searching for rabbit warrens, and sending her ferret down into them, spreading her nets to catch and kill the unwary rabbits as they tried to bolt for freedom.

TWENTY-SEVEN

The fire started, it seems, when a hot tungsten lamp, left burning in the private chapel once used by Queen Victoria, touched a curtain behind the altar. The curtain smoldered, then burst into flame. Soon the entire chapel was ablaze, black smoke began pouring from the eastern end of the Windsor Castle complex. As fire alarms sounded and firefighters rushed in, the carved timbers and wooden rafters of Saint George's Hall burned, the high temperature generated by the flames caused other rooms and ultimately the roof to combust, sending bright orange fire leaping into the night sky.

Windsor was burning, the ancient castle

on its hill surrounded by parkland and over-looking the town. Windsor where Lilibet, Margaret and their parents had lived, first at Royal Lodge and then, during the arduous war years, in the state apartments and the basement shelter.

As soon as she heard the news the queen threw on a raincoat and scarf and came from Buckingham Palace, Andrew accompanying her, to supervise the efforts to save the castle from complete destruc-tion. She had a cold, she had been spend-ing a quiet night alone until informed of the sudden outbreak of fire. It was her forty-fifth wedding anniversary, November 20, 1992, a chilly night. She stood in the lower ward of the castle, a small, aging figure, inconspicu-ous amid the coming and going of the 250 firefighters, the servants removing valu-ables, the play of water hoses and the bil-lowing thick smoke that made her cough.

Television cameras arrived to record the spectacular event. Andrew told the re-porters that his mother was "absolutely devastated." She looked lost, when she tried to speak her throat was hoarse. She watched, in horror, while portions of the roof surrounding the castle quadrangle collapsed and room after precious room was given over to the advancing flames.

Charles arrived from Sandringham, stayed a few hours, then left again. As his mother had good reason to know, only days earlier Charles had come to the painful decision that he had to end his marriage. He had talked to her about it, the decision was fresh and he dreaded the public announcement and the legal arrangements that would have to be arrived at.[1] He was under much strain, and could not stay at Lilibet's side or help in the work of salvaging valuables from the castle. Andrew, however, remained, and continued to oversee the fifteen-hour-long firefighting effort.

No one was injured, and many of the castle treasures, including hundreds of precious art works, were spared damage, being safely in storage. But some of the most magnificent of Windsor's grand rooms were gutted: the King's Drawing Room, Saint George's Hall, the Grand Reception Room, the Waterloo Chamber. Debris twelve feet deep clogged the charred hallways. Water damage ruined much of what the flames had failed to reach. Fine art and craftsmanship centuries old—elaborate painted and gilded ceilings, Grinling Gibbons carvings, rare tapestries and carpets, magnificent antique chandeliers—were gone forever, and with them, a lifetime of memories.

Had the fire occurred at any other time, Britons might have been willing to subsidize all or part of the cost of repairing the uninsured historic castle. But coming as it did on the heels of deepening royal scandal, and public disgust and alienation, with widespread calls for accountability, especially in the area of finance, on the part of the ruling family, there was sure to be resistance to using tax revenues to pay the sixty-million-pound restoration bill.* And tax revenues were much on the minds of critics of the monarchy, for the queen paid no tax and was under pressure to alter that time-honored custom. Arrangements had in fact been under way for months to end her exemption from tax, and shortly after the fire it was announced that henceforth she and Charles would both pay tax on their private incomes. The announcement appeared to be a capitulation, a response to coercion

---

* The cost of repairing Windsor Castle was later revised downward to forty million pounds.

from a hostile populace; it had the effect of worsening the royals' image, and dealing the queen's already lowered spirits another blow.

The ending of the Waleses' marriage (announced December 9), the shock of the devastating fire, more warnings from the press of embarrassing revelations yet to come about the younger royals, above all the worry that the secrets of the palace would no longer be protected: it was a great deal for Lilibet to endure, come to terms with, and try to surmount.[2]

More than ever, she was having to be the strong one in the family, providing a stable emotional fulcrum around which all the whirling conflict, anger and turmoil revolved.

Lilibet retired to Sandringham for the Christmas season in a sorrowful mood. She was grieving for Windsor, and for the loss of her intact family. (Diana was spending the holiday at Althorp with her relatives, Sarah was staying nearby, on the Sandringham estate grounds, but was not invited to come to Christmas dinner or join in any social activities.) The queen's pleasure at Anne's wedding to Tim Laurence that Christmas season was not sufficient to counterbalance her overall dismay. And to add to her stock of anxieties, her fragile sister, who at sixty-two was contrary and cantankerous in addition to being sunk in bitter self-pity, was taken to the hospital with pneumonia.

A sad Christmas gave way to a gloomy New Year, and then to a dismal shooting season. Lilibet's usual delight in her finely trained labradors and spaniels, and in her role as picker-up of dead and dying birds, was muted, then brought to an abrupt halt by the most startling and deeply mortifying news story yet to appear.

On January 13, 1993, a day that was to become known as "Black Wednesday," the palace press secretary Charles Anson was kept busy answering calls from reporters about an explosive transcript making the rounds of press offices. The queen's adviser Robert Fellowes called her about the transcript at seven in the morning, to let her know what was in it, and to prepare her for the media onslaught to come. It was, as dreaded, the record of a very personal phone conversation between Charles and Camilla, at bedtime, with Charles at his most vulnerable and immature and Camilla at her most loving and supportive.[3] Neither made mention of his or her spouse. At one point they joked, in the silly, adoring way lovers joke, about Camilla's "living inside his trousers" and Charles being reincarnated as a tampon. Foolish, trifling, inconsequential words that were another way of saying "I love every inch of your body and I need you."

Exposed to the world, however, the words and the unforgettable images they evoked became an instant tabloid classic, eclipsing all else about the royals. No one reported that Charles, just as the story broke, was in the Shetland Islands, on an environmental mission. A leaking oil tanker had spread tens of thousands of gallons of crude oil over the pristine beaches, and the prince was attempting to bring public attention to the tragedy and to the need for more regulation in the transport of oil. But where Charles was, and what he was doing, on Black Wednesday, were irrelevant; all that mattered was the intensely embarrassing exchange he had had with Camilla several years earlier, and that the whole world was now laughing over.

The indignity was beyond expression. Charles must have wondered whether he would ever be able to live down the shame. Reportedly he was having trouble sleeping, concentrating, maintaining any sort of emotional equilibrium.

And his mother, knowing his temperament, feared that he might break under the strain and imperil his standing still further by indulging in a regrettable outburst or making an ill-judged hasty decision or lashing out at those he thought were against him.

She knew what he was capable of, how self-centered and explosively demanding he could be, and she feared that he would ignore the larger issues at stake in this crisis and focus only on himself. In particular, she feared that he would fail to weigh the peril in which the monarchy itself stood, with a large percentage of the British public telling pollsters that the scandal, which was being called "Camillagate," had damaged the heir to the throne "very badly." Many people were saying they wanted Charles removed from the succession in favor of William. Several bishops, considering Charles unsuitable as a future king because of what they regarded as his contemptible private morals, were letting it be known that they too preferred William to succeed. ("Bloody cheek!" said Charles in response.)

By one count, the Camillagate story was front-page news in more than fifty countries. The once-venerable British monarchy, already cheapened by overmuch celebritizing, and outclassed by the much-admired Princess Diana, had shrunk still further under the sheer weight of global derision.

And where Lilibet herself, faced with such an overwhelming ground shift, had the presence of mind to make wry jokes about it (her punning reference to 1992 having been an "annus horribilis"—instead of an "annus mirabilis"—was a typical tongue-in-cheek, witty coinage, widely quoted), Charles was notably lacking in presence of mind—and lightness of tone.

If only Charles could be robust and combative, instead of cowardly and depressive! If only he could stand up and declare himself at fault—for he was clearly at fault, he had brought this shame on himself through his weakness for Camilla. If only he could see, and correct, all the harm that he had done.

But Charles, when he came to a family meeting at Sandringham four days after the transcript was published, was eaten up with humiliation and misery, reeling under the repeated blows of public contumely and ridicule. What he needed was solace—and rest, for he had been sleeping badly. Reportedly he had wild thoughts of running away to Italy, leaving all his responsibilities behind. He was angry, tired, snappish, wretched.

But he was not to be spared. The old rafters of Sandringham must have shaken that terrible day, January 17, when Philip brought the full weight of his loud fury to bear on his son.[4] Philip raved, the ninety-two-year-old queen mother preached about duty and moral responsibility, the queen, icy with anger, was critical.

"Whose side are you on, Mummy?" the miserable Charles burst out at one point.

She was on the side of preserving the dignity of the monarchy, of course. But how to do that? It was the elderly queen mother, stalwart and resolute yet emollient, who came up with what she called the "order of battle." She began that very day, by talking to Charles and encouraging him to muster the courage she knew he had deep within him, to gather his inner strength in order to do justice to his birthright.

It was the queen mother, not Lilibet, who talked to Charles nearly every day thereafter on the phone, encouraging him, walking that fine line a good parent must walk between correction and approval, chastisement and praise. And it was the queen mother who managed what was leaked to the press.

Lilibet deferred to her mother, letting her take charge of handling the delicate situation. Perhaps she was simply delegating a task she knew she could not carry out very well. Or perhaps she saw a certain appropriateness in letting her mother take the lead in attempting to guide Charles along his thorny path, believing, as she did, that it was in part her mother's overindulgence that had made Charles the man he was.

As ever, her own personal strength and resilience made Lilibet myopic when it came to the vulnerabilities of others. But there were limits to her strength. In the spring of 1993, she was about to turn sixty-seven. A spry, agile sixty-seven, to be sure. But sixty-seven all the same. Try as she might to fend them off, the blows of fate and time were beginning to show on her face and body. With close friends she admitted that the conflicts in her cross-grained family were eating at her, lowering her spirits. Charles was angry at her and defiant toward his father, Diana was in limbo, still legally part of the family yet an entity apart, separated from Charles, her enmity toward him having deepened following the Camillagate revelations.

Diana was, in fact, becoming the lodestar around which all the subterranean grievances against the Windsors gathered, and the government was worried lest the separation of the Waleses lead to a public demand for a reduction in the cost and role of the monarchy. With every fresh revelation, every nuance of slander, the monarchy was lowered in esteem. In May of 1993 old stories about Philip's infidelities were spread afresh in a talebearing book. Even Diana was not immune from exploitative gossip; her image was dented, but never truly damaged, and she retained her popularity.

Britain, however, had become tarnished in the world's eyes, its authority lessened. In

August the Australian prime minister, Paul Keating, met with the queen at Balmoral and told her that the time had come for her to cease to be the Australian head of state. Australia was on its way to becoming a republic, Keating said; a remote sovereign, reigning from thousands of miles away, was no longer needed. On hearing this, Lilibet reportedly remarked, "Now I really do need a very large drink."[5]

. She was to need more than a drink the following month, when she received word that Bobo, her lifetime confidante and companion, had died at the age of eighty-nine.

No one recorded how deep was the queen's wounding grief, whether she sought solitude or company in the days following her bereavement. For the loss of Bobo must have struck her like the loss of a beloved aunt or grandmother, a dearly loved and irreplaceable member of the family. Throughout her sentient life Lilibet had been nurtured, cared for, chided, consoled, and looked after by Bobo, whose patient solicitude had seen her through many a difficult year. Now that Bobo was gone, there was no one who could take her place.

Coming as it did at the end of a year of traumas, the loss of the queen's small, frail, trusted, dear old friend was the cruelest blow of all.

TWENTY-EIGHT

The mid-nineties were a time of turmoil and confusion, of hand-wringing and worry for the queen's staff. Charles Anson, press secretary from 1990 to 1997, has said that during his tenure at the palace he was constantly thinking "What on earth is going to happen today?"

It was as if, Anson has said, "you felt . . . you were in a tiny sailing boat in a huge storm and . . . the only thing to do was to batten every hatch, go below and sit it out."[1]

Yet at the center of the storm was the unvaryingly steady figure of the queen, maintaining her resilient, blithe exterior, never losing her "dry, wry sense of humor." Her steadiness calmed others, and reportedly the unswerving guidance of Robert Fellowes, her private secretary, calmed the queen herself.[2]

She managed, though inwardly sorrowful, to cope with the decisions both Charles and Diana made to give candid television interviews in which they admitted adultery and made themselves very human and very vulnerable—and ultimately, very appealing. As individuals they put their case before the British public, and in doing so, earned a measure of newfound respect. She strongly suggested that they divorce, and they did so, in 1996, inaugurating a new season of press and public speculation. Would Charles eventually marry Camilla? Would Diana remarry?

These questions eclipsed the public's interest in the queen, though she was still joked about and widely caricatured. Shy as she is, and knowing her limitations, Lilibet backed off still further, during the nineties, from attempting to engage with the (to her) incomprehensible forces shaping the postmodern world, and intruding into her family.

Often alone, and enjoying her solitude, she cultivated her favorite pastimes: watching wrestling matches on television, reading mysteries, studying thoroughbred pedigrees, doing *The Times* crossword puzzle (reputedly in four minutes flat). She hunted, stalked and shot in season, added to her collection of excellent rifles, looked forward to the spring racing season and to the multiple pleasures of breeding, supervising and racing her horses, always watchful for promising middle-distance three-year-olds.

Sinus pain and rheumatoid arthritis bothered her, and sometimes slowed her down. She became more self-indulgent where food and drink were concerned; she ate more chocolates with her Darjeeling at teatime, put mayonnaise on her salad and enjoyed her crème brûlée or oranges soaked in cognac. Bendicks mints were kept within reach.[3] A gin drink at midday and several martinis, or a glass of white German Spätlese in the evening, were her usual drinks.[4] Bobo was no longer there to sit alongside her tub while she bathed by candlelight, or to make certain that her red furry hot water bottle was at the right temperature when she went to bed. Nor was Bobo there to supervise all when she went on state visits. But her mother and Margaret were only a phone call away, and she was said to call often.

And her grandchildren, above all sensitive William and gregarious Harry, boys developing into strong lovers of the countryside like herself, were a source of pride and hope, though she was said to regret not being able to see more of them.

If, after reading the *Sporting News* and the *Financial Times*, the queen had time or energy left to read the remarks of her critics, especially those who condemned her for failing to be more assertive in her role as queen, for failing to lead and direct, rather than simply react and respond, she did not let any distress this might have caused her show. She had been true to the goal she set for herself at the outset of her reign, to imitate her father's style of kingship, a custodial rather than a pathfinding style. In choosing this mode she had honored her father, while at the same time setting herself a task that was within her capacities rather than beyond them.

She had avoided, despite constant temptation, the delusions of grandeur, the seductions of ego, the snare of pride.

And she had, after all, left her stamp, not only on her reign but on the world in the second half of the twentieth century.

It was the stamp of a well bred, self-contained, thoroughly regal woman, sensible and prudent, reserved but never repressed. A woman who had discovered, over the years, how and where to safely, and privately, let out her anger and frustration, find solace and renewal, and keep her wellspring of humor and youthful energy filled. And who was discovering how to accept the challenges of advancing age.

Amid masses of red and pink and white roses, blooming lilacs and yellow forsythia, the queen was making her way between waiting rows of guests at one of her garden parties. It was a sunny summer afternoon, she had driven down to the site of Fotheringhay Castle in Northamptonshire and was greeting people with her customary smiling cordiality. She stopped to talk to a blind man who had a guide dog with him.

She had always had a particular empathy for the blind, and her conversation with her unsighted guest was slightly longer than the usual brief exchange of questions and answers. As the queen and her subject conversed, the guide dog moved toward her, gazing up at her, until it rested against her side. Still talking to the master, she let her hand rest on the dog's head, petting it on head and ears.[5] It was an unconscious gesture, a reflex, the same reflex that came over her whenever she was in the vicinity of kennels—and that caused dogs who had never seen her before to jump into her arms unbidden. She drew them, as she did horses, without consciously trying. Her lifelong rapport with them remained strong into her seventies.

Her ability to attract and instinctively to understand dogs and horses remained strong—but her ability to understand her own people was about to undergo its greatest test.

When early in the morning of August 31, 1997, word reached the queen at Balmoral that Diana had been fatally injured in an auto accident in Paris, she failed to anticipate the enormity of the impact this would have on her subjects.

Overwhelmed with grief, Londoners came out into the streets in their tens of thousands, buying bouquets of flowers to leave at the gates of Kensington Palace and Buckingham Palace, crying, singing, striving to find comfort in the face of an overpowering sense of loss. The outpouring was unprecedented. Not since the death of Winston Churchill in 1965 had Britons shown such heartfelt sorrow. And in their sorrow, they expected their queen to comfort them by expressing the mood of national mourning.

Diana died on a Sunday morning. When by Tuesday no formal statement was forthcoming from Lilibet, sharp questions were being asked about her silence. An inaccurate press report that the queen had been opposed to having Charles go to Paris to escort Diana's body back to England darkened the public mood still further. In actuality, following the advice of Robert Fellowes Lilibet had ordered a royal aircraft plane sent to Paris with Charles aboard to fly Diana's body home, and had arranged for the body to lie in state in the Chapel Royal. Even though Diana was no longer Charles's wife, the queen decided to depart from precedent and allow the late princess a state funeral.

Despite these gestures, public complaint mounted, even as the full extent of the worldwide grief over Diana's death became apparent.[6] SHOW US YOU CARE, said the headline in the *Daily Express*. SPEAK TO US, MA'AM, said the *Mirror*.

"There has been no expression of sorrow from the queen on behalf of the nation," wrote the *Sun* solemnly. "Not one word has come from the royal lip, not one tear has been shed in public from a royal eye."[7]

More adverse press was forthcoming. The queen, it was said, had been opposed to giving Diana a public funeral, and to allowing her body to formally lie in state to receive the respects of the public. Old stories about conflict between Diana and her mother-in-law resurfaced. All the rumored and genuine enmities and pettiness from Diana's years within the Windsor family came up again—only now, in the light of Diana's death, the royals, and especially the queen, appeared cruel and heartless.

Meanwhile the swelling crowds in London grew larger, increased by tens of thousands pouring into the capital from all across the nation. By one estimate, nearly a million bouquets had been laid before the gates of Kensington Palace. England ran out of flowers. And still there had been no further word from the queen, who had remained in faroff Balmoral—giving an impression of unconcern.

A guest who was present at Balmoral for tea on that Tuesday afternoon, two days after the accident in Paris, recalls how irritable the queen was as she went about spooning her Darjeeling blend from the jade tea caddy and supervising its brewing, while the plates of egg and watercress sandwiches, scones and chocolate were handed around. She had been cautioned over the telephone by the lord chamberlain, Lord Airlie, who was in London, that she would be well advised to lower the Royal Standard to half mast.[8] Questions were being raised about why this had not been done, and the implication was being drawn, especially in newspaper reports, that in not ordering the flag lowered, Lilibet was showing disrespect to Diana's memory.

"The editors know perfectly well why the flag is not flying," the queen remarked. "The flagpole would still be bare even if Mummy or I had died. It never flies at half-mast." She was correct, of course—but others held the view that this was no time for niceties of protocol. It was the symbolic gesture that counted. And Londoners were angry.

The queen was stubborn. The flagpole remained bare, the Royal Standard was not flown. Another day passed, and the displeasure directed at the queen mounted—until at the urgent request of the sagacious Deputy Press Secretary Robert Janvrin and the sensible new young Labour Prime Minister, Tony Blair, Lilibet reluctantly agreed to a compromise. The Royal Standard would not be flown, but the Union flag would, at half-mast. Royal honor was satisfied, and the legion of mourners indicated a begrudging satisfaction. Still, the long delay in flying the flag was a small thing compared to the queen's long delay in leaving Scotland for London. Her reasons can only be guessed at, but she was certainly concerned for William and Harry, and wanted to keep them at Balmoral as long as possible to soothe their initial grief. Beyond that, she almost certainly felt proprietary about her own vacation, and was loath to shorten it. Yet in persisting in looking on Diana's death as a family matter rather than a national issue she was misreading her people, and making a serious error of judgment.

Not until Friday, September 5, did the royal family go to London and the queen, under heavy pressure, deliver a carefully worded speech referring to the "overwhelming expression of sadness" shown in response to the princess's death.

"It is not easy to express a sense of loss," she said, "since the initial shock is often succeeded by a mixture of other feelings: disbelief, incomprehension, anger—and concern for those who remain. We have all felt those emotions in these last few days." Her own mixed feelings came through, even though she paid tribute to Diana as "an exceptional and gifted human being." She did not, and could not, say that she had loved Diana, only that Diana had "made many, many people happy."[9]

Three billion people, by one estimate, watched Diana's funeral worldwide on September 9, 1997.

She was looking older. New lines of strain creased her forehead, there was a new and grim set to her narrowed mouth and a look of disapproval in her eyes. The millennial world was displeasing to Lilibet in many ways; like many in her generation she saw it as a distasteful hash of lowered cultural standards, lost civilities, violent clashes, family discord and a pervasive crumbling of patriotism and faith. The Britain of her childhood, with its deep and reassuring insularity, had been replaced by a new, confusing and disorienting Britain, one that borrowed heavily from America and from continental culture, one in which the young wandered in a fog of ignorance, having cast off the weight of the past.

It must have been difficult for her not to recall the old Britain, smaller and dirtier, smellier and more endowed with historic quaintness, and not to regret its loss, simply out of nostalgia.

Brisk and commonsensical as Lilibet was, knowing that it did no good to seek consolation in distant memories, the seductions of nostalgia must nonetheless have gnawed at her, the sweet and sour freight of memory closing in around her, as she aged. She saw how much her mother, who was ninety-seven, was relishing old age ("Things are much more fun past eighty," the queen mother liked to say) but at the same time was aware of her elderly sister's bitterness and physical and emotional pain.

Though four years younger than the queen, Margaret looked and acted like a much older woman, querulous and demanding, quarrelsome and insulting. Aggrieved for decades over her unpopularity, feeling misunderstood, isolated save for a few longsuffering friends, Margaret had lapsed into depression and wretchedness.

Philip, in his late seventies, was crusty and tortured by arthritis, liver spots marking his ever handsome forehead, but he had successfully traded sailing and polo playing for painting and photography, and continued to travel widely; he was making an intelligent adjustment to his advancing years.[10] Lilibet continued to ignore his flirtations, but was less tolerant when he took a stick to her corgis.

Bravely, pragmatically, taking one step at a time and one day at a time, the queen walked toward the abyss of the unknown future, keeping her thoughts and emotions to herself.

TWENTY-NINE

Others shivered in the chilly forty-degree November air but the queen, in her thin black cloth coat, showed no sign that she felt the cold as she bent down to plant a small wooden cross with a scarlet poppy in the Royal British Legion Field of Remembrance in Saint Margaret's churchyard. Her small cross was one of nearly twenty thousand planted there, each one a memorial to a fallen hero.

Those who noticed, as Lilibet stood for the moment of silence, that she was having difficulty keeping her composure assumed that her cross was being planted in memory of her mother, who had died seven months earlier at the age of a hundred and one. Or that it commemorated the passing of both her mother and her sister Margaret, dead at seventy-one, a stroke victim.

The queen's tears, and her somber expression as she walked slowly through the churchyard, looking down at the thousands of crosses, seemed to betoken a profound grief, far more sobering and more penetrating than any she had previously shown. For the queen to shed tears in public was an exceedingly rare event, her superb self-control and "tremendous buttoned-upness," as one of her ladies-in-waiting put it, were a byword in the royal household. Now, it seemed, she was showing the world how she truly felt—or she had reached a point in life where she no longer had the strength to conceal her feelings.

The scene at the Field of Remembrance in that first week of November, 2002, was solemn enough to draw forth tears from even the most self-contained visitor: the thousands of small crosses, the hundreds of uniformed war veterans and war widows and widowers present, the moving music and prayers for world peace—prayers offered up at a time when the airwaves were full of talk of war in the near future, and when the prime minister was vowing to send British troops to fight alongside American soldiers in a likely invasion of Iraq.

But Lilibet's sorrow and distress were prompted, watchers suspected, by more than her grief and the pathos of the scene before her.

For several days Paul Burrell, the trusted staff member who had been a footman at Buckingham Palace and then butler to Charles and Diana at Highgrove, had been revealing more and more private information about the royals to the *Mirror*, a catastrophe the queen had fervently hoped to avoid. It was a betrayal on the order of the first great staff betrayal, that of Lilibet and Margaret's governess Marion Crawford in *The Little Princesses*, published half a century earlier. But what Burrell was saying was much more intimate, more close to the bone, than anything Marion Crawford had ever written about the royal family.

Whatever measure of truth there was in the former footman and butler's revelations, they were causing a furor. Once again, Lilibet was at the center of a maelstrom of controversy. The chill of the November day was as nothing compared to the ice-storm of public disfavor she feared she would soon face.

Only the previous day, Wednesday, November 6, 2002, the *Mirror* had published Burrell's recollections of a three-hour meeting he claimed to have had with Lilibet after Diana's death, a meeting in which he said she cautioned him that he was in danger.[1] "There are powers at work in this country about which we have no knowledge," he quoted her as saying. She urged him to be vigilant, staring at him meaningfully. "I know what all her stares meant," Burrell told the *Mirror* reporter.

The *Mirror* articles were creating the impression that Burrell, a loyal servant who had devoted his life to royal service, had been, in his words "fed to the lions." Accused of stealing Diana's private effects, he had been abandoned by the queen (who knew him to be blameless) and allowed to suffer two years of stressful legal proceedings leading up to his trial. Then, suddenly, the queen had intervened to stop the trial, not—or so it was widely believed—in order to spare Burrell false prosecution but in order to protect palace secrets.

To the world, Lilibet looked devious, manipulative, heartless, selfish and despotic. A ruthless employer who would sacrifice her faithful employee without a qualm. A malevolent dowager standing atop a crumbling monarchical structure, a structure rotting away from the inside. And paranoid as well, unless her alleged remark about the sinister, shadowy "powers at work" could somehow be proven true.

Her intervention in the Burrell trial, an intervention that led to calls for a full government inquiry, lent credence to the growing belief that the palace establishment, over which she nominally presided, was a den of corruption and even sexual exploitation where illegality flourished and went unpunished. Burrell's testimony, had it been given, could have shed light on this shady institution, and those in charge of it. The queen herself could have been called to testify.

An ugly scenario was unfolding, based on the one-sided account by Paul Burrell and a growing number of accusatory articles in the press.

"The royal meeting which halted the trial," wrote Steve Dennis ("The Journalist Who Paul Burrell Really Trusts") in the *Mir-*

ror, "has led to speculation that the queen conveniently remembered the conversation just as Paul was about to take the witness stand, armed with secrets which could embarrass or damage the Windsors."

Burrell had been acquitted, but following his acquittal, he had begun to talk to the press. His lengthy disclosures had brought back the ghost of Diana, whom he had adored, and had reawakened memories of her—memories kept alive, since the princess's death, by countless articles and books and by conspiracy theories about just how and why she died—in the minds of his readers.

The monarchy was in deep trouble once again, and only months after the joyous, harmonious celebration of the queen's Golden Jubilee the previous June. Then the entire country had taken a break from grief, gloom and monarchy-bashing and had enjoyed the rock concerts and fireworks, the singing and general mood of rejoicing, with the smiling, gray-haired Lilibet the central, jubilant figure in the festivities.

Yet with the swiftness of an unexpected ice fog descending on the capital, the mood of rejoicing had vanished, and once again there were calls for an end to the monarchy, for investigations into royal wrongdoings, or at the very least, for the queen to pay for the expensive Paul Burrell trial out of her own pocket.

It was one more hurdle to jump in a life that had known so many hurdles. Coping, adjusting, had always been possible. A way had always been found.

Only recently Lilibet had managed to confront, and begin to surmount, what had seemed an impossible obstacle on the path to smooth relations with her son. The obstacle, of course, was Camilla.

Charles and Camilla had been living openly as a couple ever since Diana's death. But the queen would not receive Camilla, and would not retreat from her position—which was the position of the Church of England, of which she was head—that if Charles attempted to marry Camilla he could not then become king.

There seemed no way out of this conundrum. Lilibet was wedded to existing protocols and rules, and felt duty-bound to uphold them. Yet the country had undergone such a shift in mores that in time, both the monarchy and the church would surely have to adjust to the new realities. Meanwhile the queen's image was suffering; as the public was coming more and more to accept Camilla, Lilibet was being seen as a crusty, unfeeling, even spiteful holdout.

The first sign of thaw came when Press Secretary Robert Janvrin met Camilla on neutral ground, at the home of a mutual friend. Then the Archbishop of Canterbury, George Carey, who despite the church's prohibitions had accepted the divorce and remarriage of one of his own children, went to see Camilla and befriended her. And finally, quite unexpectedly, the queen decided to go to Highgrove for the sixtieth birthday party of the exiled King Constantine of Greece, well aware that Camilla would be present as hostess.

The informal meeting between the queen and Camilla set the royal seal of approval on Camilla as Charles's life companion. It was not yet an official acknowledgment, an invitation to Buckingham Palace. But it was an unofficial indication that there would be no further hardened opposition from the queen.

A most serious hurdle had been surmounted—and the result was a restoration of peace between Lilibet and her son.

Charles, who had increasingly come into his own in the past several years, was, by the fall of 2002, creating an impression of greater self-confidence and ease in life. The overstrained and fretful prince who had so exasperated and disappointed his mother had given way to a more assured and sanguine persona, more master of himself, a good father, a man more in command of his position and with a positive outlook on the future.

He was portrayed less often as a recluse with New Age tendencies and more often as a thoughtful, forward-looking visionary and philanthropist, artistic in his tastes and with a lavish magnificence to his lifestyle that was reminiscent of the late queen mother (who, at the time of her death, was in the habit of overdrawing her Civil List payment by millions of pounds a year, which Lilibet paid). His garages were full of Aston-Martins and Bentleys, and a costly Vantage, looked after by three chauffeurs. Thirty personal servants attended him when he left Highgrove.[2] At one sensational four-day party at Highgrove and Buckingham

Palace in Ascot Week of 2001, Charles and
Camilla entertained hundreds of celebrity
guests. In a spectacular huge tent flooded
with warm fuchsia light, the ceiling illuminated to resemble the night sky, prominent
and wealthy visitors—from Donald Trump to
Queen Noor to Steve Forbes to Elton
John—dined on asparagus with quail's
eggs and noisettes of lamb, all from the or-
ganic Highgrove farm.[3]

The queen was not among the guests on
that memorable night, her presence would
have necessitated an unwelcome formality
and uncomfortable questions of etiquette
where Camilla was concerned. Besides, if
she had been there Charles would not have
been able to tell his rather unflattering stories about her. All were agreed, the prince
was better entertaining on his own. His lavish parties, his newfound self-confidence,
were hints that the torch was passing.
There was no more talk about the queen
abdicating or Charles stepping aside to allow William to be heir apparent. The succession would take its natural course, in
due season.

That the year 2002 marked a change of
season for the queen must have been much

on her mind as she walked through the Field of Remembrance on that raw November 7, after the memorial service had ended and all the medals had been awarded. Until this year it had always been her mother's task to preside at the annual memorial service, a fitting role for one who had nursed wounded soldiers in World War I and survived some of the worst bombing raids of World War II. Gracious and warm, her face alight with genuine affection, the queen mother had stood beside the veterans and surviving spouses with a quiet poise, year after year, her benign presence a benison. Lilibet, by contrast, was stiff, slightly remote, somehow distant and detached from the others even when at her most moved.

She could not be what her mother had been, but it was now up to her to be the female head of the family, in her own style and with her own solid gifts to offer. She had become the elderly matriarch, first in line to preside at ceremonies such as this one—and next in line to face growing enfeeblement and death.

Perhaps, as the afternoon wore on, a slight shiver passed through the queen's still sturdy frame. For the air was growing colder, and she was all too aware, standing in the shadow of the old church, that she stood alone, a small figure in a field of tiny crosses, in the middle of London, at the opening of the twentieth-first century, in a lost and uncertain time.

NOTES

CHAPTER ONE

1. Denis Judd, *King George VI, 1895–1952* (New York: Franklin Watts, 1983), p. 94.

CHAPTER TWO

1. Judd, p. 87.
2. Anne Ring, *The Story of Princess Elizabeth* (London: John Murray, 1930), pp. 23–24.
3. Lisa Sheridan, *From Cabbages to Kings* (London: Odhams, 1955), p. 36. This and other passages in Lisa Sheridan's autobiography were very likely approved by the palace before publication. Still, Sheridan was a far less tame, and far more perceptive, observer than Anne Ring.

CHAPTER THREE

1. Martin Gilbert, *Winston S. Churchill: The Exchequer Years* (1979), p. 1349.
2. Osbert Sitwell, *Rat Week* (London: Michael Joseph, 1984), p. 44.
3. J. Colville, *Strange Inheritance* (Salisbury: Michael Russell, 1983), p. 109.
4. Ring, p. 74.
5. *Ibid.*, p. 87.
6. *Ibid.*, p. 90.
7. Contemporary newspapers reported that she was given a pony at Christmas 1929, but these accounts were premature; the pony was given her either for her fourth birthday, in April of 1930, or at Christmas 1930. Horace Smith, *A Horseman Through Six Reigns: Reminiscences of a Royal Riding Master* (London: Odhams, 1955), p. 143, wrote that she received the pony at Christmas 1930, at the age of four and a half.
8. Marion Crawford, *The Little Princesses* (New York: Bantam, 1952), p. 13. Although Crawfie wrote that she came to work for the royal family in 1933, she wrote elsewhere that she began teaching Lilibet when the latter was "not yet six." Lilibet turned six years old on April 21, 1932. Crawford, *Little Princesses*, pp. 17, 14, 20.
9. *Ibid.*, pp. 49, 52, 40.
10. *Ibid.*, pp. 28–29.

11. Sheridan, p. 34.
12. Ben Pimlott, *The Queen: A Biography of Elizabeth II* (London: HarperCollins, 1996; paperback 1997), p. 29. References are to the paperback edition.
13. Marion Crawford thought Lilibet resembled her reserved, quiet father rather than her warm, ingratiating mother. Crawford, *Little Princesses*, p. 66.
14. *Ibid.*, p. 50.
15. *Ibid.*, p. 36.
16. Herbert T. Fitch, *Memoirs of a Royal Detective* (London: Hurst and Blackett, 1935), p. 123. Very likely there were other such incidents, tactfully omitted, out of deference, from eyewitness accounts of Lilibet as a child.
17. Crawford, *Little Princesses*, p. 96.
18. *Ibid.*, p. 26.
19. This description of 145 Piccadilly comes from Sheridan, pp. 66ff.

CHAPTER FOUR

1. Crawford, *Little Princesses*, p. 77.
2. *Ibid.*
3. Sheridan, p. 60. Lilibet confided this to Sheridan.
4. Crawford, *Little Princesses*, p. 20.
5. *Ibid.*, pp. 45–46.
6. Sheridan, pp. 34–35.

7. Crawford, *Little Princesses*, p. 49.
8. *Ibid.*
9. *Ibid.*, p. 33. Crawfie wrote of Uncle David, when Lilibet was three or four years old, that he was "a devoted slave to her."
10. *Ibid.*, pp. 55, 57.
11. In February of 1936, according to Ernest Simpson's friend Bernard Rickatson-Hatt, Ernest and David arrived at an agreement about Wallis's future; Ernest would allow Wallis to divorce him and David would give up other women permanently and devote himself to Wallis's welfare. It was the turning point in the royal infatuation. By June, 1936, David intended to marry Wallis and she intended to file for divorce, though she did not do so for some months, and was to have second thoughts. Michael Bloch, ed., *Wallis and Edward: Letters 1931–1937* (New York: Summit Books, 1986), pp. 200–2.
12. There may well have been another reason for distress within the royal family that spring and summer. Sir Edward Robert-Peacock, a director of the Bank of England, told the American ambassador Joseph Kennedy in June of 1938 that during Edward VIII's reign, the royals "had evidence Wallie [sic] was having an affair with a young man." (Files in the Public Record Office released just as these notes are being sent to the publisher would seem to confirm this.) Compounding their dread of Wallis's

hold over the king was their private knowledge, or at least their belief, that she was betraying him with another man. Joseph P. Kennedy, *Hostage to Fortune: The Letters of Joseph P. Kennedy*, ed. Amanda Smith (New York: Viking, 2001), p. 263.

13. Crawford, *Little Princesses*, p. 56.
14. Bloch, pp. 220, 227.
15. *Ibid.*, pp. 233–35.
16. Crawford, *Little Princesses*, p. 57.
17. Elizabeth Longford, *Elizabeth R* (London: Weidenfeld & Nicolson, 1983), p. 68 note, citing Godfrey Talbot in a 1983 radio program.
18. D. Hart-Davis, ed., *Royal Service: The Letters and Journals of Sir Alan Lascelles, 1920–1936*, Vol. 2 (London: Hamish Hamilton, 1989), pp. 201–2; Sarah Bradford, *Elizabeth: A Biography of Britain's Queen* (New York: Farrar Straus & Giroux, 1996; paperback edition, Riverhead Books, 1997), p. 56. All references to Bradford are from the paperback edition.
19. J. Bryan and C. V. Murphy, *The Windsor Story* (London: Granada, 1979), p. 273.
20. Elizabeth Longford, *The Queen Mother* (New York: William Morrow, 1981), p. 54.

CHAPTER FIVE

1. Crawford, *Little Princesses*, p. 69.
2. *Ibid.*, pp. 18–19.
3. *Ibid.* Crawfie wrote that the horse games

"went on for years," even after such childish pastimes seemed inappropriate.

4. Pimlott, pp. 44–46.
5. Crawford, *Little Princesses,* p. 74.
6. R. Rhodes-James, ed., *Chips Channon: The Diary of Sir Henry Channon* (London: Weidenfeld & Nicolson, 1967), p. 13.
7. Crawford, *Little Princesses*, pp. 39, 29.
8. *Ibid.*, p. 85.
9. *Ibid.*; Sheridan, pp. 108ff.
10. Crawford, *Little Princesses*, pp. 78–79.
11. Smith, p. 144.
12. *Ibid.*, p. 145.
13. Crawford, *Little Princesses*, p. 90.

CHAPTER SIX

1. Marion Crawford, *Queen Elizabeth II* (London: George Newnes Ltd., 1952), p. 49. Lilibet confided to the painter Pietro Annigoni that she had spent many hours in the Yellow Drawing Room of Buckingham Palace, looking out of the window. "I loved watching the people and the cars there in the Mall," she said. "They all seemed so busy. I used to wonder what they were doing and where they were all going, and what they thought about outside the palace."
2. The weekend is described in Crawford, *Little Princesses,* pp. 101–5. Crawford recalls the date as August, 1939; John Parker, *Prince Philip: A Critical Biography* (London: Sidgwick

and Jackson, 1990), pp. 72–73, dates it in July.

3. Parker, *Philip*, pp. 72–73. Mountbatten called the College Commandant, Rear Admiral Freddy Dalrymple-Hamilton, before the royal visit and suggested that Philip could be appointed captain's messenger that weekend, which would keep him close to the royal family. During the weekend itself, Mountbatten remarked that Philip might be sent "to amuse the girls."

4. Crawford, *Little Princesses*, pp. 86–87.

5. Longford, *Elizabeth R*, pp. 16–17.

6. Pimlott, p. 53.

7. Donald Spoto, *The Decline and Fall of the House of Windsor* (New York: Simon & Schuster, 1995), p. 314.

8. Kennedy, pp. 252, 329. Kennedy gave Lilibet frames from *Pinocchio,* autographed by Walt Disney, for her thirteenth birthday. She had told him "how she loved Dopey and knew his song in French," adding "Though he would look pretty funny working as an Italian." Kennedy, pp. xviii, 329. Rose Kennedy thought Lilibet was "natural" and "simple," though she had the reputation of being spoiled. Kennedy, p. 331.

9. Crawford, *Little Princesses*, pp. 43, 70–71.

10. *Ibid.*, p. 94.

11. *Ibid.*, p. 108.

12. *Ibid.*, pp. 111, 120.

13. Longford, *Queen Mother*, p. 88; Judd, pp. 185–86; Crawford, *Little Princesses*, p. 45.
14. Parker, *Philip*, citing Unity Hall, *Philip: The Man Behind the Monarchy* (London: Michael O'Mara, 1987), p. 34. Lilibet's comment is in Crawford, *Little Princesses*, p. 119.
15. Sheridan, p. 93.
16. Smith, p. 145, 148; Crawford, *Little Princesses,* p. 119.
17. George VI, who had been suspecting his brother the Duke of Windsor of "trying to stage a comeback" for three years, now had reason to be even more alarmed. British intelligence had learned that the German government had approached David in Lisbon, in the summer of 1940, to keep himself in readiness for a return to the throne, and had deposited fifty million Swiss francs in an account for his use. There was also a Nazi plot to kidnap the duke. In the end, he decided to accept Churchill's offer of the governorship of the Bahamas. Parker, *Philip*, pp. 70, 108, 259.

The abdication of Edward VIII had a very distinct political dimension. Political opposition to David's proposed marriage to Wallis was grounded in well-founded fears that the monarchy would become even more strongly pro-German. David's own outspoken right-wing views were an increasingly serious problem to the government. (The king called the League of Nations a "farce" and wanted an alliance with the Führer; when questioned about whether talks between Prime Minister Baldwin and Hitler would be advantageous, David remarked, "Who is king here? Baldwin or I? I myself wish to talk to Hitler, and will do so, here or in Germany.") Christopher Hibbert, *The Court of St. James's: The Monarch at Work from Victoria to Elizabeth II* (London: Weidenfeld & Nicolson, 1979), pp. 90–91.

David's rash and ill-considered impulses, not to mention his disregard of constitutional law, were perceived as threats to Britain's ability to cope with fascist aggression. In actuality, when after their marriage the Duke and Duchess of Windsor visited Germany they were disillusioned. Longford, *Elizabeth R*, p. 76.

18. Crawford, *Little Princesses*, p. 117.
19. Richard Overy *The Battle of Britain: The Myth and the Reality* (New York and London: W. W. Norton, 2000), p. 140.
20. Hibbert, *Court of St. James's*, pp. 128–29.
21. "Uncle Charlie," Duke of Saxe-Coburg-Gotha, was a grandson of Queen Victoria, educated at Eton and a member of the Nazi party. He was King George VI's first cousin once removed. The duke had been Hitler's emissary to the Windsor court in the 1930s. *Ibid.*, pp. 90–91.
22. Overy, p. 35.
23. *Ibid.*, p. 162. On June 30, 1940, the Royal Air

Force had twelve hundred pilots to the Luft-waffe's nine hundred; by mid-September the number of British pilots had gone up to 1,492 while the Germans had only 735. Each month the totals became more lopsided. Churchill's memorable reference to the "few" Royal Air Force pilots was effective rhetoric, but a dis-tortion of the military situation.

CHAPTER SEVEN

1. Crawford, *Little Princesses*, pp. 153–54. Crawford did not reveal his name.
2. Mabel Airlie, *Thatched with Gold: The Memoir of Mabel Countess of Airlie*, ed. J. Ellis (London: Hutchinson, 1962), p. 223.
3. Helen Cathcart in *The Daily Mirror*, November 9, 1970. Philip maintained that he wrote regularly, but others noted that the letters were infrequent.
4. Parker, *Philip*, pp. 86–87. Helene Cordet became pregnant in March, 1943, and her son Max was born at an expensive nursing home in Maidenhead, an arrangement well beyond her means. Max's paternity is uncertain and there are lingering suggestions that Philip may have been the father.
5. Sheridan, p. 115.
6. *Ibid.*, pp. 115ff.
7. Crawford, *Little Princesses*, p. 163.
8. Smith, pp. 146–47.

9. Sheridan, pp. 107–8.

10. Crawford, *Little Princesses*, p. 155.

11. *Ibid.*, pp. 157, 154–55.

12. *Ibid.*, pp. 156–57.

13. *Ibid.*, p. 66. Marion Crawford wrote that this was the only time she observed Lilibet let down her guard emotionally. Her grandmother Cecelia, Lady Strathmore had died in 1938 at the age of seventy-six.

14. Crawford, *Little Princesses*, pp. 197, 182; Airlie, *Thatched with Gold*, p. 225; Longford, *Elizabeth R*, p. 96. Margaret told an interviewer during the sixties that in her childhood, Lilibet was perceived as the "goody-goody one" while she was characterized by the press as "wicked as hell." A. Duncan, *The Reality of Monarchy* (London: Heinemann, 1970), p. 124. But it wasn't only a press perception; Marion Crawford found Margaret to be all but ungovernable, and as she got older, unteachable.

15. John W. Wheeler-Bennett, *King George VI: His Life and Reign* (New York: St. Martin's Press, 1958), p. 749.

16. By law all descendants of Electress Sophia of Hanover, whose son George was the first Hanoverian monarch of Great Britain, were British citizens; Philip was among Sophia's descendants. Mountbatten's eagerness to expedite an engagement between Philip and Lilibet is evident in the contemporary letters

and documents. His hurry may have resulted from worries that if the couple did not become engaged before the end of the war, embarrassing revelations about Philip's Nazi brothers-in-law would prevent an engagement from ever coming about. Parker, *Philip*, p. 91.

CHAPTER EIGHT

1. Crawford, *Little Princesses*, p. 182.
2. *Ibid*., pp. 167–68.
3. Ann Morrow, *The Queen* (London: Granada, 1983), pp. 135–36, describes how Lilibet's course was one specially designed for her, less than a month long, omitting such topics as camouflage, gas and "domestic economy." "We didn't want to make her look a fool," one of Lilibet's fellow-"students" recalled, "but we got ticked off after the first two or three lectures because we weren't asking questions. You felt a bit silly asking about plugs when you had been telling students about these things for a couple of years." The same informant told Ann Morrow that the other girls had a bad opinion of Margaret, who somehow showed up from time to time, finding her to be "a jealous, tiresome little girl, always needling her older sister."
4. Bradford, *Elizabeth*, pp. 107–8.
5. Morrow, *The Queen*, p. 137.
6. Parker, *Philip*, pp. 45–47.

7. Christopher of Hesse died in a plane crash in 1942. Mountbatten asserted that Christopher, an ardent Nazi, had become disenchanted with Hitler and that a bomb had been put aboard his plane by the Germans in order to eliminate him. There is no evidence to support this view. Parker, *Philip*, p. 91.

8. *Ibid.*, p. 103.

9. Sarah Bradford, *King George VI, A Life* (London: Weidenfeld & Nicolson, 1989), p. 420.

10. Crawford, *Little Princesses*, p. 174.

11. *Ibid.*, p. 171.

12. Smith, p. 151.

13. Crawford, *Little Princesses*, p. 189.

14. *Ibid.*, pp. 188–90.

15. *Ibid.*, pp. 193–94.

CHAPTER NINE

1. Crawford, *Little Princesses*, pp. 177–78.

2. Pamela Mountbatten-Hicks, in an interview in the 1990s, recalled being "sure" that her father actually proposed to George VI that Philip marry Lilibet. Deborah Hart Strober and Gerald S. Strober, *The Monarchy: An Oral Biography of Elizabeth II* (New York: Broadway Books, 2002), p. 66. According to Philip Ziegler, Mountbatten liked to say that he had orchestrated Lilibet's marriage to Philip. "He was an ardent matchmaker," Ziegler said. "He devoted a large part of his prodigious energies to

arranging marriages, particularly of royalty. . . .
He had undoubtedly tried to claim the credit
for having organized the royal marriage."
Ziegler added that George VI thought that
Mountbatten was doing everything he could to
push the relationship between Philip and Lilibet along. Strober and Strober, p. 71.
3. Philip Ziegler, *Mountbatten* (London: Collins,
1985), p. 457.
4. Crawford, *Little Princesses*, p. 203.
5. Parker, *Philip*, p. 113; Hugo Vickers, *Alice:
Princess Andrew of Greece* (London: Hamish
Hamilton, 2000), p. 324.
6. Parker, *Philip*, p. 121.
7. Crawford, *Little Princesses*, p. 214.

CHAPTER TEN

1. *The Wedding of Her Royal Highness Princess
Elizabeth and Lieutenant Philip Mountbatten,
R.N., Souvenir Programme*, p. 6.
2. Crawford, *Little Princesses*, p. 235.
3. At some point in the honeymoon, the couple
returned to Buckingham Palace to get a special dog leash. Morrow, *The Queen*, p. 37.
4. Parker, *Philip*, p. 130.
5. S. G. Bocca, *Elizabeth and Philip* (New York:
Henry Holt & Co., 1953), p. 56.
6. Kitty Kelley, *The Royals* (New York: Warner
Books, 1987), pp. 81–82.
7. Parker, *Philip*, pp. 138–39.

8. Crawford, *Little Princesses*, p. 242.
9. Vickers, p. 332, quotes Philip's Aunt Louise telling Philip's mother Alice that Lilibet had "a hard time," thirty hours of labor.
10. Anthony Holden, *Charles, Prince of Wales* (London: Weidenfeld & Nicolson, 1979), p. 53.
11. Stanley Clark, *Palace Diary* (New York: Dutton, 1958), pp. 40–41.
12. *Ibid*., pp. 42–44.
13. Kelley, p. 92.

CHAPTER ELEVEN

1. Strober and Strober, p. 6. Mike Parker's account is in Strober and Strober, pp. 4–5. My account of the events of February 6, 1952, draws on Dorothy Laird, *How the Queen Reigns* (London: Pan, 1959), pp. 19ff; Clark, pp. 69–70; and Longford, *Elizabeth R*, pp. 137–140, which contains some inaccuracies.
2. Strober and Strober, p. 125, Bishop Michael Mann's recollection.
3. *Ibid*., p. 24.
4. Longford, *Elizabeth R*, p. 157.
5. Spoto, p. 334.
6. Laird, pp. 47–48.
7. Strober, p. 194.
8. Spoto, p. 335.
9. Ann Morrow, *The Queen Mother* (New York: Stein and Day, 1985), pp. 225–26.
10. Cited in Bradford, *Elizabeth*, p. 157.

11. Clark, p. 82, lists 140 engagements carried out by the queen between her accession in February, 1952 and June 1, 1952; between June 1 and December 31 of that year she carried out 308 more. Presuming another 40 to 50 appearances in January, 1953, this brings the total for the first year of her reign to approximately five hundred.

CHAPTER TWELVE

1. In his *Selected Speeches*, Prince Philip discusses the queen's long days of official activity and rehearsals ending in tears of nervous exhaustion. Parker, *Philip*, p. 162.
2. Parker, *Philip*, p. 162.
3. Though it is often stated that the queen was in favor of having television cameras present at the coronation, unpublished records indicate that she was initially opposed to the idea. Bradford, *Elizabeth*, pp. 181–83; Pimlott, pp. 205–6. Even after the coronation Lilibet remained wary of television broadcasting.
4. K. McLeish and V. McLeish, *Long to Reign Over Us: Memories of Coronation Day and of Life in the 1950s* (London: Bloomsbury, 1992), p. 133.
5. Elizabeth Longford, *The Pebbled Shore: The Memoirs of Elizabeth Longford* (New York: Knopf, 1986), p. 286.
6. Clark, p. 115 and *passim*.

7. *Ibid.*, p. 118.
8. Cecil Beaton, *The Strenuous Years: Diaries 1948–1955* (London: Weidenfeld & Nicolson, 1973), p. 148.

CHAPTER THIRTEEN

1. Bill Curling, *All the Queen's Horses* (London: Chatto & Windus, 1978), p. 30.
2. One modern historian has noted that "Churchill's lack of grasp on ordinary business was becoming embarrassing even to those of his colleagues whose names he could remember." Peter Clarke, *Hope and Glory: Britain 1900–1990* (London: Allen Lane, The Penguin Press, 1996), p. 246.
3. Margaret has said that the precise constitutional situation where her potential marriage was concerned was never fully explained to the couple and that if it had been, along with the hopelessness of any change if she waited to marry until she reached twenty-five, Townsend would have "departed" and the relationship would have ended. Longford, *Elizabeth R*, p. 151.
4. Parker, *Philip*, p. 139. Adler told Parker that from the earliest years of his marriage Philip moaned regularly about his "moral straitjacket" and felt bitter about the outward signs of his subordination, such as having to walk behind his wife. "He didn't like that; he just

didn't like it at all." According to Donald Spoto, p. 333, Philip, looking back over the course of his life, said "I'd much rather have stayed in the navy, frankly."

5. Charles Higham and Roy Moseley, *Elizabeth and Philip: The Untold Story of the Queen of England and Her Prince* (New York: Doubleday, 1991), p. 207; Parker, *Philip*, p. 141.

6. Strober and Strober, p. 109.

7. Kelley, p. 154.

8. Strober and Strober, p. 109.

9. Higham and Moseley, p. 186.

10. Larry Adler told his interviewers that "At first I thought he [Philip] was in love with her. I think then the job got to him. I think it was inevitable that he could not sustain that love. It evolved. I believe he still [in the late 1990s] respects the queen. And he does everything else correctly, except for those gaffes he makes when he goes overseas." Strober and Strober, p. 72.

11. Dorothy Laird, a journalist who spent a great deal of time with Lilibet in the early years of her marriage, wrote that "particularly in the early days of Princess Elizabeth's public appearances, there was a marked difference in her ability to be at ease according to whether her husband was, or was not, with her." Laird, p. 46.

12. Morrow, *The Queen*, p. 35.

13. Bocca, p. 101.

CHAPTER FOURTEEN

1. Churchill's comment is in Keith Kyle, *Suez* (New York: St. Martin's Press, 1991), p. 40; Eden's is in Evelyn Shuckburgh, *Descent to Suez* (London: Weidenfeld & Nicolson, 1986), 12 March 1956.
2. Philip Ziegler, cited in Strober and Strober, p. 192, recalled in an interview that the queen "found Eden difficult—who didn't?"
3. Pimlott, p. 255, citing a confidential interview with a former palace aide. Eden's overexcited, nervous state was an indication of how serious the crisis was, and to what extremes the government was prepared to go to achieve its aims. According to the Egypt Committee of the cabinet, the government's goal was to bring about the downfall of Nasser's regime. Kyle, p. 148.

   Peter Wright, a scientist with MI5 in 1956, writes in his book *Spycatcher* that plans to assassinate Nasser were considered on two occasions during the months following the Egyptian president's seizure of the canal. *Spycatcher: The Candid Autobiography of a Senior Intelligence Officer* (New York: Viking Penguin, 1987), pp. 84–85, 160–61.
4. Kyle, pp. 68–69.
5. *Ibid*.
6. One of those close to the queen told biographer Sarah Bradford that her private view was

that the invasion was "idiotic." Bradford, *Elizabeth*, p. 234. Martin Charteris recalled that she had a "less than neutral position," on the negative side. Pimlott, p. 255.

7. Pimlott, p. 255, citing a confidential interview.
8. "When her majesty is unwell, madam," said a palace footman to an ill guest at one of the queen's banquets, "she sometimes finds that Malvern water helps." Morrow, *The Queen*, p. 123.
9. Parker, *Philip,* p. 176.
10. *Ibid*.
11. There were stories of Philip sharing a London apartment with actor Richard Todd and two other married men, the three calling themselves the "Three Cocketeers." Also of Philip making use of Parker's South Street apartment for private meetings. Kelley, pp. 152–53.
12. Longford, *Elizabeth R*, p. 181.
13. Parker, *Philip*, p. 171, repeats gossip that Margaret hurled slander at Philip, revealing a current story that he had had a car accident when driving with a woman, and that news of the accident had been suppressed. According to Parker, Lilibet refused to believe the slander and was angry at her sister. The account is plausible, given the attitudes and past history of the personalities involved, but cannot be verified. Margaret had been at odds with Philip ever since 1953, and probably earlier;

Philip hated Townsend and was vehemently opposed to Margaret's marrying him.

14. This account of the commotion in Crathie churchyard during the fête of August 1955 is based on Clark, p. 176, and Helene Cathcart, *Her Majesty the Queen* (New York: Dodd Mead, 1962), pp. 180–81.

CHAPTER FIFTEEN

1. Bocca, pp. 5–6.
2. Clarke, p. 263. On British and French collusion with Israel at the time of the Suez invasion, Clarke, pp. 260–61, and Kyle, pp. 516–17.
3. This digest of criticisms is drawn from Lord Altrincham, in *The National and English Review* (August, 1957), Malcolm Muggeridge, in *The New Statesman* (1956), and John Osborne, in *Encounter* (August, 1957).
4. Letters to the *Daily Mirror* showed that the public agreed with Lord Altrincham by a proportion of four to one. Letters to the *Daily Mail* ran 55% against Altrincham, 45% for him. A national opinion poll revealed that 35% of the population—40% of men—were on Altrincham's side in the debate over the queen's defects. Philip Ziegler, *Crown and People* (London: Collins, 1978), p. 131.
5. Longford, *Pebbled Shore*, p. 299.
6. Kennedy, p. 253. The queen mother's sister

was Mary Frances Bowes-Lyon, wife of Sidney Herbert, 16th Baron Elphinstone.

7. Pimlott, p. 242.

8. Details of Buckingham Palace etiquette and minutiae are drawn from Hibbert, *Court of St. James's*, pp. 174, 178 and *passim*; Andrew Morton, *Inside Buckingham Palace* (New York: Summit Books, 1991), p. 56; Morrow, *The Queen*, p. 94; Laird, p. 82; and Bradford, *Elizabeth*, p. 150.

9. Lady Cynthia Colville, lady-in-waiting at the palace in Queen Mary's time, cautioned her son Jock Colville to stay away from royal service, which she called a "gilded cage." Those who enter the royal household, she said, lose contact with reality and the world outside. Longford, *Elizabeth R*, p. 115.

10. Hibbert, *Court of St. James's*, p. 218.

11. "When she is deeply moved," wrote Richard Crossman, "and tries to control it she looks like an angry thundercloud. So, very often when she's been deeply touched by the plaudits of the crowd she merely looks terribly bad-tempered." *Ibid.*, p. 218.

12. Interview in Strober and Strober, p. 139.

13. Morrow, *The Queen*, p. 98.

14. *Ibid.*, p. 2.

15. Hibbert, *Court of St. James's*, p. 162; Strober and Strober, p. 142, citing an anonymous military official.

CHAPTER SIXTEEN

1. Graham Turner, *Elizabeth: The Woman and the Queen* (London: Telegraph Books, 2002), pp. 71–74.
2. Lilibet regretted that Charles's nanny destroyed those letters; future biographers, once the queen's papers are made available, will regret it too.
3. Crawford, *Little Princesses*, p. 241.
4. Laird, p. 52.
5. Strober and Strober, pp. 438–39. "She treated Charles very nicely," a member of the royal household told Graham Turner, "but she was never warm. There were no open arms, no hugs. I can hardly ever remember her kissing him." Turner, p. 115. "She didn't spend anything like enough time in the family," a former private secretary of the queen confided. A retired courtier summed up Lilibet's mothering as "utterly, utterly lacking." Turner, p. 114.
6. Parker, *Philip*, p. 238.
7. Turner, p. 107, citing the queen's friend and secretary Martin Charteris.
8. *Ibid.*, p. 11, citing an unnamed retired courtier.
9. Kenneth Rose, *Kings, Queens and Courtiers* (London: Weidenfeld & Nicholson, 1985), p. 236. Although the surname Mountbatten-Windsor was intended to apply only to the queen's descendants in the male line, and only to begin in the third generation—i.e., to

come into use by Charles's and Andrew's (and later Edward's) grandchildren—in actuality Anne, who is, of course, a Royal Highness, adopted the name when she married in 1973.

10. See note 2, Chapter 24.

CHAPTER SEVENTEEN

1. A. N. Wilson, *The Rise and Fall of the House of Windsor* (London: Sinclair-Stevenson, 1993), p. 79.
2. Cited in Hibbert, *Court of St. James's* p. 161. Hibbert, who knew Crossman personally, thought that he lacked a sense of humor.
3. *Ibid.*, p. 163.
4. Strober and Strober, p. 198.
5. Joe Haines said that more than once, the prime minister returned from his weekly audience having "had a whiskey or two too many with [the queen]—she liked to drink, and she liked to gossip; they were both gossips." *Ibid.*, pp. 198–99.
6. Morrow, *The Queen*, p. 166.
7. Philip's remark to the queen's shoemaker is in Rose, p. 238. The queen's hand-wringing is described by Morton, *Inside Buckingham Palace*, p. 41. At some point Elizabeth began to suffer from rheumatoid arthritis in her finger-joints.
8. Morton, *Inside Buckingham Palace*, p. 37.
9. Curling, p. 74.

10. Strober and Strober, p. 140.
11. Hibbert, *Court of St. James's*, p. 171.
12. Laird, pp. 88–89.
13. Rose, p. 89.
14. Morrow, *The Queen*, p. 102.
15. Laird, p. 48.
16. Parker, *Philip*, p. 226. Between 1960 and 1972, European newspapers reported, by one count, that Elizabeth was about to abdicate (sixty-three times), that she was on the verge of divorcing Philip (seventy-three times) and that she was pregnant (ninety-three times).
17. *Ibid.*, pp. 240ff. Philip hired the celebrated American PR man Henry Rogers to try to improve his much besmirched reputation, and Nigel Nielson was hired to work on the image of the heir to the throne. The monarchy had embarked on the slippery slope of self-conscious celebrity.

CHAPTER EIGHTEEN

1. Kelley, p. 160, wrote, citing no source, that in 1957 Lilibet consulted a psychiatrist three times. If the queen did visit a psychiatrist, it would appear that either she became disillusioned with the process or decided she didn't need further consultations. A friend of Lilibet's told the journalist Ann Morrow that "she is herself and, of all the people in that age group,

less of a mess—the queen knows herself."
Morrow, *The Queen*, p. 6.
2. Morrow, *The Queen*, p. 114.
3. Queen Elizabeth has done a remarkable job of "seeing and being seen." Of the many Britons and Canadians I have met over the years—and quite a few Australians—a surprisingly large number have anecdotes to tell about when the queen came to their town or city and they saw her, or spoke with her briefly on one of her walkabouts, or had relatives who spoke with her. She has made a personal impression on countless numbers of people in many parts of the world.
4. Details of the queen's visit to Nigeria are in Cathcart, *Her Majesty the Queen*, p. 187. Her traveling entourage is described in Morrow, *The Queen*, pp. 111, 118.
5. Cathcart, *Her Majesty the Queen*, p. 187.
6. *Ibid*.
7. *The Sunday Times* magazine, in November of 1966, had listed Philip's impressive inventory of boats, planes and trains, which included the yachts *Bluebottle*, *Coweslip*, *Fairey Fox* and *Bloodhound*, a racing dinghy and a catamaran, four Rolls-Royces and a Triplex Reliant Scimitar, plus two aircraft of the Queen's Flight, which he flew regularly, and two Westland helicopters and considerable rolling stock. Cited in Parker, *Philip*, p. 198.

8. Susan Crosland, *Tony Crosland* (London: Cape, 1982), p. 345.

9. Morrow, *Queen Mother*, p. 163.

10. Pimlott, p. 441.

11. *Ibid.*

12. Piers Brendon and Phillip Whitehead, *The Windsors: A Dynasty Revealed* (London: Hodder & Stoughton, 1994), pp. 186–87.

CHAPTER NINETEEN

1. Morrow, *The Queen*, pp. 211–12, describes the queen's ritual of presiding at afternoon tea.

2. *Ibid.*, p. 70.

3. According to Turner, pp. 125–26, the number of the prince's affairs was "well into double figures." Sarah Spencer, Diana's older sister whom Charles dated for a time, thought that the prince was "a romantic who falls in love easily." Spoto, p. 396.

4. Charles felt caged and trapped by his fate as Prince of Wales. He has been quoted as saying that when he realized that he would one day have to be king the idea came to him "with the most ghastly inexorable sense." Hibbert, *Court of St. James's*, p. 226. That he lacked the emotional stamina for the throne was widely apparent; courtiers at St. James's and Buckingham Palace are in agreement, at the turn of the new century, that "they have

seldom met anyone who has as little real con-fidence as Prince Charles." Turner, p. 202. "Charles really must learn to be tougher," Lili-bet remarked in the 1970s. Bradford, *Elizabeth,* p. 420.
5. Higham and Moseley, p. 252.

CHAPTER TWENTY

1. In the Jubilee Year of 1977, Elizabeth spent a hundred days on tour in the UK, fulfilling some eight hundred engagements, and traveled fifty-six thousand miles to Commonwealth countries. Philip Ziegler, *Elizabeth's Britain 1926–1986* (London: Country Life Books, 1986), p. 332.
2. Ziegler, *Crown and People*, p. 181.
3. Turner, p. 181; Strober and Strober, p. 213, citing Peter Jay; Longford, *Elizabeth R*, p. 279.
4. When Sonny Ramphal, former Secretary-General of the Commonwealth, was asked whether his longtime friend the queen mim-icked the prime minister, he grinned knowingly and responded "I won't answer that ques-tion." Turner, p. 62.
5. Thatcher's outburst is quoted in Strober and Strober, p. 209, attributed to Lady Longford.
6. Pimlott, pp. 459–60, 495, writes that between the queen and Mrs. Thatcher it was "never possible to detect the slightest degree of warmth on either side." Bradford, *Elizabeth*, p.

381, concludes that "in her heart of hearts [the queen] did not like her," which was the view of others close to the queen. Though the palace and the government continued to protest that there was nothing but harmony and cordiality between monarch and prime minister, the best evidence points in a contrary direction. In Thatcher's defense it must be noted that many observers find that the queen tends to ignore or trivialize women in general, and to disregard their opinions. Turner, p. 174.

CHAPTER TWENTY-ONE

1. *Time*, September 10, 1979.
2. Hibbert, *Court of St. James's*, p. 228.
3. Morrow, *The Queen*, p. 131.
4. "If he's got a mistress, so what?" the queen remarked to an anonymous "senior cleric" about Charles. The churchman added, "She'd run a mile before she'd do anything about it. She'd run to the red boxes instead." Turner, pp. 125–26. She had known about Charles's involvement with Camilla since 1973 at least. Turner, p. 125.
5. Spoto, pp. 404–5.
6. Turner, pp. 133–34.
7. The reunion is described in Morrow, *The Queen*, p. 138.
8. Diana was the granddaughter of Ruth Fermoy, the queen mother's close friend and principal

lady-in-waiting. Lady Fermoy herself had serious reservations about Diana's suitability as Princess of Wales, but apparently kept them to herself. Spoto, p. 402. Early in the Waleses' marriage, Diana took offense at something Lady Fermoy did or said and ordered her out of Highgrove, telling her never to come back. Turner, p. 142.

To an extent, Charles's choice of a wife was affected by the longstanding struggle for influence within the royal family, between Mountbatten and the dowager queen, who had always been deeply suspicious of Lord Louis. Mountbatten had wanted Charles to marry his granddaughter Amanda Knatchbull, Patricia's daughter, while the queen mother's choice was Diana Spencer. Amanda removed herself from consideration, and after Mountbatten's death the queen mother's influence became dominant in Charles's life; he ultimately proposed to the woman she favored. Lilibet seems to have remained aloof from all this intrigue.

9. During the 1970s there had been at least one bomb scare on the Shetland Islands, when a boat, the *St. Clair*, came under suspicion by the Royal Navy. After many hours of detention the boat was escorted out to sea.

10. "Those two idiots came up behind me," the queen told several members of her household afterward, "and asked if I was all right. I said, 'I

was until you came—you're upsetting my horse!' " Turner, p. 67. According to Turner, the phrase the queen used was "a good deal more pungent than 'push off.' " Several possibilities come to mind.

11. Accounts of the June 13, 1981, incident, including some of the queen's thoughts while it was happening, and her statements afterward, are in Longford, *Elizabeth R*, pp. 1–2; Morrow, *The Queen*, p. 130; and Higham and Moseley, pp. 432–33.

12. Morrow, *The Queen*, p. 131.

13. *Ibid.*, p. 7.

14. *Ibid.*, pp. 170, 174.

CHAPTER TWENTY-TWO

1. By early 1982, three million Britons were without work. In the 1970s, a million unemployed had seemed shocking and unacceptably high. "The sum of human misery and degradation represented by the statistics was incalculable," one commentator has written.

2. A guest room where Charles and Diana stayed after they returned from their honeymoon was in a shambles from their fighting, with wallpaper stained, bedclothes ruined, a broken chair and cracked mirror. Strober and Strober, p. 455, Unity Hall and Ingrid Seward, *Royalty Revealed* (New York: St. Martin's Press, 1989), pp. 87, 106, 18.

3. Hall and Seward, p. 5.
4. Bradford, *Elizabeth*, p. 444. Bradford implies that Diana may have "slipped."
5. Turner, pp. 144, 138.
6. *Ibid.*, p. 144.
7. The queen almost never enters the palace kitchens. Philip barges in on occasion to complain about the food. Charles once tried to descend into the kitchens to find the chef, to thank him for his efforts, but forgot the way and never arrived. Hall and Seward, p. 52.
8. Admiral Sir Sandy Woodward speculates that the captain of the *Invincible*, Captain Block, may "have been told by the senior management of the Navy to be extra careful." "I expect he was," Woodward told interviewers some years after the Falklands conflict, "but I don't know that. But I assume he was." Strober and Strober, p. 425.
9. *Ibid.*, p. 423. Sir Rex Hunt's interview with the queen is in Strober and Strober, p. 424.
10. *Daily Telegraph*, June 26, 1982.

CHAPTER TWENTY-THREE

1. This account of Michael Fagan's intrusion into Buckingham Palace in July of 1982 is drawn from a variety of sources, chiefly Morton, *Inside Buckingham Palace*, pp. 80–84; Morrow, *The Queen*, pp. 231ff; Longford, *Elizabeth R*, pp. 4–6; and Higham and Moseley, pp.

448–50. Other secondary accounts are derivative and gloss over contradictory details.

Accounts of the break-in vary considerably. After the incident was over, both the intruder and the queen told their own versions of events, neither, one suspects, entirely veracious.

2. Morton, *Inside Buckingham Palace*, p. 80.
3. Fagan, in his comments after the break-in, made contradictory statements about his purpose in smashing the ashtray and drawing his own blood. He said both that he intended to kill himself in Lilibet's presence and that he needed the broken glass to cut some pigeon netting he had noticed on his way up the drainpipe; thinking ahead, he realized that the netting might impede his escape, and he wanted to be able to slash his way through it. In his disturbed frame of mind, both thoughts may have coexisted.
4. Fagan recalled that Lilibet "just hopped out of the bed, ran across the room and went out of the door. I say 'hopped' because I was quite surprised at how nimble she was. She hopped out and ran across the room like a girl. That was when I spotted her height, that she was only small." "It was all over within thirty seconds," according to Fagan. "Everyone goes on about this conversation that we had. It simply never took place."

CHAPTER TWENTY-FOUR

1. Turner, p. 111; Morrow, *The Queen*, p. 234; Higham and Moseley, p. 448; Bradford, *Elizabeth*, p. 448.
2. The consensus among journalists and biographers of Elizabeth is that Philip has had many extramarital liaisons, though none of the women with whom he has allegedly been intimate have come forward to describe their experiences. Palace staff are said to be fiercely protective of what goes on in the royal marriage—which is, after all, no one's business but that of wife and husband.

   Having said this, no biographer of the queen can avoid concluding that, to all appearances, Lilibet has chosen, or been forced by circumstances into, an awkward but tenable position as the wife of a serial philanderer who makes certain that his dalliances do not become the stuff of tabloid scandal—at least not in the UK. He is discreet, his partners are discreet, and although everyone in the privileged social circles surrounding the court is aware of what is going on, no one speaks publicly about it.

   Yet the emotional dimension of Lilibet's role is strangely ignored, or underplayed, in accounts of her life.

   It is sometimes said that in aristocratic marriages, there is a tacit understanding that a graceful "arrangement" will prevail, with both parties free to explore other relationships. But Elizabeth was not raised amid such conventions; her parents had a monogamous, loving marriage in which there was never so much as a hint of adultery on either side. It was that sort of marriage—a conventional, monogamous one—that the youthful Lilibet expected to have with Philip, and when he disillusioned her, her pain and heartbreak must have been deepgoing indeed.

For adultery invariably causes pain, heartbreak and humiliation, not to mention distrust and loathing. Unless the spouses are indifferent to one another—and Lilibet has never been indifferent to Philip—or are so jaded or distanced from all feeling as to be emotionally empty, the constant leaching away of affection by recurring infidelity is corrosive in any marriage. It seems safe to conclude that Lilibet, however emotionally tough and resilient she has been, and however well she has learned to cope with her husband's behavior toward other women—denying it, rising above it, regally ignoring it—has had more than her share of hurt. Whether, as is sometimes asserted, there remains a strong and affectionate underlying bond between the queen and her husband is impossible to say. Parker, *Philip*, pp. 206–7; Turner, pp. 109–10; Spoto, p. 326; Bradford, pp. 399–401; Strober and

Strober, pp. 213, 215–16; Higham and Moseley, pp. 281, 253. Kitty Kelley, whose strong animus against the royal family is evident throughout *The Royals*, discusses the issue of Philip's extramarital activities on pp. 186, 192–196, 422–26 and 511. *The New Yorker, Vanity Fair, People, The Tatler, The National Review* and the *Sunday Times*, among many other publications, allude to the presence of other women in the prince's romantic life.

3. Morrow, *The Queen*, p. 76.
4. Hall and Seward, pp. 65, 67.
5. Morrow, *The Queen*, p. 78; Laird, p. 54.
6. Strober and Strober, p. 128.
7. *Ibid.*, p. 463.
8. Nigel Dempster and Peter Evans, *Behind Palace Doors: Marriage and Divorce in the House of Windsor* (New York: G. P. Putnam's Sons, 1993), pp. 265–66.
9. *Ibid.*, p. 201. Andrew, says the queen's cousin the Earl of Lichfield, "was the favorite in his mother's eyes. He could do no wrong." *Ibid.*, p. 170.
10. Bradford, *Elizabeth*, p. 451.
11. Strober and Strober, p. 459, citing Philip Ziegler in an interview.

CHAPTER TWENTY-FIVE

1. There were stories of a male prostitution ring run out of the palace. Morton, *Inside Bucking-*

ham Palace, p. 85. The resignation of Lilibet's detective, Michael Trestrail, seemed to lend weight to these stories; his resignation followed revelations made by Michael Rauch, a prostitute, to the *Sun* newspaper concerning Rauch's affair with Trestrail. Gay staff members were at risk of blackmail, some were threatened with exposure or forced to resign. Members of the crew of the royal yacht were fired for sexual misconduct. And there was at least one accusation of rape, which was investigated "internally" and not by the police. The alleged victim left royal service having been paid £30,000. The allegation was made in the mid-1980s, and Princess Diana, wanting there to be some record of the circumstances, made a tape of the alleged victim and his accusations; Diana's butler Paul Burrell was in possession of the tape at the time of his criminal trial. In view of what has been revealed, rumored or alleged, it seems safe to assume that more must have gone on—how many people were paid off, or hushed up, or persuaded, out of loyalty to the sovereign to keep silence?

2. Morton, *Inside Buckingham Palace*, p. 86. The thief spoke confidentially to Morton and said that household officials put a stop to his being questioned by the police (after three days of interrogation) because he threatened to tell what he knew about prostitution at the palace.

3. *Ibid.*, p. 87.
4. Hall and Seward, p. 51.
5. Morrow, *The Queen*, p. 195.
6. See note 1 above.
7. Bradford, *Elizabeth*, p. 466.
8. Sarah Bradford writes that by the time of Prince Harry's birth in September of 1984, Charles and Camilla had resumed their intimacy. *Ibid.*, p. 454. The affair was "a scandal being discussed . . . openly in London" in 1984. Dempster and Evans, p. 154. Graham Turner asserts that by 1985 the Prince and Princess of Wales had been sleeping apart for some time. Turner, p. 137.
9. Dempster and Evans, p. 130. According to a "senior cleric," the queen mother was "far more tolerant of Charles's weaknesses and timidity than she was of such weaknesses in their own children. She coddled Charles," the cleric said, "much to the annoyance of the queen," who "felt thoroughly irritated." Turner, p. 149.
10. Turner, p. 149.

CHAPTER TWENTY-SIX

1. Hall and Seward, pp. 4–6.
2. The argument that Charles sought in Camilla an understanding mother-substitute seems quite plausible. Lilibet was fond of Charles—in an arm's length, distant sort of way—but as Charles approached middle age, mother and

son were no closer than they had been in Charles's childhood. "I have never seen any sign of closeness between them," says a former courtier who served the Windsors for three decades. Turner, p. 167.

Charles and Philip, perpetually at odds, were even more so, it would seem, by the late 1980s.

One of the queen's closest friends told Graham Turner that she and her husband were convinced that Lilibet and Philip blamed Charles for his marriage's failure. They tried to defend Charles, saying he had tried his utmost to "do his best." *Ibid.*, p. 149.

3. Hall and Seward, p. 40.
4. According to Paul Burrell, Diana asked him to smuggle her lover James Hewitt into Highgrove in the trunk of his car. *The Mirror*, November 9, 2002.
5. Morton, *Inside Buckingham Palace*, p. 34.
6. Bradford, *Elizabeth*, p. 469.
7. We now know, as of this writing in fall 2002, that Diana, aware of wrongdoing among palace staff, tried to prevent at least one of the scandals from being kept secret; according to Paul Burrell, Diana made a tape of one purported victim describing his alleged rape by another staff member.
8. According to Dempster and Evans, p. 26, "informed leaks" indicated that the queen was "imperious" with Charles and Diana, and un-

comprehending when Diana indicated that she needed "space." "Kensington Palace isn't a cottage, is it?" she is said to have asked drily when telling a friend later about Diana's request for "space."

9. *Ibid.*, p. 213.
10. Turner, p. 9.
11. *Ibid*.
12. Tom Nairn, *The Enchanted Glass: Britain and Its Monarchy* (London: Radius, 1988).
13. Turner, p. 9.

CHAPTER TWENTY-SEVEN

1. Jonathan Dimbleby, *The Prince of Wales: A Biography* (London: Little Brown, 1994), pp. 488–89.
2. In November of 1992 the *Daily Mirror* announced that its editors were in possession of embarrassing proof of an "intimate phone call" between the Prince of Wales and Camilla Parker-Bowles, and that this phone call was even more personal and more damaging than Diana's taped conversation with James Gilbey. Dempster and Evans, p. 17.
3. Transcript of the "Camillagate" tape published in the *Irish Times*.
4. Dempster and Evans, pp. 11–12, 228–29.
5. Turner, pp. 53–54.

CHAPTER TWENTY-EIGHT

1. Turner, p. 9.
2. One of Robert Fellowes's colleagues has said that Fellowes "was the person who was actually managing the royal family" in the early nineties. "The queen is better at following advice than taking the initiative herself." *Ibid.*, p. 155.
3. Morton, *Inside Buckingham Palace*, p. 47.
4. *Ibid.*, p. 8; Bradford, *Elizabeth*, p. 502.
5. Strober and Strober, p. 260.
6. In the small town in Hawaii where I live, with its multi-ethnic, polyglot population, half a world away from Kensington Palace, there was much sorrow when news of Diana's death reached us. On the morning of August 31— our time being eleven hours behind London time—we woke to hear that the princess had not survived her accident. That day, it was not possible to go into a shop or walk along a street without encountering people in tears, sharing their grief and comforting one another. Diana was indeed greatly loved.
7. William Shawcross, in *Vanity Fair*, June 2002.
8. The incident at the Balmoral tea is in Turner, p. 158.
9. The queen's speech can be accessed at http://gos.sbc.edu/e/elizabeth.html.
10. Philip was still, however, venomous and rude. "I don't seem to be able to say nice things to

people, though I would like to," he told a friend. "Why is that?" Turner, p. 27. Some observers say he has mellowed somewhat, but others insist that he continues to make himself sharply disliked by, among others, his children and the queen's ladies-in-waiting, who consider him to be a hateful bully.

CHAPTER TWENTY-NINE

1. *The Mirror*, 6 November, 2002.
2. Turner, p. 97.
3. *Vanity Fair*, October 2001.

LIST OF
WORKS CITED

Note to reader: The following brief bibliography includes only works cited in notes.

Airlie, Mabel. *Thatched with Gold: The Memoir of Mabel Countess of Airlie*. Ed. J. Ellis. London: Hutchinson, 1962.

Beaton, Cecil. *The Strenuous Years: Diaries 1948–1955*. London: Weidenfeld & Nicolson, 1973.

Bloch, Michael, ed. *Wallis and Edward: Letters 1931–1937*. New York: Summit Books, 1986.

Bocca, S. G. *Elizabeth and Philip.* New York: Henry Holt and Co., 1953.

Bradford, Sarah. *Elizabeth: A Biography of Britain's Queen*. New York: Farrar Straus & Giroux, 1996; paperback edition, Riverhead Books, 1997.

————. *King George VI, A Life*. London: Weidenfeld & Nicolson, 1989.

Brendon, Piers, and Phillip Whitehead. *The Windsors: A Dynasty Revealed*. London: Hodder and Stoughton, 1994.

Bryan, J., and C. V. Murphy. *The Windsor Story*. London: Granada, 1979.

Cathcart, Helen. [Pseudonym of Harold Albert] *Her Majesty the Queen*. New York: Dodd Mead, 1962. ·

Clark, Stanley. *Palace Diary*. New York: Dutton, 1958.

Clarke, Peter. *Hope and Glory: Britain 1900–1990*. London: Allen Lane, The Penguin Press, 1996.

Crawford, Marion. *The Little Princesses*. New York: Bantam, 1950.

————. *Queen Elizabeth II*. London: George Newnes Ltd., 1952.

Crosland, Susan. *Tony Crosland*. London: Cape, 1982.

Curling, Bill. *All the Queen's Horses*. London: Chatto & Windus, 1978.

Dempster, Nigel, and Peter Evans. *Behind Palace Doors: Marriage and Divorce in the House of Windsor.* New York: G. P. Putnam's Sons, 1993.

Dimbleby, Jonathan. *The Prince of Wales: A Biography.* London: Little Brown, 1994.

Duncan, A. *The Reality of Monarchy*. London: Heinemann, 1970.

Fitch, Herbert T. *Memoirs of a Royal Detective*. London: Hurst and Blackett, 1935.

Hall, Unity. *Philip: The Man Behind the Monarchy*. London: Michael O'Mara, 1987.

Hall, Unity, and Ingrid Seward. *Royalty Revealed*. New York: St. Martin's Press, 1989.

Hart-Davis, D., ed. *Royal Service: The Letters and Journals of Sir Alan Lascelles, 1920–1936*. Vol. 2. London: Hamish Hamilton, 1989.

Hibbert, Christopher. *The Court of St. James's: The Monarch at Work from Victoria to Elizabeth II*. London: Weidenfeld & Nicolson, 1979; New York: Morrow, 1983.

Higham, Charles, and Roy Moseley. *Elizabeth and Philip: The Untold Story of the Queen of England and Her Prince*. New York: Doubleday, 1991.

Holden, Anthony. *Charles, Prince of Wales*. London: Weidenfeld & Nicolson, 1979.

Judd, Denis. *King George VI, 1895–1952*. New York: Franklin Watts, 1983.

Kelley, Kitty. *The Royals*. New York: Warner Books, 1997.

Kennedy, Joseph P. *Hostage to Fortune: The Letters of Joseph P. Kennedy*. ed. Amanda Smith. New York: Viking, 2001.

Kyle, Keith. *Suez*. New York: St. Martin's Press, 1991.

Laird, Dorothy. *How the Queen Reigns*. London: Pan, 1959.

Longford, Elizabeth. *Elizabeth R*. London: Weidenfeld & Nicolson, 1983.

————. *The Pebbled Shore: The Memoirs of Elizabeth Longford*. New York: Knopf, 1986.

————. *The Queen Mother*. New York: William Morrow, 1981.

McLeish, K., and V. McLeish. *Long to Reign Over Us: Memories of Coronation Day and of Life in the 1950s*. London: Bloomsbury, 1992.

Morrow, Ann. *The Queen*. London: Granada, 1983.

————. *The Queen Mother*. New York: Stein & Day, 1985.

Morton, Andrew. *Inside Buckingham Palace*. New York: Summit Books, 1991.

————. *Inside Kensington Palace*. London: Michael O'Mara Books, 1991.

Nairn, Tom. *The Enchanted Glass: Britain and Its Monarchy*. London: Radius, 1988.

Overy, Richard. *The Battle of Britain: The Myth and the Reality*. New York and London: W. W. Norton, 2000.

Parker, John. *Prince Philip: A Critical Biography*. London: Sidgwick and Jackson, 1990.

Pimlott, Ben. *The Queen: A Biography of Elizabeth II*. London: HarperCollins, 1996; paperback 1997.

Rhodes James, R., ed. *Chips Channon: The Diary of Sir Henry Channon*. London: Weidenfeld & Nicolson, 1967.

Ring, Anne. *The Story of Princess Elizabeth*. London: John Murray, 1930.

Rose, Kenneth. *Kings, Queens and Courtiers*. London: Weidenfeld & Nicolson, 1985.

Sheridan, Lisa. *From Cabbages to Kings*. London: Odhams, 1955.

Shuckburgh, Evelyn. *Descent to Suez*. London: Weidenfeld & Nicolson, 1986.

Sitwell, Osbert. *Rat Week*. London: Michael Joseph, 1984.

Smith, Horace. *A Horseman Through Six Reigns: Reminiscences of a Royal Riding Master*. London: Odhams, 1955.

Spoto, Donald. *The Decline and Fall of the House of Windsor.* New York: Simon & Schuster, 1995.

Strober, Deborah Hart, and Gerald S. Strober. *The Monarchy: An Oral Biography of Elizabeth II*. New York: Broadway Books, 2002.

Turner, Graham. *Elizabeth: The Woman and the Queen.* London: Telegraph Books, 2002.

Vickers, Hugo. *Alice: Princess Andrew of Greece*. London: Hamish Hamilton, 2000.

Wheeler-Bennett, John W. *King George VI: His Life and Reign.* New York: St. Martin's Press, 1958.

Wilson, A. N. *The Rise and Fall of the House of Windsor*. London: Sinclair-Stevenson, 1993.

Wright, Peter. *Spycatcher: The Candid Autobiography of a Senior Intelligence Officer*. New York: Viking Penguin, 1987.

Ziegler, Philip. *Crown and People*. London: Collins, 1978.

———. *Elizabeth's Britain 1926–1986*. London: Country Life Books, 1986.

———. *Mountbatten*. London: Collins, 1985.

INDEX